Education between Speech and Writing

This unique book explores how graphocentrism affects Chinese education and culture. It moves away from the contemporary educational practices in China of following the Western model of phonocentrism to demonstrate that each perspective interacts and counteracts with each other, creating a dialogue between Eastern and Western thought.

The chapters explore the consonances and dissonances between the two, problematising the educational practices of Chinese tradition and proposing a dialectical thinking of post-graphocentrism, based on the concepts of Dao and deconstruction. The volume creates a unique area in the field of philosophy of education by questioning the writing/speaking relationship in Chinese tradition, complete with educational ideas and practices that consider the uniqueness of Chinese character writing.

A pioneering study of its kind, *Education between Speech and Writing* provides a valuable source for students of philosophy of education, as well as students and academics in the field of Chinese Studies. The book will also appeal to anyone interested in dialogues between Chinese and Western thoughts, especially negotiating between Daoism and deconstruction.

Ruyu Hung is Professor of Education of Philosophy at National Chiayi University, Taiwan.

New Directions in the Philosophy of Education
Series Editors
Michael A. Peters, University of Waikato, New Zealand; University of Illinois, USA
Gert Biesta, Brunel University, UK

For more information about the series, please visit www.routledge.com.

This book series is devoted to the exploration of new directions in the philosophy of education. After the linguistic turn, the cultural turn, and the historical turn, where might we go? Does the future promise a digital turn with a greater return to connectionism, biology, and biopolitics based on new understandings of system theory and knowledge ecologies? Does it foreshadow a genuinely alternative radical global turn based on a new openness and interconnectedness? Does it leave humanism behind, or will it reengage with the question of the human in new and unprecedented ways? How should philosophy of education reflect new forces of globalisation? How can it become less Anglo-centric and develop a greater sensitivity to other traditions, languages, and forms of thinking and writing, including those that are not rooted in the canon of Western philosophy but in other traditions that share the 'love of wisdom' that characterises the wide diversity within Western philosophy itself? Can this be done through a turn to intercultural philosophy? To indigenous forms of philosophy and philosophising? Does it need a post-Wittgensteinian philosophy of education? A postpostmodern philosophy? Or should it perhaps leave the whole construction of 'post'-positions behind?

In addition to the question of the intellectual resources for the future of philosophy of education, what are the issues and concerns that philosophers of education should engage with? How should they position themselves? What is their specific contribution? What kinds of intellectual and strategic alliances should they pursue? Should philosophy of education become more global, and, if so, what would the shape of that be? Should it become more cosmopolitan or perhaps more decentred? Perhaps most importantly in the digital age, the time of the global knowledge economy that reprofiles education as privatised human capital and simultaneously in terms of an historic openness, is there a philosophy of education that grows out of education itself, out of the concerns for new forms of teaching, studying, learning, and speaking that can provide comments on ethical and epistemological configurations of economics and politics of knowledge? Can and should this imply a reconnection with questions of democracy and justice?

This series comprises texts that explore, identify, and articulate new directions in the philosophy of education. It aims to build bridges, both geographically and temporally: bridges across different traditions and practices and bridges towards a different future for philosophy of education.

In this series

Heidegger and Executive Education
The Management of Time
Toby Thompson

Education between Speech and Writing
Crossing the Boundaries of Dao and Deconstruction
Ruyu Hung

Education between Speech and Writing

Crossing the Boundaries of Dao and Deconstruction

Ruyu Hung

LONDON AND NEW YORK

First published 2018 by Routledge

2 Park Square, Milton Park, Abingdon, Oxfordshire OX14 4RN
52 Vanderbilt Avenue, New York, NY 10017

Routledge is an imprint of the Taylor & Francis Group, an informa business

First issued in paperback 2019

Copyright © 2018 Ruyu Hung

The right of Ruyu Hung to be identified as author of this work
has been asserted by her in accordance with sections 77 and
78 of the Copyright, Designs and Patents Act 1988.

All rights reserved. No part of this book may be reprinted or reproduced or
utilised in any form or by any electronic, mechanical, or other means, now
known or hereafter invented, including photocopying and recording, or in any
information storage or retrieval system, without permission in writing from
the publishers.

Notice:
Product or corporate names may be trademarks or registered trademarks, and
are used only for identification and explanation without intent to infringe.

British Library Cataloguing-in-Publication Data
A catalogue record for this book is available from the British
Library

Library of Congress Cataloguing-in-Publication Data
A catalog record for this book has been requested

ISBN: 978-1-138-84638-8 (hbk)
ISBN: 978-0-367-36793-0 (pbk)

Typeset in Bembo
by Apex CoVantage, LLC

Contents

Preface and acknowledgements   vii
Prologue: seeing is believing?   xi
The wordaholic society and ocularcentric education xi
Overview of the book xiv

1   Thinking education through the spoken and the written word   1
Voice, logos, and bias 2
Writing/word matters 7

2   Chinese graphocentrism: a search through texts   16
The rise of writing and the dismissal of speech 17
Appellation as legitimation and the words of sage kings 28
The graphocentric worldview 35

3   Graphocentric education: the cultivation of the writing subject   44
The discipline of writing calligraphy 46
*The institutionalisation of writing through the imperial civil
   examination* 54
The cultivation of the moral writing subject 61
The end of the writing subject as the end of humans? 80

4   The paradox of graphocentrism: Dao–logocentrism   89
Logos in writing and in speech: the Chinese prejudice 89
Logocentrism and graphocentrism 94

5   Post-graphocentrism: Dao–deconstruction   108
The dao 111
Myriad daos 116
The post-graphocentric thrust 124

vi Contents

6 Post-graphocentric education   127

Wú-practices 128

Becoming daofully otherwise 134

Crossing the boundaries of dao and deconstruction 146

Epilogue: playing the word   151

Index   154

Preface and acknowledgements

In this book, I seek to answer the question of whether there is a particularly Chinese way of thinking, as I have sensed the phenomenon of word obsession (or wordaholism) prevalent among Chinese-speaking societies. Underpinning this wordaholism is a set of beliefs with a history both in literature and in practice. This set of beliefs in Chinese culture and tradition, which pays particular attention to the written language, is what I called 'graphocentrism'. The awareness of the wordaholic phenomenon is generated from comparing the East and the West on the individually experiential level as well as on the theoretical level. Therefore, the process of this project starts with considering my personal experience and then dwells on the theoretical exploration of literature. The sources of inspiration include Chinese and Western literature, especially those in Daoist philosophy and the philosophy of deconstruction. The concepts of deconstruction and dao lead the train of thought through the writing. Because Jacques Derrida considers writing throughout the Western philosophical tradition in a very new and creative way in *Of Grammatology*, he provides a fulcrum of thought in this book.

This book explores how the graphocentric view is gradually built up on the levels of theory and practice in the history of imperial China. The discussion inevitably involves some special Chinese terms and translation. Conventional translation always creates a huge difficulty in my reading because it does not indicate intonation. Intonation in Chinese is inevitable. There are four tones in Mandarin Chinese. Syllables with different tones create different words and, thus, different meanings. For example, the syllable *shi*: *shi* with first tone can be 'lose' (失) or 'teacher' (師); *shí* with second tone, 'eat' (食) or 'stone' (石); *shǐ* with third tone, 'history' (史); and *shì* with fourth tone, 'city' (市). There are many homonyms, with or without tone marks. To overcome my own reading disorder, I add tone marks on the vowel. To the readers who can make sense of the conventional translation, it is feasible to ignore the tone marks. However, this also causes another problem – that is, the spelling of the translated terms may not be consistent throughout the manuscript. Some Chinese terms are already familiar to the Western world, e.g., *Dao* (道). Yet, 道 is pronounced with the fourth tone. In my writing, it should be *dào*. Dao with the first tone could be 'knife' (刀). Nevertheless, most authors use the conventional translation – without intonation. I must respect their original texts and do not add tone marks when I cite or quote their works. In addition, there are different systems of spelling translation. For example, the word 趙 can be translated as Chao (Chào) or Zhao (Zhào). The references contain different spelling translation systems. Therefore, the consistency of the translated terms is not firmly fastened. I apologise for this new way of spelling and for any inconsistencies of spelling.

Most Chinese classical texts used are based on the online open-access digital library Chinese Text Project. To help readers access the original source easily, I use the number marked on the website Chinese Text Project. For example, the statement 'Fine words and an insinuating appearance are seldom associated with true virtue' is cited from the third section of the first chapter (Xúe Ér) of the *Analects*. The source will be specified as follows: (*Analects, Xúe Ér*, 1:3). As for the *Mencius*, the chapters of this text are organised and numbered in a distinctive way: there are 14 chapters in total with seven titles. Two chapters are given a same title with different marks: the former (normally translated as Part One) and the latter (Part Two). For example, the first two chapters are titled 'Liang Hui Wang I' and 'Liang Hui Wang II'. If I cited a quotation from the third section of the chapter 'Liang Hui Wang I', the reference is written as 'Mencius, 1A3'.

★   ★   ★

Many people and organisations lent their help to this project by kindly providing comments and encouragement. I particularly thank Michael Peters, Gert Biesta, Chung-Ying Cheng, Morimichi Kato, Xu Di, Chia-Ling Wang, Tsao-Ling Fong, Yung-Ming Shu, and Cheng-His Chien for their very considerate and thoughtful comments. The book's contents served as the basis of public lectures and oral presentations I gave at the University of Luxembourg (2013), the Institute of Education, University of London (2013), the fourth Meeting on Educational Aesthetics in Taiwan (2017), the conferences of the Philosophy of Education Society of Australasia (2014), the Society for Asian and Comparative Philosophy (2016), the Philosophy of Education Society (2017), the Taiwan Philosophy of Education Society (2017), and the academic workshops of Asian Link of Philosophy of Education (ALPE) held at Seoul National University (2014) and the University of Zurich (2016). These lectures and presentations helped me to elaborate and reflect on my ideas over time. I owe a special debt to ALPE, created by Duck-Joo kwak, Morimichi Kato, and me in 2012. Since then, more and more scholars and colleagues have joined in, including Roland Reichenbach, Mika Okabe, and Yasushi Moriyama. Through ALPE, we are trying to address our own issues, particularities and identities in terms of Eastern Asia in the global or, indeed, Westernised world. Collaborating with these colleagues helps me to rethink and re-examine the cultural and philosophical background that I have been immersed in and taken for granted without reflection and criticality and led me to the question that launched the project.

I also acknowledge the support of the Ministry of Science and Technology (MOST 104-2410-H-415-016-MY2) of Taiwan and the Foundation for Scholarly Exchange (Fulbright Taiwan).

Prologue: seeing is believing?

孔子曰：「君子有三畏：畏天命，畏大人，畏聖人之言。小人不知天命而不畏也，狎大人，侮聖人之言。」

（論語季氏）[1]

If supplementarity is a necessarily indefinite process, writing is the supplement par excellence since it marks the point where the supplement proposes itself as supplement of supplement, sign of sign, taking the place of a speech already significant.

—(Derrida, 1976, p. 281)

The wordaholic society and ocularcentric education

Sometimes, we are unaware of the things or practices that powerfully influence our lives and are deeply embedded in our beliefs until we are away from and maintain distance from them. The distance creates a break from what we are accustomed to so that the absence strikes us suddenly. This is how I felt about my experience with the 'word', especially the written word, when I was in foreign countries.

Many international students suggested that watching television was helpful for improving the learning of a foreign language, so I bought a television set soon after I arrived in England. However, when I turned on the television, I was surprised by the absence of subtitles on the screen. After some time, I realised that additional steps were required to set up the subtitles. Subtitles are not an embedded part of the programme. Yet in my home country, Taiwan, it is taken for granted that television programmes are played with subtitles. Almost all television programmes – whether news, dramas, reality shows, or talk shows – are played with captions or subtitles. The captions or subtitles are always displayed on the screen automatically. These words are supposed to be an essential and indispensable part of the programmes.

In addition, I noted that the written (or printed) words on the streets are not as conspicuous as those in my hometown. In Taipei or any other city in Taiwan, the streets are full of huge, colourful, shining shop signs. During the evening, many dazzling signs are bright enough to blind the eyes. The words on the signs draw the eyes of passersby in a powerful and forceful way.

When I visited public spaces such as schools or governmental offices, I also sensed a big difference between the public spaces in my home country and those in foreign countries. Again, this difference was related to the written word. In Taiwan, it is normal for posters or couplets – which are not only decorative but are also, and more importantly, informative and educative – to be hung or pasted on the walls of public spaces. Placards, posters, or plaques are everywhere in schools, constantly educating about recycling, energy saving, improving moral character, maintaining good hygiene, and the like. A few decades ago, school posters displayed the central Chinese ideologies of nationalist solidarity, respect for national leadership, and traditional morality. To me, the written word plays a mystical and vital role in my home society, my home culture. For example, a shelter community called Dàài, meaning Great Love, was built by an influential religious charity in southern Taiwan after a typhoon destroyed an entire village in 2009. Spread throughout the shelter community are wood and stones engraved with appraisal of and appreciation for the organisation and its leader. The inscriptions educate the residents through the power of words.

Let me think more boldly and imaginatively. That the written word in Chinese culture plays a profound role in daily life could have deep roots in culture, history, and tradition. Since ancient times, during the Chinese New Year Festival, people have pasted a single-character poster on their walls or doors written or printed with blessing words such as Fú (福 blessing, happiness), Shòu (壽 longevity), Lu (祿 prosperity), or Chun (春 spring, joy) and have placed the chunlían (春聯 spring couplet), a pair of lines of poetry, at the entrance of their homes to express auspicious blessing or wishes. Nowadays, posting the words at the entrance or on the walls is simply a cultural conventional practice. In the old times, however, words were believed to be magical – powerful enough to carry out people's wishes and to expel devils. In Chinese Daoist religion, Daoshì (道士), the priest of religious Daoism, has the magical power to tell the future or to change one's fortune by communicating with deities or demons. The Daoshì writes mysterious words on a piece of paper to create a talisman or amulet to cast the spell (McCreery, 1995). Practices of this kind still exist in many folk religion temples in Taiwan. In the Chinese tradition, the written word has magical power. The Chinese heritage cultures, in my observation, have a general inclination to obsess about written words, which is called wordaholism.

Wordaholic symptoms are found in Taiwan as well as in China. The written word was an important means for political leaders to exercise control. In the mid-1960s, Mao and his Red Guard followers employed mini-posters (小字報) and big character posters (大字報) as important weapons to attack political enemies (Barmé, 2012). During the Chinese Cultural Revolution, the written word played an important role in serving the political purpose in many aspects, 'from the widely distributed "Little Red Book" of Chairman Mao's thoughts and the publicly displayed big character posters proclaiming the latest political slogans, to the privately written "confessions" of political undesirables' (Erickson, 2001, p. 34). The cult of the written word endured the Cultural Revolution and has flourished. In 2012, the Chinese government hosted a month of celebration to mark the seventieth anniversary of Mao Zedong's 'Talks at the Yánan Forum on Literature and Art'. One product of this observance was the publication of the book *One Hundred Writers' and Artists' Hand-Copied Commemorative Edition of the Yánan Talks* (Abrahamsen, 2012, June 6). One hundred prestigious writers and artists copied Mao's words in their own handwriting in both collective and individual ways. They embodied Mao through their own hands, their own writing. It is apparent that writing and the written word play a critical role in many aspects of Chinese tradition.

These phenomena make clear that Chinese and Taiwanese cultures depend heavily on both visual and written words. I characterise this dependence as the 'wordaholic symptom' or 'wordaholic obsession'. This, then, raises a question for me: what makes my home culture, my home country, a wordaholic society?

In addition to the wordaholic scenarios mentioned, another word-related phenomenon is worth noting: the absurd bilingual signs in public spaces, such as shops or streets, in Taiwan and China. In recent years, bilingualism seems to be assumed as part of globalisation and internationalisation. Thus, signs in many places are bilingual, whether in officially administered facilities such as border checkpoints or international institutions, business areas such as shops or tourist attractions, or stations, schools, or roads. Yet, ridiculous translations appear frequently in both Taiwan and in mainland China. For example, in many shops in China, the term '干货' (simplified Chinese, '乾貨' in traditional Chinese) on a sign is often (mis-)translated as 'f★★k food'. The word '干' or '乾' and the F word in Chinese are homographs. This term, in fact, refers to 'dried food'. Similarly, 'café latte' is usually translated as '拿鐵咖啡' (ná tiě ka fei) because the pronunciation of '拿鐵' is very similar to 'latte' and '咖啡' to 'coffee'. The Chinese term '拿鐵咖啡' has become more popular than 'café latte'. The term '拿鐵咖啡' is reversely translated as 'take iron coffee' (Jiang, 2006) because '拿' in Chinese means 'take', while '鐵' means 'iron'. In another example: the sign 殘疾人专位 in mainland China (殘障專用 in Taiwan), meaning 'Designated Space for the Disabled' or 'Priority Space for the Disabled', has been inappropriately translated as 'Deformed Man End Place'. A tourist attraction民族園 in China has been mistranslated as 'Racist Park'. The word 民 means 'people'; 族 means 'clan, race, or nationality'. In Chinese, 民 and 族 are usually combined as a two-character term, 民族, which indicates 'race, race group, or ethnicity'. The word 園 means 'a park'. A more appropriate translation of 民族園 would be 'Park of Multi-nationalities'.

Mentioning these lost and ridiculous translations is done neither for fun nor to highlight the difficulties or insurmountable limitations of translation

(Derrida, 2001). What begs notice is that the Chinese way of thinking about ordinary language assumes correspondence between ideas and terms in different languages. This naïve view of language is more prominent in Chinese-speaking cultures. Although different languages may use different 'names' (signs) to refer to the same thing, translation as an activity of communication is done to substitute one 'name' in one language for the corresponding 'name' in another language. This assumption of one-to-one correspondence is what Ong (1982) describes as the 'chirographic and typographic bias'. As Ong (1982, p. 162) states, the bias assumes a one-to-one correspondence between 'items in an extramental world and the spoken words, and … between spoken words and written words'. On this assumption, 'the naïve reader presumes the prior presence of the extramental referent which the word presumably captures and passes on through a kind of pipeline to the psyche' (Ong, 1982, p. 162). To a certain degree, the chirographic and typographic bias manifests in the ridiculous bilingualism in the sense that the Chinese way of translation assumes an equivalent and interchangeable relationship between 'names' or 'signs' across different languages. The assumption of the Chinese view of translation – of the equivalent and interchangeable relationship – is grounded in the belief that 'names' in different languages are able to represent a common idea or object. Does it imply a reified realist perspective? What metaphysics, then, underpins the Chinese view of translation? If the ocularcentric orientation in the Chinese language system is taken into consideration, does the Chinese way of thinking not merely assume a correspondence between words in different languages but also a correspondence between words and images – assumed ideas or reality? Does the Chinese view of language imply a deeper belief that the 'name' or the signifier is present 'in' and 'of' itself, or, borrowing Derrida's term (1982, p. 11), 'in a sufficient presence that would refer only to itself'? All in all, these examples and questions reveal that the word – especially the written word – is supposed in Chinese to be self-sufficient and self-contained. Observing the Chinese preference for the written word and my ensuing questions spurred me to conduct an inquiry deep into the origin and the process of this particular way of thinking – graphocentrism, as contrasted with the Western phonocentrism that prioritises speech over writing.

Overview of the book

Through *Education between Speech and Writing*, I wish to present an innovative and exciting view of human subjects and education based on the interplay of dao and deconstruction. This book questions and repositions the established relationship between speech and writing, ears and eyes. I argue that the speech–writing relationship is crucial for distinguishing Chinese and Western ways of thinking and thus coin the term 'graphocentrism' as the underlying principle of Chinese thought.

Prologue: seeing is believing? xv

One goal achieved through the exploration in this book is the meaning that graphocentrism brings to the formation of the human subject through education. The significance of education lies in the formation of the human subject. Traditional education places emphasis on helping students find their own voice. The focus on voice or speech occupies the most prominent place in most educational discourse. Writing is thus viewed as a skill of literacy or a device of capturing voice. In Derrida's terms, writing is the mere supplement to speech. Phonocentrism prioritises speaking over writing. In contrast, Chinese language shows a very different relationship between writing and speech. In Chinese, words have richer and more spontaneous meaning when viewed than when heard. The understanding through written words occurs prior to the understanding through spoken ones. The very opposite view of phonocentrism is what I call graphocentrism. Within the Chinese tradition, codes and rules about writing were imbued with educational practices with deep ethical-political implications. This is due to graphocentrism, which fosters beliefs in close relationships with the present predicament of education, such as beliefs in standards, measurements, and the reified human subject.

While Western thinkers seek inspiration from Chinese thought to counter phonocentric problems, I search for insights from the West to bring graphocentric education out of this impasse. I argue that there is a dialectic between phonocentrism and graphocentrism, one that entails a way of thinking that crosses boundaries of Chinese and Western cultures. I propose that, with inspiration from dao and deconstruction, we can conceive a view that transcends Chinese graphocentrism and implied reified humanism: the post-graphocentric approach.

Chapter 1 examines and investigates wordaholic symptoms to reveal the heavy dependence on visual and written language in Chinese culture and education. Wordaholic symptoms can be seen in many aspects of Chinese social life, including ubiquitous advertising signs and slogans, ridiculous bilingualism, and the mainstream schooling system that translates educational activity as hearing, speaking, reading, and writing (tin, shuo, dú, xǐe, 聽, 說, 讀, 寫). The written or printed word greatly influences the Chinese lifeworld, both implicitly and explicitly. For Chinese, visual words are omnipresent. What can be discovered from the fetishism of written words or the obsession with words is an episteme that is closely related to ocularcentric consciousness and the dominance of the written word. This view is what I call graphocentrism.

Chapter 2 explores the graphocentric episteme by examining and discussing Chinese classics to reveal how graphocentrism is built up in Chinese philosophy and how it influences Chinese educational ideas and practices. The Western vision-centred view is the epistemological privileging of sight that starts from the metaphor of light as truth in Greek philosophy, continues in the Renaissance with the invention of printing, and develops with observing and objective subjects in modern science (Jay, 1988, 1993, 2002). In contrast, Chinese graphocentrism begins with the legends of invention of writing furnished by the metaphors of imitation of natural phenomena. The investigation reveals that Chinese graphocentrism exists in the characteristics of visibility, inalterability, and verifiability of visual and written words. Intriguingly, the identification of Chinese graphocentrism reveals its congruity and disparity with Western phonocentrism. It reveals that opposite judgements about writing and speech are addressed for similar reasons between these two modalities of episteme. For me, there is a profound connection between Chinese graphocentrism and Western phonocentrism. In order to clarify this relationship, I return to an age-old but contemporarily high-profile debate concerning the nature of Chinese characters. I will pursue this issue in Chapter 3. In addition, these characteristics of visual and written words – visibility, inalterability, and verifiability – contribute substantially to the beliefs in appellation, measurements, and standards that render to a great degree the examination – and credential-orientation – of educational ideas and practice in Chinese culture, from past to present. The relationship between the graphocentric episteme and the educational system under mainstream Chinese political-ethical tradition will be explored in the next chapter.

Chapter 3 offers a new way of thinking about politics and pedagogy with respect to graphocentrism. As some scholars put it, early China is the 'empire of writing' (Lewis, 1999). Writing is used to command assent and obedience. The core question in politics and pedagogy is the education of citizens – usually undertaken in the name of humanistic education, or the education for humanism. In terms of graphocentrism, the invention of words, the structure, the writing, and the way of using words (i.e., the regime of writing) have deep implications for politics and pedagogy. The difference between the literate and the illiterate creates social division. In ancient China, the imperial examination system cannily played the role of strengthening and fortifying social division and hierarchy. Overall, four aspects will be discussed in terms of words: the discipline of writing, the taboo of writing, the institutionalisation of writing (meaning the imperial examination system as the means of differentiating the literate from the illiterate), and the fundamental ideas of graphocentrism. This examination displays how Confucian orthodoxy builds on onto-political foundational beliefs and how these ideas fortify the Chinese hierarchy.

Chapter 4 returns to debates about 'Chinese prejudice' mentioned in Chapter 1. This debate began in the seventeenth and eighteenth centuries and bas intensified in contemporary times, especially after Derrida's discussions of the issue in his books. Derrida views phonocentrism as the crux of Western metaphysics. Does this critique, then, suggest that graphocentrism – which seems to be the opposite way of thinking about voice and writing – holds the solution? Unpacking the strains interwoven in this issue is to re-evaluate the limitations and possibilities of dialogues between Eastern and Western boundaries. This chapter shows that Western phonocentrism and Chinese graphocentrism conspire in the sense that they share very similar elements – logocentrism and ethnocentrism – despite working in different ways. Both ways of thinking may result in injustice and violence in different forms, for they possess biases and prejudices within different cultural and intellectual contexts.

This discovery leads to a dilemma: graphocentrism was initially suggested to counter the tyranny of the trio of logo-phono-ethnocentrism in light of Derrida. It turns out that even graphocentrism cannot escape the snare of Dao as Logos. How can human beings be liberated from the endless desire for binary and hierarchical thinking that are underpinned by centrism? Chapter 5 explores the concept of dao(s) in a comparison with deconstruction. I will argue that, in the West, Derrida aptly identifies the problems of logo-phonocentrism and proposes deconstruction as a breakthrough. In the East, the Daoist philosophers are also aware of the predicament of thought and language and suggest the dao or daos as a solution. The dao implies not only the consonance of the logos but also the dissonance, which shows the paradoxical ambiguity of dao and the possibility of overcoming the problems of graphocentrism or post-graphocentrism. The dialogue between deconstruction and daos contributes to an alternative thinking regarding human subject and education, which is called post-graphocentrism.

The next chapter considers the educational implications in terms of post-graphocentrism. With the intention of breaking the boundary, the thinking experiment of post-graphocentric pedagogy takes inspiration from the Daoist Wú-practices and modern arts. As Richard Rorty (1978) comments, 'there is no way in which one can isolate philosophy as occupying a distinctive place in culture or concerned with a distinctive subject or proceeding by some distinctive method' (p. 142). Likewise, education needs incentives and excitements from fields other than education. In art, words, letters, characters, writing, and voices are able to interweave a horizon for thinking and acting alternatively and thus give the world new meaning. The Chinese word has provided rich inspiration for the art of the Western world. For example, the Soviet Russian film director and theorist Sergei Eisenstein (1898–1948) admits that Chinese ideographs influenced his pioneering use of montage in 'filmic writing' (Kenner, 1971; Gu, 2000). The visual poetry of American imagist poet Ezra Pound (1885–1972) is well known for incorporating Chinese ideographs (Kenner, 1971; Fenollosa & Pound, 1936; Gu, 2000; Öztürk, 2012). More fascinating are some Chinese contemporary artworks that edge and rebel against the graphocentric tradition from the interior to the limit. The artistic deconstruction and reconstruction of the conventional division between graphic and phonetic language both disturbs and excites our soundscape and our viewscape.

The final chapter summarises the overall exploration of the graphocentric philosophy of education and concludes with the post-graphocentric view of connecting daos and deconstruction. This book aims for education to be an invitation to a kaleidoscopic view, a multifaceted horizon, a heteroglossia where one is able to write, speak, express, sign, and be listened to and be read with respect and regard.

xviii Prologue: seeing is believing?

Before delving into the exploration of graphocentrism, let me clarify the position and the aim of this book. It is not about making a philosophical argument based on any particular school of Chinese philosophical thought. As a philosopher of education, I am interested in the discussion of how certain cultural elements or beliefs influence our current educational ideas and practices. Generally, influential cultural elements or beliefs are not products of a single school of thought but are achievements of interactions of multiple cultures. In Chinese cultural circles, Confucianism, Daoism, and Buddhism coexist in a complementary way. These three perspectives are, simultaneously, religions and philosophical thoughts. The religious and the philosophical aspects are not entirely identical but are highly interactive and interdependent. Of course, there are divergences and conflicts between the philosophical doctrines and value systems of these three perspectives. Yet, it is normally the case that ordinary people do not strictly obey teachings of a particular school. The teachings of Confucianism, Daoism, and Buddhism have been valued and have coexisted in Chinese thinking and life. Philosophically, there are differences between these schools of thought, but this could oversimplify and overstate the contrast in between (Hall & Ames, 1998). In daily life, the saints of Confucianism, Daoism, and Buddhism are worshipped and offered incense together in some temples (Ching, 1993; Li, 1999). In Chinese heritage cultural societies (CHCs), 'a person can be a Taoist, Confucian and Buddhist more or less at the same time' (Berthrong, 1994, p. 178). People accept and practice teachings of Confucianism, Daoism, and Buddhism simultaneously and in a complementary way. Li Chengyang (1999, pp. 148–152) calls such a phenomenon 'multiple religious participation'. The 'multiple religious participation' is the basic position that I take to launch the exploration of this book. In Chinese history, many scholars claimed to be Daoist-Buddhist-Confucian.[2]

In normal daily life, in schools in CHCs, people have taken lessons not only from Confucius, Mencius, Laozi, Zhuangzi, and Buddha, but from prestigious Confucian scholars, Daoist practitioners, Buddhist monks, etc. Nowadays, Western religions, thoughts, and cultures have entered CHCs and influenced almost every aspect of life. These global interactions neither simplify nor homogenise, but instead diversify and intensify different modes of life and value systems around the world. There are still distinctions between cultures of the CHCs and the West. Hence, I wish to specify the distinction of CHCs with regard to writing to explore the way Chinese character writing hinges on the deep-seated elements of philosophy in history and to investigate the potential in articulating education in a different way brought about by unique and age-old writing in the postmodern era.

In discussing the ancient classics, I do not intend to refer to the texts with archaeologically proven authorship. Many Chinese classics are compilations of texts over hundreds of years. Every classic, whether the *Daodejing* (or *Laozi*) or the *Zhuangzi*, represents a tradition that a system of thought is formed by the contributions of many, even though there may be incoherence and inconsistencies under philosophical scrutiny. This is just how the classics become a part of culture and life and receive influence in return.

Notes

1 Confucius said, 'There are three things of which the superior man stands in awe. He stands in awe of the ordinances of Heaven. He stands in awe of great men. He stands in awe of the words of sages. The mean man does not know the ordinances of Heaven, and consequently does not stand in awe of them. He is disrespectful to great men. He makes sport of the words of sages' (*Analect, Ji Shi*, 16.8; trans. Legge, 1861).
2 Chengyang Li has given a number of scholars who self-claimed to be Daoist-Buddhist-Confucian. The famous and admired poet Táo Qián (陶潛 365–427 CE) is typical. See Li (1999), pp. 152–156.

References

Abrahamsen, E. (2012, June 6). Chairman Mao, in their own hand. *The New York Times*. Retrieved March 15, 2017, from http://latitude.blogs.nytimes.com/2012/06/06/chairman-mao-in-their-own-hand/?_r=0

Barmé, G. R. (2012). History writ large: Big-character posters, red logorrhea and the art of words. *Journal of Multidisciplinary International Studies, 9*(3), 1–35.

Berthrong, J. (1994). *All under heaven: Transformation paradigms in Confucian-Christian dialogue*. Albany, NY: State University of New York Press.

Ching, J. (1993). *Chinese religions*. Maryknoll, NY: Orbis Books.

Derrida, J. (1976). *Of grammatology*. Trans. G. C. Spivak. Baltimore, MD: John Hopkins University Press.

Derrida, J. (1982). *Margins of philosophy*. Chicago, IL: University of Chicago Press.

Derrida, J. (2001). What is a "relevant" translation? *Critical Inquiry, 27*, 174–200.

Erickson, B. (2001). *The art of Xu Bing: words without meaning, meaning without words*. Washington, DC: Arthur M. Sackler Gallery.

Fenollosa, E., & Pound, E. (1936). *The Chinese written character as a medium for poetry*. San Francisco, CA: City Lights Books.

Gu, M. D. (2000). Reconceptualising the linguistic divide: Chinese and Western theories of the written sign. *Comparative Literature Studies, 37*(2), 101–124.

Hall, L. D., & Ames, T. R. (1998). *Thinking from the Han: self, truth, and transcendence in Chinese and Western culture*. Albany, NY: State University of New York Press.

Jay, M. (1988). The rise of hermeneutics and the crisis of ocularcentrism. *Poetics Today, 9*(2), 307–326.

Jay, M. (1993). *Downcast eyes: The denigration of vision in twentieth-century French thought*. Berkeley, CA: University of California Press.

Jay, M. (2002). Cultural relativism and visual turn. *Journal of Visual Culture, 1*(3), 267–278.

Jiang, X. 江迅 (2006). The irony is not only "making mistakes". 透視：啼笑皆非的不只是"錯誤百出" (**1**), 透視中國, BBC中文網2006年2月22日. Retrieved August 30, 2013, from http://news.bbc.co.uk/chinese/trad/hi/newsid_4730000/newsid_4739500/4739576.stm

Kenner, H. (1971). *The Pound era*. Berkeley, CA: University of California Press.

Legge, J. (Trans.). (1861). *Confucian analects: The Chinese classics, volume 1*. D. Sturgeon (Ed.), *Chinese text project*. Retrieved November 10, 2013, from http://ctext.org/analects www.sacred-texts.com/cfu/conf1.htm

Lewis, M. E. (1999). *Writing and authority in early China*. Albany, NY: State University of New York Press.

Li, C. (1999). *The Tao encounter with the West: Explorations in comparative philosophy*. Albany, NY: State University of New York Press.

McCreery, J. L. (1995). Negotiating with the demons: The use of magical language. *American Ethnologists, 22*(1), 144–164.

Ong, W. (1982). *Orality and literacy: The technologizing of the word*. London, UK: Routledge.

Öztürk, A. S. (2012). The influence of the Chinese ideogram on Ezra Pound's *Cathay*. *Epiphany: Journal of Interdisciplinary Studies, 5*(1), 83–94.

Rorty, R. (1978). Philosophy as a kind of writing: An essay on Derrida. *New Literary History, 10*(1), 141–160.

Chapter I

Thinking education through the spoken and the written word

草木之生, 華葉青葱, 皆有曲折, 象類文章, 謂天為文字, 復為華葉乎?宋人
或刻木為楮葉者, 三年乃成

(論衡, 自然篇)。[1]

Reading maketh a full man; conference a ready man; and writing an exact man!
— *Francis Bacon, Of Studies, Essays,* 1996

Are there differences in thinking and understanding between different languages? What does this difference mean to education? In real life, I experienced a 'cultural shock' related to 'words' when I entered the Western world from a Chinese-speaking society. While it is reckless to infer anything general from personal experiences, what intrigues me is that societies that speak different languages have different ways of dealing with spoken and written languages. This divergence is particularly conspicuous between Western societies and the Chinese-speaking world, or between phonetic language societies and the ideographic language world. Hence, I modified my question thus: what is meant by the difference between Chinese and Western ways of thinking in terms of the relationship between spoken and written language?

Before examining the relationship between speaking and writing, let me first clarify the meaning of the terms 'Western' and 'Chinese'. By using the term 'Western', we run the risk of considering all Western societies uniform; further, the concept of 'Chinese' is even more unclear. Therefore, we can say that these two concepts are rather used in a loose and relative sense. Further, by the term 'Chinese', I refer to Chinese societies as having a history of influence from ancient Chinese culture, especially from the history of using the Chinese language – the logographic or ideographic language. In contrast, the Western way of thinking, concerning language, is characterised by alphabets and phonetic languages. It is certain that the Chinese language is different from Western languages, but I am not interested in how they differ from each other in terms of grammar or syntax. What interests me is a deeper difference that lies

2 Thinking education

in the relationship between speech and writing; in other words, the difference between the spoken word and the written word. This difference ignites the journey of exploration throughout this book.

Voice, logos, and bias

What is the difference between speech and writing? Is writing not a record of speech and speech, in turn, a record of inner thinking expressed aloud? We might answer these questions by considering the views of the Swiss linguist Ferdinand de Saussure (1966). Saussure (1966) considers writing subordinate and external to speech, referring to it as 'unrelated to its inner system' (p. 23). He also asserts that '[l]anguage and writing are two distinct systems of signs; the second exists for the sole purpose of representing the first' (Ibid., p. 23). As for the differentiation between languages, Western languages are considered to belong to the phonetic language system group, whereas Chinese belongs to the logographic system group. Saussure (1966) claims that the world's writing systems can be divided into two types: ideographic and phonetic. He states,

1) In the ideographic system each word is represented by a single sign that is unrelated to the sounds of word itself. Each written sign stands for a whole word and, consequently, for the idea expressed by the word. The classic example of an ideographic system is Chinese.
2) The system commonly known as 'phonetic' tries to reproduce the succession of sounds that make up a word. Phonetic systems are sometimes syllabic, sometimes alphabetic, i.e. based on the irreducible elements used in speaking (Saussure, 1966, pp. 25–26).

Saussure also mentions a quantitative difference in a tendency of Chinese language compared with Western languages:

> The statement that the written word tends to replace the spoken one in our minds is true of both systems of writing, but the tendency is stronger in the ideographic system. To a Chinese, an ideogram and a spoken word are both symbols of an idea; to him, writing is a second language, and if two words that have the same sound are used in conversation, he may resort to writing in order to express his thought.
>
> (Saussure, 1966, p. 26)

Although Saussure claims that Chinese as an ideographic language has a stronger tendency to use the written word than do Western languages, he still takes the written word as subordinate or secondary to the spoken one. This view, wherein speech or voice is prioritised over writing, is what Derrida calls phonocentrism.

Phonocentrism, Derrida (1976, 1978, 1982, 2016) argues, has dominated Western intellectual history. The study of language throughout Western intellectual history devalues writing and considers it an appendage to speech, a mere technique, and even a menace (Spivak, 1976). Western intellectual history, from the ancient pre-Socratic Greeks to contemporary times, is a history of giving 'privilege of sound in idealisation, the production of the concept and the self-presence of the subject' (Derrida, 2016, p. 12). In his many works, Derrida discusses the meaning of phonocentrism (and logocentrism) by examining some key thinkers. At the beginning of *Of Grammatology* (2016), he provides three statements about phonocentrism and its complicities – logocentrism and ethnocentrism. He writes,

1   *the concept of writing* in a world where phoneticisation of writing must dissimulate its own history as it produces itself;
2   *the history of the metaphysics*, which, in spite of all differences, not only from Plato to Hegel (even including Leibniz) but also, beyond their apparent limits, from the pre-Socratics to Heidegger, has always assigned the origin of truth in general to the logos: the history of truth, of the truth of truth, has always been, except for a metaphorical diversion that we shall have to consider, the debasement of writing, and its repression outside 'full' speech.
3   *the concept of science* or the scientificity of science – what has always been determined as *logic* – a concept that has always been a philosophical concept, even if the practice of science has constantly challenged the imperialism of the logos, by invoking, for example, always and ever increasingly, non-phonetic writing (Derrida, 2016, pp. 3–4).

In other words, Western intellectual history is founded on the logos, which is transmitted and communicated primarily through voice, in terms of phonetic expression. Non-phonetic expression is a derivative of phonetic expression and therefore is secondary, auxiliary, and supplementary to it. Furthermore, the trilogy of phono – logo – ethnocentrism determines the meaning of the signifiers and thereby produces distinction and exclusion, hierarchy and violence.

As Derrida reveals, the voice has been perceived as inseparable from the mind/soul/thought/logos in the Western philosophical tradition. Derrida (2016, p. 13) writes: 'What is said of sound in general is a fortiori valid for the *phone* by which, by virtue of hearing – (understanding) – oneself-speak – indissociable system – the subject affects itself and is related to itself in the element of ideality'. The voice is the inner thought, the presence of the cogito, consciousness, subjectivity. Thus, 'all signifiers, and first the written signifier, would be derivative. The written signifier would always be technical and representative' (ibid., p. 12). This line of thought has a history – the tradition of phonocentrism and, simultaneously, logocentrism – that ranges from Plato to Aristotle, Hegel to Husserl, and Rousseau to Saussure. Within this tradition is

4 Thinking education

an 'absolute proximity of voice and being, of voice and the meaning of being, of voice and the ideality of meaning' (ibid., p. 12).

Derrida points out that phono-logocentrism implies an ethnocentrism that prefers a phonetic language system to non-phonetic systems. The non-phonetic system is perceived as a system within which the signs are secondary and backward, immature and inadequate, inaccurate and weak, to express the inner thoughts. Further, non-phonetic signs have the potential to menace and abuse the meaning of the language. In Western intellectual history, Hegel is considered by Derrida as a key contributor to the construction of phono – logo – ethnocentrism. For Hegel, rational thinking and logical thinking are the essence of humanity, distinguishing humankind from beasts. Yet, logical thinking must be communicated through logical language, which is phonetic language:

> Into all that becomes something inwards for man, an image or conception as such, into all that he makes his own, language has penetrated and everything that he has transformed into language and expresses in it contains a category – concealed, mixed with other forms or clearly determined as such, so much is Logic his natural element, indeed his own peculiar nature.
>
> (Hegel, 2001, p. 5)

What distinguishes a human being from an animal is the ability of logical speech. As a result, a fully developed language that can express logical thoughts is fundamental to human existence. A language that possesses many logical expressions, such as prepositions and articles, is good for thought because the abundance of logical expressions can adequately express any thought. For Hegel, Chinese is not a fully developed language because 'the Chinese language is supposed not to have developed to this stage or only to an inadequate extent' (Hegel, 2001, p. 5). Hegel is not the only scholar who views the Chinese language with disdain. The earliest systematic Chinese studies, or sinology, began in the sixteenth century in the West with the Jesuits gaining entrance into China (Zurndorfer, 1995). The Jesuits' studies about China covered a wide range of fields, from geography, history, botany, and medicine, to Confucianism and language. For the Westerners, the Chinese characters were strange and nonsensical at first sight. In 1668, John Wilkins (2002), one of the founders of the Royal Society, writes:

> These Characters are strangely complicated and difficult as to the *Figures* of them . . . Besides the difficulty and perplexedness, of these Characters, there doth not seem to be any kind of Analogy . . . betwixt the shape of the Characters, and the things represented by them, as to the Affinity or Opposition betwixt them, nor any tolerable provision for necessary derivations.
>
> (pp. 450–451)

Seventeenth-century Western scholars viewed Chinese as a set of characters written as incomprehensibly weird figures. In addition, Chinese phonology does not make sense due to its vast arbitrariness. Even a century and a half later, Hegel shows similar scorn towards the Chinese language, describing Chinese as 'imperfection' and lacking 'the objective determinacy that is gained in articulation from alphabetic writing' (Hegel, 1894, p. 243).

As Derrida reveals, the 'Chinese prejudice' (p. 86) is paradoxical. On the one hand, it is shown in the contempt of phonocentrists such as Hegel. On the other, it is expressed in the hyperbolic admirations of some, like Leibniz (1981), who is eager to determine a model of universal script from Chinese because it 'seems to have been "invented by a deaf man" (*New Essays*)' (Derrida, 2016, pp. 85). Indeed, the seemingly contradictory disdain and admiration are both effects of ethnocentrism.

In addition to the 'Chinese prejudice' or the 'European hallucination' that demonstrates ethnocentrism in conspiracy with phonocentrism, another example is found in Derrida's discussion about Leví-Strauss's 'writing lesson'.

In the chapter titled 'A Writing Lesson', Leví-Strauss (1974) describes an interesting story or an 'extraordinary incident' about the anthropologist's meeting and exchange of gifts with natives living in the Amazon – the Nambikwara. As Leví-Strauss (1974) notes, the Nambikwara neither have a written language nor know to draw signs, aside from 'making a few dotted lines or zigzags on their gourds' (p. 296). During his earlier visits, the anthropologist had handed out sheets of paper and pencils to the natives and observed that

> [a]t first they did nothing with them, then one day I saw that they were all busy drawing wavy, horizontal lines. I wondered what they were trying to do and then it was suddenly borne upon me that they were writing, or to be more accurate, were trying to use their pencils in the same way as I did mine.
>
> (Leví-Strauss, 1974, p. 296)

What happened next is of great interest. The chief asked Leví-Strauss for a writing pad. This request and the following performance of the chief showed that, among the Nambikwara people, the chief was 'the only one who had grasped the purpose of writing' (Leví-Strauss, 1974, p. 296). The chief and the anthropologist were working together. This was a very interesting scene in the book. The chief said nothing but presented wavy lines that he drew on the pad and showed to the anthropologist, as if they could read and communicate with each other through 'writing'.

The chief had a certain experience of 'writing' as depicted. Then, in the meeting when the 'extraordinary incident' occurred, the chief was described as doing something more ambitious, because, perhaps, he had his fellow men there.

> . . . he took from a basket a piece of paper covered with wavy lines and made a show of reading it, pretending to hesitate as he checked on it the list of objects I was to give in exchange for the presents offered me.
>
> (Leví-Strauss, 1974, p. 296)

6 Thinking education

This drama sets Leví-Strauss (1974) thinking deeply about the chief's intention: was the chief deluding himself or trying to astonish his companions regarding his role as an intermediary agent or in alliance with the white men and sharing their secrets? After the meeting and the exchange of gifts, Leví-Strauss gained a clearer perspective on writing. Nevertheless, as Derrida deliberates on the Nambikwara episode in 'A Writing Lesson', he argues that Leví-Strauss' view implies a deep-seated phono–logo–ethnocentrism.

First, Leví-Strauss claims that no writing is involved in the Nambikwara language. As a matter of fact, it is. Derrida (2016, p. 133) cites a passage from Leví-Strauss: 'In that they imitated the only use that they had seen us make use of our notebooks, namely writing, but without understanding its end or scope. They called the act of writing *iekariukedjutu*, namely: "making stripes"'. Since the Nambikwara have a name for writing, it means they understand and perceive what writing means. It is an evasion, due to the ethnocentrism, to translate it as 'making stripes' or 'making lines'. Derrida argues that whatever term we use to translate *iekariukedjutu*, e.g., 'to scratch', 'to engrave', 'to claw', 'to scrape', 'to incise', 'to trace', 'to imprint', etc., cannot deny its implication of the signification of writing in Nambikwara language (Derrida, 2016, pp. 133–134).

Derrida then returns to the anecdote regarding the chief and the writing pad. He reiterates and elaborates upon Leví-Strauss's afterthoughts about the 'extraordinary incident' with the comments that each element, each sementeme of the story, 'refers to a recognised function of writing: hierarchisation, the economic function of mediation and of capitalisation, participation in a quasi-religious secret' (Derrida, 2016, pp. 136–137). All these elements are evidence of writing. More important are two significances drawn from the afterthoughts, which verify the arche-writing – the 'very thing that cannot be reduced to the form of *presence*' (p. 61), a language working 'in the form and substance of graphic but also in those of nongraphic expression' (p. 65), 'the movement of the *sign-function* linking a content to an expression, whether it be graphic or not' (p. 65), 'the play of difference' (p. 118), and 'that opens speech itself' (p. 138). First, '[t]he appearance of writing is *instantaneous*. It is not prepared for. Such a leap would prove the possibility of writing does not inhabit speech, but the outside of speech' (p. 137).

Second, Leví-Strauss makes a distinction between the sociological and the intellectual ends of writing. For Derrida (2016), an ultimately profound sense of writing drawn out of this distinction is that 'writing cannot be thought outside of the horizon of intersubjective violence', and therefore nothing, even science, can radically escape it. Yet, as Derrida criticises, Leví-Strauss did not do justice to the Nambikwara act of writing. Nor does he do justice to the writing itself. This is due to the implied ethnocentrism presumed by Leví-Strauss.

Derrida's discussion on the Chinese prejudice and the writing lesson demonstrate the conspiracy of phonocentrism, logocentrism, and ethnocentrism that has dominated Western metaphysics. For non-phonetic language users, what can we learn from or respond to the critique? Returning to the original question, if thinking in different languages – phonetic and non-phonetic, or phonetic and ideographic languages – makes a difference, what does the difference mean? Following Derrida's critique that phonocentrism, logocentrism, and ethnocentrism inseparably conspire, and that phono–logo–ethnocentrism is typically Western, what can we find in a different field, where the language used is not phonetic and the language is more ocularcentric than phonocentric (e.g., Chinese-speaking societies)? Can we find a way out of this trap set by the trilogy: phono–logo–ethnocentrism? Or, what profundity is revealed in terms of the tradition and culture from the perspective of non-phonetic language as contrasted with phonetic language?

Writing/word matters

Can we find a way out of the trap deployed by the collusion of phonocentrism, logocentrism, and ethnocentrism by means of thinking in non-phonetic language? Before seeking the answer, let me clarify something specific and interesting about the word *word* in Chinese and its implications for education.

The preceding discussion focuses on speaking and writing, or the related objects: the spoken word and the written word. The word *word* in English indicates both the spoken word and the written word. In Chinese, the spoken word is 言 (yán) or 話 (hùa), whereas the written word is 字 (zì) or 文字 (wénzì). As we look more closely, we understand that in ancient Chinese, the spoken word is 言 (yán), and the written word is 文 (wén). In modern times, 話 (hùa) is more often used for the spoken word, while 字 (zì) is used for the written word. According to the first Chinese character dictionary, *Shuowén Jiĕzì*, 話 (hùa) means 'to be good at speaking' (善言) (Xŭ, n.d.). As for the two-character word 文字 (wénzì), its origin etymologically implies a rich visual sense. As written in the *Shuowén Jiĕzì*,

> Tsang Chíeh at the beginning of the invention of *writing* depicts according to the natural figures and so the 'vein' or 'venation' (wén) is grasped. Then forms and sounds are added to the figures to make 'words' (字 zì). The vein is the basis of realistic depiction; the word (字 zì) is named as it is generated (孳 zi) [from proliferating veins or venation]. Writing on bamboos or silk is named 'script' (shu). 'Script' (shu) means [to script] whatever as it is.
>
> (*Shuowén jiĕzì*, preface 1:2; my translation)[2]

The original written word is 文, meaning stripes, lines, patterns, or threads, which can be found in the natural environment. With the progression of time, the number of written words is increasing. At a certain point in the past, the written word 字 (zì) was formed by borrowing the word 'increase' (孳 zi). The etymology of the written word 文字 interestingly displays the close relationship

8 Thinking education

between Chinese character and vision. Derrida is also aware of this point. He cites from the French sinologist Jacques Gernet:

> The word *wén* signifies a conglomeration of marks, the simple character of writing. It applies to the veins in stones and wood, to constellations, represented by the strokes connecting to the stars, to the tracks of birds and quadrupeds on the ground (Chinese tradition would have it that the observation of these tracks suggested the invention of writing), to tattoo and even, for example, to the designs that decorates the turtle's shell.
>
> (cited from Derrida, 2016, p. 134)

Drawing on Gernet, Derrida casts doubt on the phonocentric assumption that speaking precedes writing. Furthermore, writing is the mediator not of voice but of sight. This might provide us with a clue towards thinking of writing and speaking in terms of education.

Unlike speaking, writing as a state of being literate is highly educational. To recognise, read, and write the word, one must go through a process of institutionalisation. 'The process of putting spoken language into writing is governed by consciously contrived, articulable rules' (Ong, 1982, p. 81). Learning to write takes effort. It is an intentional, conscious, and strenuous task. In contrast, learning to speak, the mother tongue in particular, is natural and spontaneous. 'Oral speech is fully natural to human beings in the sense that every human being in every culture who is not physiologically or psychologically impaired learns to talk' (Ong, 1982, p. 81). The situation of being illiterate means that one is able to speak a language but is unable to read and write it. Sometimes, the opposite situation occurs: one is able to read and write a language but is unable to speak it. In the former case, one can speak but not read or write a language for a particular reason – for example, where immigrants or the underclass have not received proper formal education and are illiterate. They learn the spoken language in a natural and spontaneous way but can neither read nor write. In the latter case, people who can read and write one language but not speak it must have learnt the language on purpose, through a designed and planned process, i.e., education. This situation can be found in second-language learners who are not confident about their ability to pronounce correctly or address in sound grammatical constructions; thus, they avoid speaking in this second language. It is noted that writing is an epoch-making technology (Coulmas, 1996, 2003; McLuhan, 1962; Ong, 1967, 1982). The so-called literate and non-literate cultures are distinguished by the presence (or lack thereof) of visual linguistic signs, i.e., written scripts. Therefore, the issue of writing as well as the written word are fundamental to education. Learning to write and recognise written words can be viewed as the core focus of education in any civilisation. For literate cultures, the process of mastering writing is a cardinal part of the education process. Moreover, what distinguishes writing educationally from speaking is its relationship with study (Ong, 1982). For a study to be conducted, there must be something that can be cultivated, analysed, examined, and investigated in detail, i.e., written words or written texts. The spoken word alone cannot sustain study because 'after the speech was delivered, nothing of it remained to work over' (Ong, 1982, p. 9). Overall, the concept of writing is essentially educational. The ability to write is central to the whole task of education. The cultivation of a writing subject – one who is able to write – is the goal of educational task.

The written word as the human artefact varies across cultures and incorporates large parts of cultural particularities from each civilisation, from the invention and formation of the word, to the institutionalisation and the code of writing, to the style and formality of writing, etc. Writing enables and, in turn, is enabled by education. Communication and translation between different language systems generate new meanings because words, phrases, and terms that have never appeared in one culture must be presented in another. Among the languages with written systems, Chinese characters could be some of the most difficult to learn to write. In comparison with Western languages, the Chinese language system requires visual orientation for using ideographic signs. In this view, it is fascinating to explore the relationship between the visually oriented Chinese writing and the Chinese way of thinking, as doing so will surely illuminate our understanding of education in Chinese-speaking societies.

As mentioned, writing is the cultural artefact and is incorporated as part of education. The Chinese language is very different from most of the world's phonetic language systems with respect to the features of written words and empirical phenomena within the lifeworld. First, the Chinese spoken system uses monosyllabic words, and the written sign is the character. In the case of Western languages, the spoken systems are mainly phonetic, and the writing systems are alphabetic. The recognition of a word consists of pronouncing it according to the corresponding alphabet. It is possible for one to pronounce a word without knowing its meaning. People who have learned phonics can pronounce words without knowing what the words refer to. Having phonic knowledge about the relationship between the sounds and the spelling patterns representing the sounds enables one to read, but not to understand, an unfamiliar word. In contrast, the use of Chinese characters heavily relies on visual ability since characters originating from pictograms are ideograms. It is barely possible to pronounce an unknown Chinese word, let alone perceive its meaning. The Chinese written system imports much more visual dependence than Western systems. We may conclude that vocality is to phonetic languages as visuality is to Chinese. Thus, similarly, phonocentrism is to Western thinking as ocularcentrism is to Chinese.

In a debate on the Chinese visual written word in eighteenth-century Europe, Hegel debases Chinese language and philosophy. Hegel scorns the Chinese language and describes Chinese as 'imperfection' and as lacking 'the objective determinancy that is gained in articulation from alphabetic writing' (Hegel, 1894, p. 243). For Hegel, a language that possesses many logical expressions, such as prepositions and articles, is good for thought because the abundance of

10 Thinking education

logical expressions can express thought adequately. Compared with the German language, 'the Chinese language is supposed not to have developed to this stage or only to an inadequate extent' (Hegel, 2001, p. 5). In contrast, Leibniz (1981, p. 290) highly praises Chinese characters simply because they are capable of 'speaking to the eyes', a powerful description that shows the value of vision-dependence.

The signification of the word 'word' in Chinese has nuances not present in Western languages. The term 'word' in ordinary linguistic usage – both in Chinese and in English – is a single unit of language that has meaning and can be used to refer to either a spoken or a written word. The perplexing distinction is that in English the 'word' lays stress on the 'spoken word', whereas Chinese emphasises the 'written word'. For example, in his discussion on the signification of words, John Locke (1975) makes the point that thoughts and ideas are in the human mind, 'invisible, and hidden from others' (p. 405). Internal ideas are made external and apparent to others by sounds as words. A human being is, by nature, able to use his or her mouth to frame articulate sounds – 'which we call Words' (Ibid., p. 402). Locke (1975, p. 405) says that '[t]he use . . . of Words, is to be sensible Marks of *Ideas*; and the *Ideas* they stand for, are their proper and immediate Signification'. Locke continues to say,

> *Words in their primary or immediate Signification, stand for nothing, but the* Ideas *in the Mind of him that uses them*, however imperfectly soever, or carelessly those *Ideas* are collected from the Things which they are supposed to represent.
>
> (1975, p. 405)

One articulates words to express one's ideas and thoughts to another – the hearer – by sounds. The word is the auditory and audible mark – the spoken word. What differentiates the word from the noise lies in the 'constant connexion between the Sound and the *Idea*' (Locke, 1975, p. 408). A meaningful sound is a word, whereas a meaningless sound is simply a noise. Locke does not mention writing at all. We may assume this is because writing, in Locke's view, is nothing but the visual mark, the secondary sign of recording of the sound. Locke discusses imperfection and abuse of words. However, he focuses on the relationship between sounds and ideas rather than on that between speech and writing. It is obvious that the word as a signifier stands more for the spoken word than for the written word. Western intellectual history places obvious importance on the spoken word over the written word.

The Western mentality of the word as the spoken word is also manifest in many other philosophers' thoughts. The French philosopher and sociologist Jacques Ellul, in his *The Humiliation of the Words* (1985), shows his angst about visual reality superseding words (which are verbal) with the aid of modern technology. Ellul agrees that the human experience includes the universe of the word (hearing) and the universe of the image (seeing), both of which are related. The relationship between seeing and hearing should not be severed because these two senses are parts of the human existence. Nevertheless, he insists to 'side with the entire current thought that makes *spoken* language the basis of human specificity' (Ellul, 1985, p. 3). In his view, human spoken language transcends the written language: 'Human spoken language is characterised precisely by these elements we have mentioned: overflowing of limits, going beyond, and destructuring what can be conveyed in tactile and visual language' (Ibid., p. 3). There is one decisive reason for Ellul to assert the superiority of spoken language over written language: written language is a set of collections of visible signs that stabilise meanings, whereas human spoken language cannot be reduced to the coherent collection of signs. The meaning of spoken language is ambiguous and shifting. Hungarian critic Aron Kibédi Varga's (1989) assertion may be taken as a provisional conclusion: the word was assumed to belong to the mere domain of being heard. Since writing was invented, the word has been assigned to the additional domain of being seen. Overall, the term 'word' in Western language indicates both the spoken word and the written word. More often, though, 'word' stands for the spoken word.

In contrast, in Chinese, 'word' gives a direct hint of the written word. 'Word' is generally translated as 字 (zì). In Chinese, a literate – a person able to read and write – is translated as '識字者' (shìh zì zhě), meaning one who recognises words. Yet, an illiterate person can speak well, using a lot of words in one's speech without knowing how to write. The 'word' (字) in the Chinese context is closely related with visual recognition.[3] But those who cannot read and write do speak. In Chinese, the ability to speak is not to have words but to address utterance (說話, shuo huà). In English, the 'word' indicates both spoken and written words, whereas in Chinese, 字 (zì, word) indicates the written word and 話 (hùa, utterance or speech) the spoken word. Thus, the term 'word' (zì) in Chinese connotes the visual aspect rather than the aural. This is a subtle difference in the use of 'word' between Chinese and Western ways of thinking. Again, it vindicates the trend of ocularcentrism in the Chinese language system.

In addition to being found in Chinese culture and social life, the ocularcentric tendency is gaining support in brain research. Abundant research in neurolinguistics strongly supports the idea that Chinese characters are processed as graphics and are thereby vision dependent (Gu, 2000; Hansen, 1993; Koyama, Hansen & Stein, 2008; Sasanuma, 1974, 1975; Sasanuma & Fujimura, 1971, 1972). Japanese language has two different types of characters: kanji (ideograms) and kanas (phonograms). Neurologists discovered that one Japanese aphasic patient shows different abilities in writing or reading kanji and kanas. This difference indicates that ideographic words and phonographic words are processed in different areas of the human brain.[4] I do not mean to propose that biological determinism further fortifies cultural determinism. Neurological studies have shown that the human brain is not a physiologically static organ but is the centre of the nerve system with neuroplasticity. The neurolinguistic research reveals that different language systems may represent different modes of operation of linguistic behaviours that are activated and controlled by different parts of the brain.

12 Thinking education

If we examine ancient Chinese texts, we will discover that the ancients regarded the written word and writing with great respect. According to the oldest Chinese dictionary, *Shuowén Jiezì* (說文解字, by Xū Shèn, 許慎 58–147 CE), the word plays a tremendously significant role in politics, ethics, education, and metaphysics:

> The overall written language (wén zì, word) is the foundation of classics and arts and the initiation of sovereignty of kingdom. It is what the former generations relied on to transmit culture to later ages. Men of later times will rely on it to understand antiquity. Therefore, it is said, 'The upholding of the foundation generates the foremost principle'.
>
> (*Shuowén Jiezì, preface* 1:13; trans. Connery, 1998, p. 39; my modification)[5]

According to Xū Shèn, writing is highly regarded, both as the source of principal truth and as the basis for developing and passing canons and doctrines to later generations. The canons and doctrines have been connected with the justification of political authority. In addition, the statement 'The upholding of the foundation generates the foremost principle' means that the establishment of script is necessary for bringing forth the truth. The script is taken as the most fundamental to worldly affairs. The practices are executed within the limits of script, or word. This is an apparent truth that has been confirmed by the wordaholic phenomenon. As the way of acting and doing is de facto regulated by the script, will the way of thinking, the way of philosophising, be bound to the script? To what extent, and in what sense, is the way of thinking bound to the word? The written word is a reservoir that holds the legacy and unique characteristics of culture. As the Chinese written word may be one of the most unique and original signs,[6] the inquiry into written characters could reveal some of the particularities that indicate the 'Chinese' way of thinking.

Two characteristics that can be derived from the wordaholic scenarios mentioned previously are visual primacy and written words (characters) orientation. These characteristics distinguish Chinese ocularcentrism from Western visual cultures in that the visible written words dominate the Chinese eye, while linguistic or conceptual metaphors – such as 'the light of truth', 'darkness as innocence', or 'the enlightenment' – are likely to be the focus of Western visual culture.[7] It seems that Chinese ocularcentrism aims at concrete objects, whereas Western ocularcentrism targets abstract concepts. In Western and Chinese cultures are different versions of ocularcentrism with different preferences. I do not mean that there is no metaphor related to vision in Chinese language or philosophy. Nor do I assert that Western visual culture is all about metaphors, as some critics (Ellul, 1985; Ong, 1982) have asserted. Modern technologies do play an important role in visual culture. What I argue is that Chinese ocularcentrism has a relatively stronger inclination to emphasise concrete objects, especially the written word, than does Western ocularcentrism. There are visual metaphors and rhetoric in Chinese language. The epistemic view of ocularcentrism and orientation with the written word is coined 'the Chinese graphocentrism'.

Thinking education 13

Notes

1 'When plants and trees grow, their flowers and leaves are onion green and have crooked and broken veins like ornaments. If Heaven is credited with having written the above mentioned characters, does it make these flowers and leaves also? In the State of Song a man carved a mulberry-leaf of wood, and it took him three years to complete it' (*Lùnhéng*, 54; trans. Forke, 1907).

2 倉頡之初作書，蓋依類象形，故謂之文。其後形聲相益，即謂之字。文者，物象之本；字者，言孳乳而寖多也。著於竹帛謂之書。書者，如也。(說文解字卷一序1:2)

3 The 'word' here is understood in the current context of ordinary language usage, not in the etymological context. In ordinary language, the one-character word zì (字) and the two-character word wén zì (文字) are interchangeable, both referring to 'word'. Yet from the perspectives of etymology and lexicography, wen and zi may indicate two slightly different scripts. Wen means the form of writing without the mediation of sound; zi may indicate the form of writing with consideration of sound. See Bottéro, F. (2002). Revisiting the Wén 文 and the Zì 字: The great Chinese character hoax. *Bulletin of the Museum of Far Eastern Antiquities, 74*, 14–33. Nowadays, the word wén is more often used to refer to a piece of literary composition, e.g., an essay or a treatise. Moreover, the Southern Sòng Dynasty (1127–1279 CE) scholar Dài Tóng (戴侗) makes a comparison between míng (名) and zì (字) in terms of the aural/visual contrast in his *Liushugu* (六書故), which shows the visual orientation of zi. See Jane Geaney (2010) Grounding 'language' in the senses: What the eyes and ears reveal about míng 名 (names) in early Chinese texts. *Philosophy East & West, 60*(2), 251–293.

4 In a case report, Sasanuma (1974) describes that a patient who exhibited the syndrome of alexia with transient agraphia caused by a cerebrovascular accident showed different strategies in reading and writing Japanese kana (syllabic symbols) and kanji (ideographic symbols). In the case of the kanji system, the patient used the strategy of a direct graphic-meaning association. In the case of the kana system, he used an indirect graph-meaning association. The finding indicates that 'the process of *kana* and *kanji* represents distinctively different modes of operations of linguistic behaviour' (p. 96).

5 蓋文字者，經藝之本，王政之始。前人所以垂後，後人所以識古。故曰：「本立而道生。」(說文解字卷一序:13).

6 As William G. Boltz (2001, p. 1) points out, in human history, writing was invented *ex nihilo* four times, and only four times: in Egypt, in Mesopotamia, in Mesoamerica, and in China. See Boltz, W. G. (2001). The invention of writing in China. *Oriens Extremis, 42*, 1–17.

7 In Western intellectual history, there has been a long-term dispute between discourse privileging sight and discourse in favour of voice. From this perspective (when the reference is a language other than Chinese), Western thought can be seen as visually oriented. According to scholars such as Dewey (1960), Jay (1988, 1993, 2002) and Kavanagh (2004), European philosophy since Plato has been strongly dominated by the visual paradigm – or in Dewey's words, 'the spectator theory of knowledge'. Plato's well-known cave allegory imports the value of the ideas of light, sight, and vision (Irigaray, 1985; Nye, 1993). The sun, the light, is described as the absolute truth and intellect although it can only be seen by reason – the eyes of the soul or the eyes of the mind – but not by eyes as organs – the eyes on the head (Kavanagh, 2004). After centuries, Descartes and the Enlightenment thinkers use a lot of models and precepts based on vision such as 'objectivism, reflection, critical rationality and subjectivism' (Kavanagh, 2004, p. 448). According to Kavanagh (2004), the philosophy of this group is underpinned by a certain 'spectatorial epistemology'. Yet, since the time of Bergson, there has been an intellectual trend against privilege of sight and for vocal primacy, which can be seen as the 'linguistic turn'. A number of philosophers, linguists, and theorists in many different fields, such as hermeneutics, critical theory, literary criticism, postmodernism, structuralism, etc., who have turned against Cartesianism and Enlightenment thought, take the position of safeguarding the primacy of orality (Jay, 1988; Kavanagh, 2004). The notion of privileging sight has been criticised

14 Thinking education

as 'fetish or idol Western culture' (Jay, 2002; Mitchell, 1987). As Arendt (1978, p. 122) states, 'Since Bergson, the use of the sight metaphor in philosophy has kept dwindling, not surprisingly, as emphasis and interest have shifted entirely from contemplation to speech, from nous to logos'. An echo of the vocal primacy in the field of educational research can be found from a lot of works pleading for 'voice' and 'discourse'. Many works of educational research have been published with voice-derivative words in their titles, such as discourse, dialogue, conversation, narrative, communication, and so on in recent decades. Nevertheless, the appeal for speaking and the using of sound metaphors is a reaction to the visual paradigm, which can be seen as an association with phonocentrism. I am not aiming to solve the debate between visual and voice orientations with this book. The point in the contrast between phonocentrism and ocularcentrism in the Western intellectual world is that the opposition between vision priority and voice primacy is in relation to the contrast between writing and speaking, because 'writing is largely a visual exercise, in contrast to speaking, which is centered on the sense of hearing' (Kavanagh, 2004, p. 449).

References

Arendt, H. (1978). *The life of the mind*. New York, NY: Harcourt brace Jovanovich.

Bacon, F. (1996). *Essays: The essays or counsels, civil and moral, of Francis Ld.* Verulam Viscount St. Albans. Project Gutenberg. Retrieved March 14, 2017, from www.gutenberg.org/files/575/575.txt

Boltz, W. G. (2001). The invention of writing in China. *Oriens Extremis, 42*, 1–17.

Bottéro, F. (2002). Revisting the wén 文 and the zì 字: The great Chinese character hoax. *Bulletin of the Museum of Far Eastern Antiquities, 74*, 14–33.

Connery, C. L. (1998). *The empire of the text: Writing and authority in early imperial China*. Lanham, MD: Rowman & Littlefield Publishers.

Coulmas, F. (1996). *The Blackwell encyclopaedia of writing systems*. Oxford, UK: Blackwell.

Coulmas, F. (2003). *Writing systems: An introduction to their linguistic analysis*. Cambridge, UK: Cambridge University Press.

Derrida, J. (1976). *Of grammatology*. Trans. G. C. Spivak. Baltimore, MD: John Hopkins University Press.

Derrida, J. (1978). *Writing and difference*. Chicago, IL: University of Chicago Press.

Derrida, J. (1982). *Margins of philosophy*. Chicago, IL: University of Chicago Press.

Derrida, J. (2016). *Of grammatology*. Trans. G. C. Spivak. Introduction by Judith Butler. Baltimore, MD: John Hopkins University Press.

Dewey, J. (1960). *The quest for certainty* (Gifford Lectures, 1929). New York, NY: Putnam.

Ellul, J. (1985). *The humiliation of the word*. Grand Rapids, MI: William. B. Eerdmans Publishing.

Forke, A. (Trans.). (1907). *Lun-heng*. London, UK: LUZAC & Co. Retrieved March 29, 2017, from: https://archive.org/stream/lunheng01wang#page/n0/mode/2up

Gu, M. D. (2000). Reconceptualising the linguistic divide: Chinese and Western theories of the written sign. *Comparative literature studies, 37*(2), 101–124.

Geaney, J. (2010). Grounding language in the sense: What the eyes and ears reveal about ming 名 (names) in early Chinese texts. *Philosophy East & West, 60*(2), 251–293.

Hansen, C. (1993). Chinese ideographs and Western ideas. *The Journal of Asian Studies, 52*(2), 373–399.

Hegel, G. W. F. (1894). *Hegel's philosophy of mind. A revised version of the Wallace and Miller*. Oxford: Clarendon Press: Project Gutenberg. Retrieved March 29, 2017, from www.gutenberg.org/files/39064/39064-h/39064-h.html

Hegel, G. W. F. (2001). *Science of logic*. Hegel.net. Retrieved March 29, 2017, from www.hegel.net/en/pdf/Hegel-Scilogic.pdf

Hegel, G. W. F. (2001). *Science of logic*. Hegel.net. Retrieved March 29, 2017, from www.hegel.net/en/pdf/Hegel-Scilogic.pdf

Irigaray, L. (1985). *Speculum of the other woman*. Ithaca, NY: Cornell University Press.

Jay, M. (1988). The rise of hermeneutics and the crisis of ocularcentrism. *Poetics Today, 9*(2), 307–326.

Jay, M. (1993) *Downcast eyes: The denigration of vision in twentieth-century French thought*. Berkeley, CA.: University of California Press.

Jay, M. (2002). Cultural relativism and visual turn. *Journal of Visual culture, 1*(3), 267–278.

Kavanagh, D. (2004). Ocularcentrism and its others: A framework for metatheoretical analysis. *Organization Studies, 25*(3), 445–464.

Kibédi Varga, A. (1989). Criteria for describing word-and-image relations. *Poetic Today, 10*(1), 31–53.

Koyama, M. S., Hansen, P. C., & Stein, J. F. (2008). Logographic Kanji versus phonographic Kana in literacy acquisition. *Annals of the New York Academy of Sciences, 1145*(1), 41–55.

Leibniz, G. W. (1981). *New essays on human understanding*. Ed. by P. Remnant & J. Bennett. Cambridge, UK: Cambridge University Press.

Levi-Strauss, C. (1974). *Tristes Tropiques*. Trans. J. Weightman and D. Weightman. New York, NY: Atheneum.

Locke, J. (1975). *An essay concerning human understanding*. Oxford, UK: Oxford University Press.

McLuhan, M. (1962). *The Gutenberg galaxy: The making of typographic man*. London, UK: Routledge & Kegan Paul.

Mitchell, W. J. T. (1987). Nature and convention: Gombrich's illusions. In *Iconology: Image, text, ideology* (pp. 75–94), Chicago, IL: University of Chicago Press.

Nye, A. (1993). Assisting at the birth and death of philosophic vision. In D. M. Levin (Ed.), *Modernity and the hegemony of vision* (pp. 361–378). Berkeley, CA: University of California Press.

Ong, W. (1967). *The presence of the word: Some prolegomena for cultural and religious history*. New Haven, CT: Yale University Press.

Ong, W. (1982). *Orality and literacy: The technologizing of the word*. London, UK: Routledge.

Sasanuma, S. (1974). Kanji versus kana processing in alexia with transient agraphia: A case report. *Cortex, 10*(1), 89–97.

Sasanuma, S. (1975). Kana and kanji processing in Japanese aphasics. *Brain and Language, 2*(3), 369–383.

Sasanuma, S., & Fujimura, O. (1971). Selective impairment of processing phonetic and non-phonetic transcriptions of words of aphasic patients: Kana and Kanji in visual recognition and writing. *Cortex, 7*(1), 1–18.

Sasanuma, S., & Fujimura, O. (1972). An analysis of writing errors in Japanese aphasic patients: Kanji versus kana words. *Cortex, 8*(3), 265–282.

Saussure, F. de. (1966). *Course in general linguistics*. New York, NY: McGraw-Hill Book Co.

Spivak, G. C. (1976). Translator's preface. In J. Derrida, *Of grammatology* (pp. ix–xc). Baltimore, MD: John Hopkins University Press.

Wilkins, J. (2002). *An essay towards a real character, and a philosophical language*. Bristol, UK: Thoemmes Press.

Xū, S. 許慎 (n.d.) *Shuowén Jiězì*. 說文解字. Retrieved March 29, 2017, from D.Sturgeon (Ed.), *Chinese text project*. http://ctext.org/shuo-wen-jie-zi

Zurndorfer, H. T. (1995). *China bibliography: A research guide to reference works about China past and present* (Vol. 10). Leiden, The Netherlands: Brill.

Chapter 2

Chinese graphocentrism
A search through texts

《書》曰：「紳之束之。」宋人有治者, 因重帶自紳束也。人曰：「是何也?」對曰：「書言之, 固然。」

—(韓非子外儲左上, 32:45)[1]

To name, to give name, to five names that it will possibly be forbidden to pronounce, such is the originary violence of the language [*langage*] which consists in inscribing within a difference, in classifying, in suspending the vocative absolute.
—(Derrida, 2016, p. 121)

In the previous chapter, I identified the wordaholic phenomena prevalent in Chinese heritage cultural societies. Chinese societies tend to be obsessed with words, particularly the written word. What makes the Chinese mind prefer written words rather than voice and compliance with what these written words command? What creates the mindset that prioritises writing over speaking? I do not intend to perform genealogical or archaeological studies to specify the origin of Chinese graphocentrism. Graphocentrism is a widely influential but rarely noticed tendency affecting the Chinese way of life and thought. It would be difficult to identify a specific factor or factors that determine the direction of culture or history. My aim is to look for general ideas in relation to wordaholic symptoms by means of theoretical exploration. As one of the world's most enduring cultures, and through its use of a non-phonetic language system, Chinese culture contributes many elements, practices, and conceptions to graphocentrism, and vice versa. The conceptual sources for nurturing graphocentrism are hidden in the classics. I will examine two types of texts: those concerning the legends of origin of writing and those concerning the uses of writing.

According to the texts of the legends, writing is generated from imitation of nature. Paradoxically and interestingly, as documented, writing has the power to control nature and the supernatural world. The legends concerning the invention of writing lay the groundwork for the graphocentric worldview. Literature that focuses on the uses of writing further reinforces the graphocentric worldview. Inquiry into Chinese classical texts will reveal one significant idea of graphocentrism: the distrust and debasement of spoken language and the admiration of writing. Although I cannot be certain of the specific time and place that writing gained its authority through history and the regime of writing was built (Connery, 1998), I will argue first that graphocentrism was already imminent in the Chinese worldview, way of thinking, and education and, second, that graphocentrism provides a powerful lens to re-examine the Chinese worldview.

The rise of writing and the dismissal of speech

According to philological and archaeological research, the earliest writing known in China dates to about 1200–1050 BCE (Boltz, 1986, 2001). Yet ancient Chinese scholars throughout history have their own stories about writing. The Chinese written word was, according to many ancient literary texts such as *Húinánzǐ* (淮南子 by Liu An 劉安 179–122 BCE), *ShuowénJiězì* (說文解字), *Lùnhéng* (or *Critical Essays* 論衡 by Wáng Chong王充 27–91 CE), and *Yìwén-Lèijù* (or *Collection of Literature Arranged by Categories* 藝文類聚 Tang Dynasty, 624 CE), invented by a legendary figure, Cang Jié or Tsang Chíeh (倉頡), who was described as an official historian of the Yellow Emperor (黃帝) some 5,000 years ago (Bottéro, 2006; Kane, 2006). In the legendary account of the origin of Chinese script, the invention imitates the 'pattern of the traces left by birds and animals on the ground or by natural phenomena' (Zhang, 1985, pp. 395–396). The invention of scripts is also a starting event in the world:

> In ancient times, when Cang Jíe invented writing, Heaven rained down millet and ghosts wailed at night ... The more that knowledge increased, the less concern was shown for inner virtues.
>
> (*Húainánzǐ, BěnJinXùn* 8:4; cited from Bottéro, 2006, p. 140)[2]

According to the text, heaven and ghosts are worried by the invention of writing because it develops knowledge and, at the same time, has inner virtues less attended. However, the statement is vague. What do the concepts of knowledge and inner virtue mean? Moreover, the term 能 is translated as 'knowledge'. Indeed, the noun 能 in Chinese can be used to refer to 'ability', 'capability', 'strength', and 'craftiness'. Less concern shown for the relationship between increasing knowledge (or ability or craftiness) and inner virtue in the former case could be different from that in the former. In my view, the quotation above transmits a crucial message: knowledge, ability, or craftiness corrupts virtue. Various interpretations have been proposed to explain why the appearance of writing in the human world frightened ghosts and heaven. Gao Yòu (高誘), a

18 Chinese graphocentrism

critic of the Eastern Han Dynasty (25–220 CE), made the following commentary on *Húinánzǐ*:

> Ts'ang Chíeh, upon observing the patterns to the tracks of birds, invented written documents, whereupon deceit and artifice sprouted forth. Once deceit and artifice sprouted forth, people ignored the basics and busied themselves with the peripheral. They gave up the occupation of farming and turned their attention instead to the gains from awl and blade. Heaven knew of their impending hunger, and so made it 'rain millet' for them. Ghosts feared they would be impeached by written records, so they 'wailed in the night'.
>
> (Gao, 1965; trans. by Boltz, 1994, p. 132)[3]

According to Gao Yòu, writing and written records produce knowledge that brings forth further deceit and artifice. Deceit is the act and practice of concealment and distortion of the truth for the purpose of misleading. Artifice means the clever or cunning devices or expedients used to mislead or deceive people. In this vein, writing leads not to truth but to untruthfulness. It can be found in Gao Yòu, a Daoist reproach, that the manmade corrupts truthfulness and morality. In addition, supernatural beings have two different reactions to the invention of writing. One is to feel regret for the sake of humans. The heaven is concerned that human beings will concentrate too much on artifice and will ignore the 'basics', such as farming for livelihood. Therefore, the heaven rained down grains of millet for feed. Conversely, the ghosts are concerned about themselves. Writing has the power to 'impeach' the ghosts. We can find an explanation of the power of impeachment of writing in the works of later scholars.

The Táng dynasty (618–907 CE) painter and theorist Chang Yèn-Yuǎn (張彥遠) asserts that writing reveals the secrets of the supernatural and the demons could never hide from the human world. In the chapter 'On the Origin of Painting' of the book *A Record of Famous Paintings of the History*, Chang (n.d.) writes:

> By imitating the footprints of birds and of tortoises, [Tsang Chíeh, or Cang Jíe] determined the forms of the written characters. Then creation could no longer hide its secrets, and therefore showers of grain fell from the sky: supernatural beings could no longer conceal their presence, therefore the demons howled at night.
>
> (Chang, n.d.; my translation)[4]

It has been a firm belief in the magical power of writing through the history. On the one hand, writing reveals the hidden secrets of creation, of the universe, and of nature and makes visible the invisible beings. On the other, it is the 'magical' tool to 'demystify' or 'disenchant' the world. The belief in the magical powers of writing is not a simple superstition but implies a collusion by many power-holders – the violence of arche-writing – in terms of Derrida. As Derrida (1976) discusses, a very interesting example can be found in Lévi-Strauss's (1974) masterpiece *Tristes Tropiques*.

Lévi-Strauss (1974) has described stories about the Nambikwara – an indigenous people living in the Amazon – who have no written language. One such description recounts the moment when the visitors and the Nambikwara tribal people met and exchanged gifts – an 'extraordinary incident' happened (Derrida, 2016, p. 132). The chief 'took from a basket a piece of paper covered with wavy lines and made a show of reading it, pretending to hesitate as he checked on it the list of objects I was to give in exchange for the presents offered me . . . acting as an intermediary agent for the exchange of the goods' (p. 296). Without knowing about the written words, the chief mimics writing, pretends that he knows how and what to write. The acting shows that, even though the chief does not comprehend the word itself, he grasps the 'profoundly enslaving function' of writing, which is a political manipulation (Derrida, 2016). There is much more to be explored concerning the 'writing lesson', which I will suspend for now and return to later. However, this episode shows the profound intrigue of writing – be it a function, a technique, an ability, or a power – not only to the Chinese, but to humankind.

In the Chinese mind, writing was esteemed with great value and honour, whereas spoken language was regarded as of little value. 'The less one speaks, the better morality one has' has almost become a firm ethical code in Confucianism. More than once, Confucius advises his pupils to hold their tongues.

> The Master said, 'The superior man wishes to be slow in his speech and earnest in his conduct'.
>
> > (*Analects, Lǐ Rén* 4:24; trans. Legge, 1861a)[5]

> Si Ma Niu asked about perfect virtue. The Master said, 'The man of perfect virtue is cautious and slow in his speech'. 'Cautious and slow in his speech!' said Niu, 'Is this what is meant by perfect virtue?' The Master said, 'When a man feels the difficulty of doing, can he be other than cautious and slow in speaking?'
>
> > (*Analects, Yán Yuan* 12:3; trans. Legge, 1861a)[6]

The virtue that Confucius values is to speak cautiously and, more importantly, to let action speak louder than words. The classic Confucian thinkers endorse discretion and prudence in word and deed. Furthermore, glib talk is devalued in relation to deficiency of rén – the comprehensive virtue highly regarded in Confucianism. Verbal eloquence is not a necessary virtue to be a Confucian junzǐ (君子, meaning noble person or gentleman or superior man) – the moral exemplar. Mencius (372–289 BCE), the most famous interpreter of Confucius's

20 Chinese graphocentrism

doctrines, also says, 'Words which are simple, while their meaning is far-reaching, are good words' (*Mencius, Jìn Xīn* 7B:78; trans. Legge, 1985).[7] I agree that simple words can convey truly significant meanings. Yet the ancient philosophers' view about simple utterance is partially taken and interpreted as inarticulateness and quietness. Meanwhile, eloquence and articulacy are equated to glib talk. The discouragement of verbal eloquence may be valorised into mistrust. That is why Confucius considers that one who is good at glib talk is short of rén and is therefore untrustworthy.

> The Master said, 'Fine words and an insinuating appearance are seldom associated with true virtue [rén]'.
> (*Analects, Xùe Eŕ 1*:3; trans. Legge, 1861a)[8]

Moreover, speech in Confucian doctrines is an important criterion to judge people. Confucius ranks people according to what they attempt to avoid. Those who do not hold back their speech are allocated the lowest ranking.

> The Master said, 'Some men of [great] worth retire from the world. Some [of less] retire from particular states. Some [of much less] retire because of disrespectful looks. Some [of least] retire because of contradictory language'.
> (*Analects, Xiàn Wèn 14*:37; trans. Legge, 1861a)[9]

Thus, people who possess the greatest virtue keep themselves away from the greatest range of vice – the ordinary world – because it is full of mediocracy, vulgarity, and corruption. In some sense, the noblest people live like secluded hermits – nearly a Daoist life. People of second-order respectful quality steer clear of areas where conflicts take place. However, they cannot completely withdraw themselves from the worldly affairs as the most virtuous people do. People of less virtue keep themselves from certain controversial issues and areas. Then, people of less value avoid displaying unpleasant looks and manners. They do not know how to keep themselves away from conflicts and fights with other people. The only merit they have is to maintain good manners. Finally, people of the least respected virtue can only know to avoid speaking.[10] People who do not know how to hold speech do not even deserve the consideration of ranking. In Confucius's teaching, verbal utterance is nothing more than a vehicle that carries meaning as concisely as possible. As the Master said, 'In language it is simply required that it convey the meaning' (*Analects, Wei Ling Gong 14*:41, trans. Legge, 1861a).[11] Another short anecdote in the *Analects* shows the insignificance of speech:

> The Master said, 'I would prefer not speaking'. Zǐ Gòng said, 'If you, Master, do not speak, what shall we, your disciples, have to record?' The Master said, 'Does Heaven speak? The four seasons pursue their courses, and all things are continually being produced, but does Heaven say anything?'
> (*Analects, Yáng Hùo 17*:19; trans. Legge, 1861a)[12]

Chinese graphocentrism   21

In this short story, Confucius takes a negative attitude towards human speech by showing the limits of language and human beings' incompetence in using it. As he notes, every being in the world lives and dies according to the order of Heaven (or nature). Without verbalising any mandate, Heaven tacitly gives commands, takes care of everything and every being, and keeps them in order. The order is not guaranteed by verbal language. The redundancy and dispensability of speech somehow indicate disparagement and mistrust of the spoken word in the Confucian tradition. The mistrust of verbal eloquence, of voice, and of phonetic expression is not only the distinctiveness in Confucianism but also a general sentiment that can be discovered in all major schools of Chinese thought (Xu, 2004).

Spoken language is perceived as less virtuous than written language in Chinese philosophical tradition. In the sixth century, Yán Zhitui (or Yen Chih-T'ui, 顏之推, 531–591 CE), in his *Family Instructions for the Yen Clan* (*YenShis chia-Hsün*, 顏氏家訓), advises his descendants that the references of learning, past or present, must be mediated through the eyes instead of the ears. He says, 'All these are faults caused by learning by ear. Characters are the foundation of writings. Nowadays many students cannot recognise the characters' (Tèng, 1968, pp. 78–79).[13] The contemporary sinologist Tèng Ssu-yŭ (鄧嗣禹) remarks that Chinese literary tradition always keeps scholars on alert by addressing the problem of learning through orality and spoken language. Spoken language as orality – hearsay – has less value in culture because it is 'an inferior version of textual culture' (Connery, 1998). Orality is taken as inferior to script in terms of education; writing is what people can count on to learn about the ancients and the utmost principle. In the *Analects*,

> The Master said, 'I could describe the ceremonies of the Xia dynasty, but Qi cannot sufficiently attest my words. I could describe the ceremonies of the Yin dynasty, but Song cannot sufficiently attest my words. (They cannot do so) because of the insufficiency of their records and wise men. If those were sufficient, I could adduce them in support of my words'.
> (*Analects, Ba Yî 3:9*; trans. Legge, 1861a)[14]

Confucius is willing to provide explications on the ceremonies of ancient dynasties, but he is concerned about the lack of 文獻 to verify his views. 文獻 is translated as 'records and wise men' by Legge, which indicates 'documents and elders'. The literal translation of the term 文獻 is 'literature'. This term is composed of two characters 文 (wén) and 獻 (xiàn). 文 has many meanings, including appearance/characters, words/books, works/Confucian doctrine/civilian, non-military/drum (musical instrument)/measure word for money. The single character 獻 is often used as a verb, meaning 'to offer, to present, to show, or to display'. The two-character term 文獻 (wénxiàn) usually indicates literature, documents, and records. The significance of the above anecdote is that the elders and the documents play the role of 'script', the purpose of which is to testify and ensure the truthfulness of legacy from ancient sage kings. For Confucius, the person or the object that can be 'the script' to guarantee, secure, and conserve the truth is someone or something that can be physically and immediately accessed and contacted. The direct and immediate contact with this person or object as script raises the credibility of the truth in pursuit. It is the 'physicality' that makes a genuine record or a genuine script from forgery.

The Confucian classical text *Lǐ Jì* or *The Book of Rites* (禮記) clearly expresses the conviction that writing is able to record and preserve spoken words faithfully and thereby brings forth rules and order for others to follow. According to *Lǐ Jì*, there was a great historiographer, Lǐu Zhuang (柳莊), serving in the State of Wèi (衛). After his death, the Duke of Wèi paid his respect to the deceased historiographer by granting him with two towns. The Duke ordered the bestowment to be written down and put into the coffin. In so doing, the bestowment and the honour would be preserved and handed down forever, 'For the myriads of his descendants, to hold from generation to generation without change' (*Lǐ Jì, Táng Gong II*, 3:174; trans. by Legge, 1885).[15] Writing has the power to fix the ephemeral and transient voice and to make words endure. Another example is in the Chapter *Zengzǐ Wèn* (曾子問) of *Li Jì*. The Master Confucius explained to Zengzǐ about the generation of mourning rituals for a foster-mother. Confucius said that, in the ancient times, there was no ritual like this. The Duke Zhao of Lǔ (魯昭公) intended to wear mourning clothes for his foster-mother. The officer dissuaded the Duke from doing this: 'According to the ancient rule, there is no mourning for a foster-mother. If you wear this mourning [clothes], you will act contrary to that ancient rule and introduce confusion into the laws of the state. If you will after all do it then we will put it on record and transmit the act to the future; will not that be undesirable?' (*Lǐ Jì, Zengzǐ Wèn*: 21; trans. by Legge, 1885).[16] What is noteworthy here is that the generation of any ritual or rite could have nothing to prove that any ritual is originally baseless. Once a ruler decides to start a new practice or to enact a new law, the command of the ruler must be preserved in physical forms. In other words, it must be written down. The act of writing approves the new practice as a part of the established rites for subjects and descendants to observe and obey. Writing has the power to command and to legitimise; the ruler has the power to author the legal codes. Writing, which communicates the ruler as the origin of rules and the subjects as the followers of the rule, overcomes the distance of space and time. Writing as inscription supports the authority of the state by spreading the order or the rule without alteration. The ruler as the author of the rule will be discussed in the next section. The rest of this section focuses on the commanding power of writing. As long as the words are written down, they turn into something out of the control of the author. Hán Fei (280–233 BCE), the philosopher of the Warring State period, expresses his anxiety about the power of writing:

> A man of Ying once wrote a letter to the Prime Minister of Yen. He wrote the letter at night. When the light was not bright, he, accordingly, said to the candle-holder, 'Raise the candle!' So saying he wrote down by mistake

the words, 'Raise the candle', although raising candles was not the gist of the letter. However, the Prime Minister of Yen on receiving the letter was glad and said: 'To raise the candle means to exalt the bright; To exalt the bright means to elevate the worthy and appoint them to office'. Therefore, the Premier of Yen spoke to the King about the policy of appointing the worthy to office, which the King was very glad to carry into effect. In consequence, the state became orderly. As regards the problem of political order, they did attain political order. But it was not the gist of the letter! Thus, scholars of the present world mostly resemble the Premier of Yen in interpreting the meaning of words.

> (*Hánfeizǐ, Chapter XXXII. Outer Congeries of Sayings, The Upper Left Series*: Annotations to Cannon III; trans. Liao, 1939)[17]

The anecdote, according to Lewis (1999), shows the problem of writing: that the original intent of the author could be lost and thereby cause misunderstanding. Yet in my view, the very point Hán Fei emphasises is that writing escapes from the author and independently exercises its power upon the reader. Writing could be a record of speech, but it is independent of its original circumstances and detached from the spoken language. Regardless of whether the intent of the author will be preserved in the text, writing exerts effects upon the readers and turns them into followers. This raises the issue that if writing has the power to command, how can we distinguish good writing from bad writing, proper writing from improper writing, or legal writing from illegal writing, in order to take the command of right, correct, legitimate writing? In the Chinese mindset, the legitimacy of writing is in the antiquity. The writing of the ancients is always better and more accountable than the writing of those who come later. Xū Shèn (許慎 58–147 CE) states,

> The *Shu* says, 'I wish to observe the images of the ancients'. This means that one must follow the old writing without distortion. Confucius said, 'I can remember when a scribe left a blank in his text. Now this is no longer done, alas'. It is not because people do not know and do not ask, but because if they all used their own private judgement, there would be no zhèng (standard) for distinguishing right from wrong, and clever opinions and heterodox pronouncements would have caused confusion among scholars. The overall written language (wénzì, word) is the foundation of classics and arts and the initiation of sovereignty of kingdom. It is what the former generations relied on to transmit culture to later ages. Men of later times will rely on it to understand antiquity. Therefore, it is said, 'The upholding of the foundation generates the foremost principle'.
>
> (*ShuowenJiězì, preface 1*:12–13; trans. Connery, 1998, p. 39; my modification)[18]

The previous passage indicates several extremely important messages about writing: 1) the legacy from the ancestors, which is scribed in writing, is an indispensable guide for learning; 2) writing has the standard for making fair and

24 Chinese graphocentrism

just judgements against private opinions and heterodox views; and 3) writing has the ground rules of governance. Overall, writing is the source of the utmost principle of education, morality, and politics.

The priority of writing over speech, or of the written word (with physicality) over the spoken word (with ephemerality), has imbued Chinese thought with an interesting characteristic: the graphocentric worldview. In the graphocentric worldview, physicality is embodied in 'visibility' and 'tactility' rather than 'orality' or 'aurality'. The object that can be seen and touched can exist beyond the limit of time. The concrete object seems to maintain its solid state. In this sense, the verifiability and credibility of the object lie in its 'unchangeableness' or 'inalterability', which, in turn, originates from the physicality or materiality. In contrast, the voice passes away over time. The moment a sound is heard is the moment it expires. The sound can only be 'recollected' by memory while memory changes all the time. Memory of one thing is susceptible to differ from person to person. Roger Chartier (1994) writes, 'Works and discourses exist only when they become physical realities and are inscribed on the pages of a book, transmitted by a voice reading or narrating, or spoken on the stage of a theatre' (1994, p. ix). Derrida's (1979) remarks on William Warburton's *Essai* echo in an inspirational way: 'The sound of voice never carries far enough. It lacks extension. Extension fails it. The scarcely paradoxical consequence – although it belongs to duration, sound never lasts long enough – duration fails it too' (p. 119). The written script endures time and space – 'writing has the function of reaching *subjects* who are not only distant but outside of the entire field of vision and beyond earshot' (Derrida, 1976, p. 281). Coulmas (1989, 2003) makes a comparison between speech and writing that includes six pairs of contrasts in dual categories: speech/writing, continuous/discrete, bound to utterance time/timeless, contextual/autonomous, evanescent/permanent, audible/visible, and produced by voice/produced by hand. The comparison reminds us to think whether the difference between speech and writing warrants phonocentrism or graphocentrism. From the Chinese perspective, these contrasts tend to uphold the superiority of writing over speech for being able to 'freeze' the presence over distance and time. For speech to function, the listener and the speaker must be present at the same time. Writing carries messages through time and space, between generations and beyond distances. That is why the 'script' as 'physical record' carries more weight than speech and voice in Chinese culture.

Paying heed to 'physicality' leads to valuing 'materiality' and 'worldliness'. In the *Analects*, Jì Lù asks Confucius about serving the spirit of the dead. This is the Master's reply:

> The Master said, 'While you are not able to serve men, how can you serve their spirits?' Ji Lu added, 'I venture to ask about death?' He was answered, 'While you do not know life, how can you know about death?'
> (*Analects, Xian Jin 11*:12; trans. Legge, 1861a)[19]

According to Confucius, service of the living is prior to the service of the dead, so much so that knowing about the world of the living is more important than knowing about that of death. Although I might dispute that knowledge of the living may not be logically related to the knowledge of the dead, the point is that, for Confucius, worldly service and knowledge shall be held in higher regard than thinking about the unknown. The world of the living is visible, concrete, and accessible, while the world of the dead is invisible and inscrutable. No matter how hard we try, it is not possible for us as living people to have direct communication with and unequivocal knowledge about the dead. In this vein, the Confucian doctrine strongly suggests that it is frivolous and useless to work on the tasks that cannot bring about visible, concrete, and practical outcomes. The concepts of visibility and concreteness outweigh those of invisibility and abstractness in traditional Chinese culture. Therefore, 'ocularcentric culture' or 'visual culture' (Marinelli, 2012) have increased in importance in China.

The favouritism towards writing over speech can be found in later literary works from the Han Dynasty. Yáng Xióng (揚雄 53 BCE–18 CE) was a well-known scholar and critic of the late Western Han Dynasty (西漢206 BCE–8 CE). In *Fǎ Yán* (法言), he writes,

> Language is not able to fully express what is in one's xin [heart/mind], and writings are not able to fully express what one wants to say. How troublesome! Only the sage is able to grasp the meaning of language and the essence of writing. It is like when the shining sun illuminates, or when the rivers cleanse – they are so great that nothing can resist them. For meeting face-to-face, exchanging letters, expressing the xin's desires, or breaking through the barriers between people – there is nothing like language. For summarizing the affairs of all under Heaven, for recording the old and explaining what is far away, for making known the darkness of antiquity and transmitting unclear matters from a thousand miles away, there is nothing like writing. Thus, language is the xin's voice. Writing is the xin's pictures. When voice and pictures take form, they are seen both by the junzǐ [noble man] and the small man [vulgar]. The voice and writing, these are what move the feelings of the junzǐ and the small man.
>
> (*Fǎyán, Asking About Shén* 5:13; trans. by Bullock, 2011)[20]

Although the first two sentences seem to be phonocentric, the succeeding parts reflect the positive emphasis on writing and written words (shu書) (Liu, 1988). Shu has two meanings: writing and written words (or books). Yáng Xióng, in my view, demonstrates great respect for the sage; a typical Confucian disposition is that only the sage has the privilege to understand the mystery and the truth of the world. Take another example – the Eastern Han Dynasty historian and poet Ban Gù (班固, 32–92 CE) in the *Hàn Shu* (漢書) lamented the neglect of writing of his contemporaneous scholars:

> In the past the scholars who edited texts didn't consider the lacunae caused by defective texts. With great irresponsibility and mindless conformity with the vulgar, they broke up passages and took graphs apart. Their

obscure pronouncements and prolix analyses multiplied. Scholars could grow old before they could fully exhaust the teaching of a single classic's commentarial tradition. They trusted oral transmission and rejected written records. They affirmed worthless teachers and denied the teachings of the ancients ... They preserved and guarded these superficial and defective texts, fearful of exposure and the spoiling of their self-interested projects. They had none of the public spirit that would lead them to follow the good and serve principles. Some were jealous at heart, and loath to examine their real feelings. But their sycophantic coteries marched in step, with their yes's and no's in unison. They shut out the Old Texts, regarded the *Shàngshu* as complete, and said that the *Zuǒzhuàn* was not a commentary on the *Spring and Autumn Annals*. What a pity!

(*Hàn Shu, Prince Chǔ Yúan*, 36:58; Connery, 1998, p. 60)[21]

The Eastern Han Dynasty author Ban Gù explicitly expressed his strong criticism of orality. Hidden in the assault is the graphocentric position with the approbation of writing and of learning from the ancients. The privileged status of the sage in Chinese thought will be further explored in the next section concerning zhèngmíng (正名, appellation). For ordinary people, it is the case that 'Language is not able to fully express what is in one's xin [heart/mind], and writings are not able to fully express what one wants to say'. Thus, they need to read the writing of the sage, who can understand the heaven and can properly put the understandings in writing.

In brief, three significant points can be drawn from the preceding discussions: first, it is difficult for ordinary people to use voice or writing to express properly and fully what is in mind – meaning. Therefore, they need the guidance of the former sages. Second, the sage kings are the rare ones who understand the principles and express them appropriately through voice and writing. Finally, the understanding and expression of the sage kings in the old times and remote areas can be recorded on the pages of a book. The physical realities secure the inalterability of the written words as well as the teachings of the sage. The meaning of the physicality of writing can be grasped from two aspects. One is about the word as pictograph; the other is about the inalterability of the text.

First, the Chinese character is invented from the imitation of natural objects. In this sense, the Chinese word is 'visually sensible'. For example, the word 'mouth' in Chinese is 口, which depicts the shape of the mouth vividly. The third-century influential commentator of *Daodejing* and *Yijing* Wáng Bì (王弼, 226–249 AD) provides ocularcentric commentary on the relationship between language and the concept of image:

The Image is what brings out concept; language is what clarifies the Image. Nothing can equal Image in giving the fullness of concept; nothing can equal language in giving the fullness of Image. Language was born of the Image, thus we seek in language in order to observe the Image. Image was born of concept, thus we seek in Image in order to observe the concept. Concept is fully given in Image; Image is overt in language.

(Wáng Bì; trans. Owen, 1996, pp. 63–64)[22]

The character 象 is translated as 'image'. In terms of Chinese nomenclature and etymology, this word can refer to the animal of 'elephant' and the idea of 'physical likeness', 'resemblance', or 'image'. According to the legalist philosopher Han Fei (280–233 BCE), 'the word 象 as image or resemblance comes from the picture of bones of a dead elephant to help people to imagine a living elephant since it is unusual to see a living elephant. Therefore, the word 象 is used to refer to something that can make sense and make visible' (*Hánfeizǐ*, 20:24, *my translation*).[23] The idea of image is to make sense of the insensible, make visible the invisible, and make present the absent. Wáng Bì's view demonstrates that visual imagery plays an important role in the Chinese tradition of language and knowledge. Writing and words capture images, whereas images capture meanings. As mentioned, writing is a visual exercise (Kavanagh, 2004). During the process of signification and expression, vision takes the key. More importantly, favouritism for the visual/mimetic model of thought is implied in Chinese graphocentrism, wherein an image of the object directs one to conceive the object itself and to project it, as it is, through the eyes to the mind. The visual resemblance between an image and an object dominates the graphocentric way of thought. No wonder Cang Jíe, the inventor of Chinese character in the legend, is described in the *Lùnhéng* (11:3; 論衡骨相:3) as having four eyes. Therefore, he has much better and greater visual ability to see and to discover the traces of creatures in the nature to invent characters.

The second aspect of the physicality of writing is inalterability and the derivative, verifiability. The presence that has been valued is what can be physically accessed, repeatedly attested, and thereby bestowed with firm trust through a certain process of externalisation, which means that the mimetic realistic depiction is not merely operated in the brain but executed in practice, to produce the written words. Writing conveys meanings of remote space and time without alteration. This is how textual existence demonstrates physicality in different forms. The materiality of the text – be it on bamboo, silk, wood, stone, or paper – guarantees the truthfulness of the meaning of the text (Connery, 1998). Writing is understood as something objective, something that will not be changed arbitrarily by the reader. The autonomous written words strengthen the observance of external standards. The external standards are the 'object' (物, wù, thing).

The third-century poet Lù Ji (陸機, 261–303 CE) writes in his *Wén Fù* (文賦, *Essay on Literature*) about the difficulty of writing (屬文, shǔwén; writing, composing, creating works). As he describes, writing is difficult because the '*meaning* [or idea] apprehended does not represent the *objects observed*; furthermore, *words* fail to convey the *meaning*' (cited from Zha, 1992, p. 390).[24] There is a hierarchy among objects (物), meaning (意), and words (文). Metaphysically, the object

28 Chinese graphocentrism

is prioritised in a subtle way. One very interesting story in *Hánfeizǐ* (韓非子) pertinently demonstrates the attitude of accrediting external visible standards.

> Once a man of Chêng wanted to buy a pair of shoes for himself. He measured his feet first and left measurements on his seat. He arrived at the market-place, but had forgotten to take the measurements along. Though he had already found the shoes for himself, he said, 'I have forgotten to take the measurements along. Let me go home to get them here'. When he came back again, the market was closed, however. He could not get the shoes after all. 'Why didn't you try the shoes with your own feet?' asked people. 'I have confidence in the measurements but not in my own feet', was the reply.
>
> (*Hánfeizǐ*, Chapter XXXII. *Outer Congeries of Sayings, The Upper Left Series*: Annotations to Cannon III, trans. by Liao, 1939)[25]

It is interesting and ironic to learn from this story that Chinese culture tends to place more weight on the created and external measurements or standards than on the creators. It is the betrayal of the creation against the creator – not in the Western Christian sense – or the betrayal of the product against the producer, or the betrayal of the sign against the sign-maker. This betrayal further points to the triumph of writing over the writer and the subjectification of writer (as speaker). The preceding discussion about Chinese graphocentrism discloses an intriguing and ambiguous view about writing: writing equivocates because it reveals the secrets of the nature, secures and verifies the truth, and, paradoxically, conceals by making deceit. In his reading of William Warburton's *Essai*, Derrida's (1979) comment resounds: 'a writing made to manifest, serve and preserve knowledge – for custody of meaning, the repository of learning and the laying out of the archive – encrypts itself, becoming secret and reserved, diverted from common usage, esoteric' (p. 124). The view of Chinese antiquity displays the paradox of writing: that it reveals and conceals, disenchants and enchants, decrypts and encrypts. Facing this paradox are two responses that can be unearthed from Chinese philosophy. One is explicitly approved in Chinese Confucianism as legitimation of naming, which will be discussed later in this chapter. The graphocentric approach is normalised in the mainstream Confucian philosophy. The other is what I term the post-graphocentric approach, which is insinuated in the Daoist concept of 'wú' ('non-' or 'de-') that can be seen as a certain undoing, unlocking, or positive invalidation. This point will be explored in later chapters.

Appellation as legitimation and the words of sage kings

Graphocentrism, which is oriented by vision and the written word, dominates the Chinese epistemic thinking. Things with high visibility, inalterability, and

Chinese graphocentrism 29

verifiability are highly esteemed, while those that are easily decomposed, transitory, and mortal are of poor or no value. What is present to the eyes can be valued – it can be physically accessed, repeatedly attested, and thereby firmly entrusted. The script with written words epitomises presence. However, as mentioned, writing does not only reveal – it also conceals. Thus, it is possible for the testament to deceive. For Chinese Confucian thinkers, one way to escape from this predicament is to accredit the writing and to bring credit to the written words by means of zhèngmíng (正名). The phrase zhèngmíng is literally translated as 'correcting names', 'rectifying names' or 'correction of names'. Zhèng (正) means 'to correct', 'to rectify', or 'to make proper'. Míng (名) means 'name' or 'appellation'. Zhèngmíng is 'the legitimation of appellation', which turns out to be the formation, construction, and defence of the order, the authority, the canon. During the process of rectifying names, using correct appellation, it is not only the canon to be established, but also the discrimination to be made.

The concept of zhèngmíng plays an extremely crucial role in Confucianism. As Hansen (1983, p. 181 n28) puts it, 'the rectification of names can be regarded as a genuine Confucian teaching *in the sense that* without it, the ethical system of Confucius would be considered less coherent'. Most important of all, it plays a key role in Chinese graphocentrism. There is only one mention of this phrase in the *Analects*, but it could be one of the core teachings of Confucianism. Zǐ Lù said, 'The ruler of Wei has been waiting for you, in order with you to administer the government. What will you consider the first thing to be done?' The Master replied, 'What is necessary is to rectify names' (*Analects, ZǐLù 13*:3; trans. Legge, 1861a).[26] Yet in another Confucian classic text, *Lǐjì* (禮記, The Book of Rites), the idea of name or appellation is mentioned several times in the word of zì. In ancient Chinese, zì and míng both are used to refer to the name, the appellation, or the title. For example,

> A son at twenty is capped, and receives his *appellation* ...When a daughter is promised in marriage, she assumes the hair-pin, and receives her *appellation*.
> (*Lǐjì, 1*:44; trans. by Legge, 1885)[27]

> The giving of the *name* in childhood, of the *designation* at the capping, of the title of elder uncle or younger uncle at fifty, and of the honorary title after death, was the practice of the Zhou dynasty.
> (*Lǐjì, 3*:62, trans. Legge, 1885)[28]

> The giving the *name* of maturity in connexion with the ceremony was to show the reverence due to that *name*.
> (*Lǐjì, 11*:33, trans. Legge, 1885)[29]

There is a slight difference between míng and zì, although both refer to the name. According to *Lǐjì*, the name of the child is called míng. When one comes of age, one will be given another formal name, or zì. According to the ancient rites, 冠字 (guànzì, to crown one with a name) means to give one a name or an appellation at his or her coming of age ceremony. As written in the *Lǐjì* (*43*:2; trans. Legge, 1885): 'When the capping was over, he received the name of his maturity. So was it shown that he was now a full-grown man'.[30] In the Confucian tradition, to crown one with a name has much significance in ethics and politics because the name is a code implying duty and obligation with which the named one should comply. This notion is one of the most important teachings in Confucian tradition. Here, the term 'word' does not indicate the basic unit of language but connotes a sign referring to a name or an appellation. To give a name (as well as to prescribe the corresponding political and moral code) has been incorporated into the idea of 'zhèngmíng', which has been put under scrutiny by a number of later Confucian thinkers. In this sense, 'zì' and 'míng' are interchangeable.

As the *Analects* describes, once Zǐ Lù asks Confucius for advice about how to serve in the state of Wei and what should be the first priority, Confucius replies with *zhèngmíng*. Zǐ Lù keeps asking the reason. Then the Master replies,

> If names be not correct, [spoken] language is not in accordance with the truth of things. If language be not in accordance with the truth of things, affairs cannot be carried on to success. When affairs cannot be carried on to success, proprieties and music will not flourish. When proprieties and music do not flourish, punishments will not be properly awarded. When punishments are not properly awarded, the people do not know how to move hand or foot.
>
> (*Analects, Zi Lu 13*: 3; trans. Legge, 1861a; my modification)[31]

'Míng zhèng yán shùn' (名正言順), meaning 'appropriate appellations, consistent language', has been widely recognised as one of the most important notions in Confucianism. According to the above passage, inappropriate names (appellations) result in non-correspondence between 'yán' (言, utterance, language, word) and the referred objects. Non-correspondence further causes the subsequent failures of doing things, accomplishing rites (lǐ, 禮) and music (yèh, 樂) (symbolising making laws), and executing laws (including inflicting punishments). In the very condensed, brief passage are wide-ranging and far-reaching implications concerning language. I ask the following four questions to initiate the discussion on the significance of the notion of zhèngmíng. What and who is the origin of the 'míng'? What is the function of the 'míng'? Why does the 'míng' need to be rectified? And, finally, in what sense does 'zhèngmíng' relate to graphocentrism?

First, the identification of appropriate names implies the correspondence of language between the terms and the truth of the referred things or the objects – that is, between the signifier and the signified. The Confucian philosophers do not limit correspondence to the linguistic level but extend the understanding of the notion of 'zhèngmíng' from the pragmatic use to the metaphysical, ethical, and political levels. Names are not invented *ex nihilo*; they are given by the sage kings – those who are gifted. Only a sage king can recognise the intrinsic nature of things in the world and thereby give them proper names. Xúnzǐ, the third and last of the classical Confucian masters, asserts that the essence of humanity lies in the ability to make distinctions that must be illuminated by the guidance of sage kings: 'What is it that makes a man human? I say that it lies in the ability to draw boundaries . . . Of such boundaries, none is more important than that between social classes. Of the instruments for distinguishing social classes, none is more important than ritual principles. Of the sources of ritual principles, none is more important than the sage kings' (*Xúnzǐ, Contra Physiognomy*, 5:4; trans. by Knoblock, 1994).[32]

Xunzi repeatedly stresses in his book that the former kings are the source of lǐ (ritual, 禮) and yì (righteousness, 義). Here are some examples.

> If you have not heard the words inherited from the Ancient Kings, you will be unaware of the greatness of learning and inquiry.
> (*Xúnzǐ, An Exhortation to Learning*, 1:2; trans. by Knoblock, 1994)[33]

> Consider the way of the Ancient Kings and the guiding principles of humanity and justice. Are they not the means by which we live together in societies, by which we protect and nurture each other, by which we hedge in our faults and refine each other, and by which together we become tranquil and secure?
> (*Xúnzǐ, Of Honour and Disgrace*, 4:10; trans. by Knoblock, 1994)[34]

> Every doctrine that is neither consistent with Ancient Kings nor in accord with the requirements of ritual and moral principles is properly described as a 'treacherous doctrine'.
> (*Xúnzǐ, Contra Physiognomy*, 5:6; trans. by Knoblock, 1994)[35]

> Such was the Way of the Ancient Kings, and the highest expression of the loyalty of the minister and the piety of the filial son.
> (*Xúnzǐ, Discourse on Ritual Principles*, 19:19.4b;
> trans. by Knoblock, 1994)[36]

In total, 'the former king' is mentioned 39 times in the *Xúnzǐ*. Every time, it appears as the origin of the virtues, rituals, principles and learning that can be obtained by Rú scholars.

Xúnzǐ insists that only the sage king is capable of understanding and discovering the essence and the purpose of things. As such, therefore, the sage king is the arbiter who determines the appropriate appellation: 'Accordingly, the way a True King institutes names [is as follows]. Because fixed names keep objects distinguished and because when his Way is practiced his goals are universally understood, he takes pains to produce uniformity [in regard to names and his way] among the people' (*Xúnzǐ, Zhèngmíng*, 22.1c; trans. by Knoblock, 1994).[37] The identification of names or appellations for the objects or affairs in the Confucian tradition is not arbitrary.[38] On the contrary, appropriate appellations must be assigned by the former sage kings because they are the only gifted ones capable of perceiving truth.

The view that the sage king assigns proper names to all things on earth can be found in many Confucian followers. As the Western Han Dynasty (206 BCE–9 CE) scholar Dǒn Zhòng Shu (董仲舒) (2011) writes, 'Appellations emerge in truth. Whatever does conform to its true state cannot be named accordingly' (*Chun Qiu Fán Lù 35*:4; *my translation*).[39] Moreover, 'All beings in the world are generated with appellations. The sage names them according to their images' (*Chun Qiu Fán Lù 82*:2).[40] According to Confucian doctrine, the sage is able to perceive the truth of all and thereby gives proper names to them. Another Confucian classic, *Lǐ Jì* (禮記), refers to 'Huáng Di [Yellow Emperor], who gave everything its right name, thereby showing the people how to avail themselves of its qualities' (*Lǐ Jì, Jì Fǎ, 23*:8; trans. Legge, 1885).[41] The sage king has a special gift to perceive the truth or the genuine essence of beings on earth and thereby assigns appropriate names to them. The names imply rules about how the named should behave, treat each other, and be dealt with. For example, a chair is something that serves as a seat. The appropriate way that it should be treated is to be sat on. If someone uses it as a desk and writes on it, this act is improper and wrong. In the Confucian tradition, the sage kings comprehend not only the truth of substances but also the truth of moral ideas, virtues, and ethical interpersonal relationships. This is the second point involved in appellation.

Second, appellation implies and defines the way that one treats and is treated by others. The name is not simply a word or a label to be arbitrarily or randomly assigned to any person or any object. Appellation is to contextualise, locate, and obligate one through the name. Once the appellation has been designated, the social norm, code, and order have been assigned. As Dǒn Zhòng Shu (2011) states, appellation is about distinguishing one from the other by making explicit the relationship between everyone. Everyone is a relational and networked being. Relationships differ between different people. The name thus prescribes interpersonal relationships.

> Appellation consists in distinguishing one from the other. [Accordingly,] the intimate is important; the distanced is unimportant; the honoured is courteous; the inferior is straightforward; the near is in details; the remote is vague.
>
> (*Chun Qiu Fán Lù 82*:2; my translation)[42]

Appellations given by the former sage kings carry meanings for regulations and social order. Appellations provide standards and criteria for living a good life in accordance with teachings of the sage kings of antiquity.

The third aspect of appellation is 'rectification'. If there is nothing wrong, it is unnecessary to 'rectify'. In the Confucian tradition, inappropriate appellation causes conflicts and fights because it results in interruption or even destruction of the norm and order ascribed by the appellation. In ancient times, there certainly were many battles and wars among states. Thus, we found in the words of Confucius, Mencius, and Xúnzǐ a strong sense of mission that the confused world should be given guidance to get out of the disorder and conflicts. The task ahead is to rectify the improper appellation or the inappropriate use of names. In other words, the former sage kings' teaching that was ignored should be highlighted and taken as criteria for keeping society in order.

It is noteworthy that the sage kings are those of past generations. For Confucius, the sage kings are Yellow Emperor (黃帝), Yáo (堯), Shùn (舜), Yǔ (禹), and the Duke of Zhou (周公). For Mencius and Xúnzǐ, in addition to the abovementioned characters, the master Confucius is esteemed as one the earlier sages. There has been a three-stage model concerning the earlier sage kings (Lewis, 1999). In the 'Chapter of *Téng Wén Gong I*' (滕文公上), Mencius discusses how the earlier sages saved people from the disorderly world. He describes three stages and marks featuring kings – the high antiquity of Yáo (堯), Shùn (舜), and Yǔ (禹); the middle antiquity of the Duke of Zhou (周公); and the recent period marked by Confucius. Xúnzǐ has a similar view. Hánfeizǐ, in his chapter *Wǔ Dú (Five Vermin)*, also suggests a three-phase history model of sages. The first phase is the remote antiquity marked by legendary figures Yǒuchaóshì (the Nest-Dweller, 有巢氏) and Suírénshì (the Flinter, 燧人氏). In the middle antiquity was a great flood. The sage king of Yǔ (禹) came out to build the channels for water control. The age of recent antiquity is marked by two kings – Emperor Tang (湯) of the Shang Dynasty, who overthrew the tyranny of the last emperor, Jíe (桀), of the Xìa Dynasty; and King Wǔ (武), the founder of the Zhou Dynasty, who ended the vicious rule of the emperor Zhoù (紂) of the Shang Dynasty. In the Chinese mindset, there is an overall strong belief in the three-stage model of history and ancient sages. The sages are regarded as the source of sacred words and writing that, in turn, set the standards and laws for later generations. The Western Han Dynasty (202 BCE–8 CE) author Yáng Xióng (揚雄) writes:

> Every five hundred years a sage appears . . . Yáo, Shùn and Yǔ were rulers and subjects to one another, all [during] the same era. Wén, Wǔ and the Duke of Zhoù, were fathers and sons, all during the same era. But Táng and Confucius were born several centuries removed from each other.
>
> (*Fǎn Yán*, 9:1; trans. by Bullock, 2011)[43]

The sage does not appear in the world all the time. Often, a sage is born every few hundred years. There are two times in history that sage kings appeared more frequently. The first was the time ruled by the ancient emperor Yáo because his crown was succeeded by Shùn and then by Yǔ. The second occurred in the late

34 Chinese graphocentrism

Shang Dynasty, when the dynasty was under the reign of the King Wén, his successor King Wǔ, and his younger brother, the Duke of Zhòu.

In general, it is difficult for one to witness sages with their own eyes or hear them with their own ears because the appearance of sages in the physical world is extremely rare. Sages leave their words for those who have no opportunities to have contact with the sages that follow. Their words, the content of which is appropriate naming, are scripted through writing. Thus, the most important ways to maintain good social order are to retrieve the correct usage of appellation and to rectify improper names. This is why ancient Confucian thinkers continuously emphasise 'correction of names', 'rectification of names', 'setting names right', or 'correction of terminology' (Boltz, 1999; Bottéro, 2002; Geaney, 2010). Correction or rectification means to remove the wrong and substitute with the right. Sometimes, incorrect names are assigned; they are not used in the sagely way. In this situation, it is necessary to change the name. For Confucian thinkers, these formerly assigned appellations are the norms and standards.

The fourth aspect of appellation is the relationship between the idea of zhèngmíng and graphocentrism. The written word has the power to command, and so does 'zhèngmíng'. The two-character term 'Zhèngmíng' means 'to rectify the name' or 'to use appropriate names' or 'to appellate proper names'. 'Zhèng' means to set something right; 'zhèng míng' is to set the míng (or the name) right. Hence, to name someone, something, or an event is to identify who or what the person or thing is. 'Zhèng míng' indicates the perfect match between the signified object and the name as the signifier. Naming is an act of identification, an act of definition by using the correct word to refer to a person or a thing or an event. To use the correct word is the exercise of writing. According to the ancient text *Gŭanzĭ* (管子, edited by Liu Xiang, 劉向, 77–6 BC), there are five kinds of 'zhèngmíng': 'the authority, the measure, the compass, the ruler and the level' (*Gŭanzĭ, Gúi Dù*, 78:2) (Liu Xiang, 2011).[44] The appellations as criteria are provided for weighing and regulating colours, tones, and people's tastes in order to manage their views and speeches.[45] Proper appellations of standards keep the world in order. On the contrary, 'Improper appellations result in confusion of duties. Then many punishments and penalties will be executed. The turmoil cannot be more serious' (*LǔshìChunqiu*, 93:4; my translation).[46] Therefore, using appropriate appellations and abiding by the implied duties is absolutely important. With respect to graphocentrism, the notion of appellation points towards the reified and normalised standards embodied in names. The standards proclaimed by sage kings can only be defended, not challenged.

Makeham (1991) points out that the ultimate justification of naming as standardisation is political rather than philosophical. What Gŭanzi suggests is how a ruler governs his state and subjects by normalising their senses in terms of assigning proper names. The process of giving appellations is not only political but also highly moralising and didactic (which could be a feature common to most Chinese classic thinkers). Abiding by the sage kings' words as defending the legitimacy of individuals and the state is the graphocentric practice on political, ethical, and educational levels.

From the perspective of ancient Chinese thinkers, 'zhèngmíng' plays an extremely important role in maintaining social order and hierarchy. Appellation is not merely to give a name, a title, or a label to a person or an object. Bestowing a name is not an arbitrary and reckless act but a cautious move with the consideration of the truth (真) of the being. If the name is inappropriately appointed, there will be turmoil and conflict. The ultimate goal of appellation is to achieve and secure harmony and order of the state by giving a proper name to every member of the society, by putting one in an appropriate position that will not be in conflict, and by obligating one with duties. Assigning proper names is to legitimate one as lawful – politically, socially, and morally, viz., to declare one's identity and duty, to specify one's relationship with others, and to announce one's acknowledged status and position. 'Zhèngmíng' is a task aimed at fortifying the canon against contamination of the impure, the excluded, the expelled, the marginalised, the dismissed, the ignored, the rejected, and the infinitesimal. Using incorrect names is to violate the order, to contaminate the purity of the canon, to produce turmoil, i.e., to transgress. 'Zhèngmíng' is an act for counteracting transgression and for maintaining order.

It is noteworthy that the ultimate legitimacy of appellation or naming lies in the earlier sage kings' words. The appellation or the name can be seen as both the fortress and the citadel of the canon and the order. The name, borrowing the words from Hope A. Olson (2002), is a means of structuring reality. Yet, only the sage kings can perceive reality and truth and thereby give proper names to persons and objects. Not everyone has the authority and the power to name. For me, this is one of the biggest myths of Chinese graphocentrism. However, the ancient Confucian thinkers have not provided enough evidence about the authority of sage kings. They simply believe in the talent and the power of the earlier sage kings.

The graphocentric worldview

As discussed, graphocentrism underpins the mainstream Chinese intellectual tradition. Chinese graphocentrism can be seen as a worldview comprising the following ideas: 1) Writing and the written word are held in higher esteem than the voice and speech, even though written words are initially records of spoken words. 2) The written word, with the characteristics of visibility (physicality), inalterability, and verifiability, registers standards and norms for social relationships and interpersonal communication. The trust in the visible and inalterable written word extends to faith in the physical and corporeal thing or object. 3) Although the written word is valued more highly than the spoken word, it is the fixation of the spoken word. However, not everyone's speech is worth keeping and writing. Only the speech of sage kings is worth writing down in order to exert the commanding power of naming and appellation to prescribe social order.

While writing is treated with great respect in the Chinese tradition, it is devalued in the Western tradition. In Plato's *Phaedrus* (257c–279c) (Hamilton & Cairns, 1961), writing is flawed. There are at least two reasons for this. First, writing destroys memory – it 'will produce forgetfulness in the minds of those who learn to use it, because they will not practice their memory' (*Phaedrus*, 275a). Second, writing is unresponsive (Ong, 1982): 'if one asks them a question, they preserve a solemn silence . . . if you question them, wishing to know about their sayings, they always say only one and the same thing' (*Phaedrus*, 275d).

Ong (1982) summarises four weaknesses about writing in Plato: writing is in-human and thing-like; writing spoils memory and the mind; writing makes no response, and writing does not defend itself. For Plato, writing or the written word is of little worth (*Phaedrus*, 278c). It is obvious that Plato's view about writing is very different from the Chinese view. Chinese values writing, whereas Plato finds little to no value.

Once a word is written, it becomes a fixed script, and its meaning is stabilised. The written word endures with physicality and inalterability. For Plato, the written word is dead. For the Chinese, paradoxically, the deadness of the written word represents truthfulness and verifiability because it no longer changes. In Ong's (1982) words, 'The paradox lies in the fact that the deadness of the text, its removal from the living human lifeworld, its rigid visual fixity, assures its endurance and its potential for being resurrected into limitless living contexts by a potentially infinite number of living readers' (Ong, 1982, p. 80). For Plato, writing results in the impairment of education. In *Phaedrus*, Socrates tells Phaedrus a story about Theuth, the inventor of numbers, arithmetic, geometry, astronomy, draughts, dice, and, most important of all, letters – meaning writing – in ancient Egypt. The Egyptian god Thamus praises Theuth for his inventions, except for writing. Theuth defends writing because it 'will make the Egyptians wiser and will improve their memories; for it is an elixir of memory and wisdom that I have discovered' (274e). But Thamus replies,

> Most ingenious Theuth, one man has the ability to beget arts, but the ability to judge of their usefulness or harmfulness to their users belongs to another; and now you, who are the father of letters, have been led by your affection to ascribe to them a power the opposite of that which they really possess. For this invention will produce forgetfulness in the minds of those who learn to use it, because they will not practice their memory. Their trust in writing, produced by external characters which are no part of themselves, will discourage the use of their own memory within them. You have invented an elixir not of memory, but of reminding; and you offer your pupils the appearance of wisdom, not true wisdom, for they will read many things without instruction and will therefore seem to know many

Chinese graphocentrism   37

things, when they are for the most part ignorant and hard to get along with, since they are not wise, but only appear wise.

(Plato, 1925; *Phaedrus*, 274a – 275b)

Within the Western phonocentric tradition, writing is taken as the product or, in Derrida's words, the supplement of spoken language. As rhetorician Walter Ong (1967, 1977, 1982) asserts in many of his works, writing is dead and artificial, whereas voice is alive and natural.

On the contrary, the Chinese graphocentric notion considers writing in no way supplementary or secondary but as fundamental to worldly affairs and emerging from nature. As mentioned previously, Xǔ Shèn (許慎 58–147 CE) states, 'The overall written language (wén zì, word) is the foundation of classics and arts and the initiation of sovereignty of kingdom. It is what the former generations relied on to transmit culture to later ages. Men of later times will rely on it to understand antiquity. Therefore, it is said, "The upholding of the foundation generates the foremost principle"' (*ShuowénJiĕzì*, preface 1:13; modification from Connery, 1998, p. 39).[47] The unchangeable highest principle is found in written – rather than spoken – language.

In *Lùnhéng* (論衡), Wáng Chong (王充, 27–100 AD) asserts that characters are the natural spontaneity: 'When plants and trees grow, their flowers and leaves are onion green and have crooked and broken veins like ornaments. If Heaven is credited with having written the abovementioned characters, does it make these flowers and leaves also?' (*Lùnhéng, 54*:6, trans. by Forke, 1907).[48] Wáng Chong compares the leaf venation of plants with characters and suggests that both are creations of the Heaven that is also referred to as nature in this essay. Unlike the Western view, the Chinese perspective sees the written word as coherent, as corresponding to nature, and as the foundation of principal truth for guiding worldly affairs.

Based on *Phaedrus*, Plato's Socrates asserts that a wise person or a true philosopher is not restrained by writing. The true philosopher 'has composed his writings with knowledge of the truth and is able to support them by discussion of that which he has written and has the power to show by his own speech that the written words are of little worth, such a man ought not to derive his title from such writings, but from the serious pursuit which underlies them' (Plato, 1925; *Phaedrus*, 278c–d). In other words, a philosopher knows the primacy of speech over writing. Those who do not understand this value do not deserve the title of philosopher but can only be a poet or a writer. As Plato writes, 'he who has nothing more valuable than the things he has composed or written, turning his words up and down at his leisure, adding this phrase and taking that away, will you not properly address him as poet or writer of speeches or of laws?' (Plato, 1925; *Phaedrus*, 278d–e). A poet or a writer is bound to writing, while a philosopher is free from the limits of writing and is able to think and speak freely and creatively.

In contrast, in the Chinese graphocentric tradition, it is not only Cang Jié, the inventor of writing, who gives proper names to all that exists in the world. So do the most honourable and respectful wise men – the sage kings of the past. Not only do their words teach about the model, the standard, and the principle for everyone to obey, but they as persons are role models to follow. Believing in and obeying the sage king is one of the most important creeds held by Confucianists. Their images and words are engraved into eternally unchangeable scripts. For the Chinese, the written word is not dead but refers instead to eternal and immortal ideals that provide standards for laypeople to follow, look up to, and learn from. The rise of writing in Chinese tradition announces at the same time the obituary of the author. Confucius modestly claims himself as a narrator but not as a writer, for he has firm belief in and love for the ancients (*Analects, Shù Ér* 7:1).[49] Confucius is humble because he attributes all the credit to the ancient sages. If Confucius the Master is too humble to be a writer, a creator, an author, who else can be? Yáng Xióng states: 'The sage casually opens his mouth and his words become maxims. He effortlessly wields his brush and his writing becomes a classic. His words can be heard but cannot be used up; his writings can be read but cannot be exhausted' (*FǎYán 9*: 18; trans. Bullock, 2011).[50] Although the truth of the sage's thought cannot be completely written down, the writing is the only relic that ordinary people rely on to access the truth – or parts of the truth. This implies an important Confucian teaching: 'One should continue to read in hope of discovering ever more meanings that have been hitherto unperceived' (Liu, 1988, p. 30). The Confucian respect for the early sage kings and their words – which shall be engraved into the script – reinforces the graphocentric episteme that cultivates reverence for the written words in Chinese folk tradition. Moreover, this exploration raises a question: divergent views about the relationship between writing and speech means that graphocentrism is ostensibly contradictory to phonocentrism.Yet both views are indeed, in terms of Derrida, the metaphysics of presence. Both pursue 'to locate a fundamental ground, a fixed permanent centre, an Archimedean point, which serves both as an absolute beginning and as a centre from which everything originating from it can be mastered and controlled' (Biesta, 2001, p. 38). The origin or the ground is thought of in the Western philosophical tradition, as Derrida (1978) states, in terms of presence, for 'It could be shown that all the names related to fundamentals, to principles, or to the centre have always designated an invariable presence' (p. 279). Derrida's remarks on the Western phonocentric metaphysics of presence aptly echo graphocentrism in Chinese philosophy and culture. Writing is venerated as pure, uncontaminated, transcendent, self-sufficient, standard, and, therefore, to make distinction, determination, discrimination, and exclusion. The 'hierarchical axiology' is therefore fabricated.

At some point, the Chinese version of metaphysics of presence at some point morphed into a religion of writing/inscription. Writing and its pertinent objects, including paper and books, were consecrated. In the old times, paper or books with written words were seen as the 'hallow'; thus, they could not be discarded or wasted freely. Since the seventeenth century, numerous non-governmental societies called 'Society for Cherishing Written Characters' (惜字會, Xí Zì Hui) have worked to collect used paper or books to burn in the Pagoda of Respectful Words (惜字亭, Xí Zì Tín) or Pagoda of Divine Relics (聖蹟亭, Shèn Ji Tín) (Leung, 1994). Used paper and books that are written with words are seen as vessels for sages' words; therefore, they are divine and sacred. Discarding the written paper as is extremely disgraceful and blameworthy. People thus need a sacred place – the Pagoda – to deal with divine written words. We must note that, overall, the written word and writing hold a venerated place in the Chinese mind and society.

Over thousands of years, there has also been a series of operations to canonise the written word and writing. These activities represent the graphocentric practice. In the next chapter, I will explore the graphocentric practice in four directions and with further explication – discipline of writing, formality of writing, institutionalisation of writing, and fundamental ideas. Through the exploration of the four aspects of writing, we may realise how the wordaholic obsession has accrued power over thousands of years.

Notes

1 It is said in an ancient book, 'Gird yourself, belt yourself!' A man of Sung, who once ran across this passage, doubled his sash and girdled himself with it accordingly. 'Why do you do that?' asked someone else. 'The ancient book saying so, so must I do', was the reply. (*Hánfeizi, Chapter XXXII. Outer Congeries of Sayings, The Upper Left Series*: Annotations to Cannon III, trans. Liao, 1939.)
2 昔者倉頡作書而天雨粟, 鬼夜哭。. . . 能愈多而德愈薄矣。(淮南子本經訓: 4) (Liu An, 2011)
3 倉頡始視鳥跡之文, 造書契, 則詐偽萌生。詐偽萌生則去本趨沒, 廢耕作之業而務錐刀之利。天知其將餓, 故為雨粟。鬼恐為書文所劾, 故夜哭也。 (藝文類聚, 卷八十五, 百穀部, 粟17) http://ctext.org/dictionary.pl?if=gb&id=548970
4 因儷鳥龜之跡, 遂定書字之形, 造化不能藏其秘, 故天雨粟, 靈怪不能遁其形, 故鬼夜哭。 (歷代名畫記: 敘畫之源流)
5 子曰: 「君子欲訥於言, 而敏於行。」 (論語里仁4:24)
6 司馬牛問仁。子曰: 「仁者其言也訒。」曰: 「其言也訒, 斯謂之仁已乎?」子曰: 「為之難, 言之得無訒乎?」 (論語顏淵12:3)
7 言近而指遠者, 善言也。(論語孟子盡心下7b:78)
8 子曰: 「巧言令色, 鮮矣仁!」 (論語學而1:3)
9 子曰: 「賢者辟世, 其次辟地, 其次辟色, 其次辟言。」 (論語憲問14:37)
10 A. C. Muller has a different version of translation of the above, as the Master said, 'A worthy becomes free of the world, then he becomes free of his land; then he becomes free from lust; then he becomes free from language'. In Muller's view, the words show a somewhat Daoist attitude in Confucianism. 'Normally Confucianism is understood as a tradition where one must remain engaged in society. However, in this case, Confucius' attitude is reminiscent of that of Zhuángzi, who always recommend that intelligent people not accept the norms of a decadent world and retire in solitude instead'. I do not

40 Chinese graphocentrism

dispute that Confucius gives his approval of Daoist view. Regarding the attitude towards speech, Muller's translation does not convey the intention of debasement of vocal language in Confucianism.

11 辭達而已。（論語衛靈公14: 41）
12 子曰：「予欲無言。」子貢曰：「子如不言，則小子何述焉?」子曰：「天何言哉?四時行焉，百物生焉，天何言哉?」（論語陽貨17:19）
13 ...皆耳學之過也。夫文字者，墳籍根本。世之學徒，多不曉字。（顏氏家訓勉學）
14 子曰：「夏禮，吾能言之，杞不足徵也；殷禮，吾能言之，宋不足徵也。文獻不足故也，足則吾能徵之矣。」（論語八佾3:9）
15 世世萬子孫，無變也。（禮記檀弓下，3: 174）
16 古之禮，慈母無服，今也君為之服，是逆古之禮而亂國法也；若終行之，則有司將書之以遺後世。無乃不可乎！（禮記曾子問，7:21）
17 郢人有遺燕相國書者，夜書，火不明，因謂持燭者曰：「舉燭。」云而過書舉燭，舉燭，非書意也，燕相受書而說之，曰：「舉燭者，尚明也，尚明也者，舉賢而任之。」燕相白王，王大說，國以治，治則治矣，非書意也。今世舉學者多似此類。（韓非子外儲左上，32:47）
18 《書》曰：「予欲觀古人之象。」言必遵修舊文而不穿鑿。孔子曰：「吾猶及史之闕文，今亡矣夫。」蓋非其不知而不問。人用己私，是非無正，巧說邪辭，使天下學者疑。蓋文字者，經藝之本，王政之始。前人所以垂後，後人所以識古。故曰：「本立而道生。」（說文解字卷一序1:12–13).
19 子曰：「未能事人，焉能事鬼?」敢問死。曰：「未知生，焉知死?」（論語先進11:12）
20 言不能達其心，書不能達其言，難矣哉。惟聖人得言之解，得書之體。白日以照之，江河以滌之，灝灝乎其莫之禦也。面相之，辭相適，捈中心之所欲，通諸人之嘿嘿者，莫如言。彌綸天下之事，記久明遠，著古昔之㖧㖧，傳千裏之忞忞者，莫如書。故言，心聲也。書，心畫也。聲畫形，君子小人見矣！聲畫者，君子小人之所以動情乎！（法言問神，5:13）
21 往者綴學之士不思廢絕之闕，苟因陋就寡，分文析字，煩言碎辭，學者罷老且不能究其一藝。信口說而背傳記，是末師而非往古 ... 猶欲保殘守缺，挾恐見破之私意，而無從善服義之公心，或懷妒嫉，不考情實，雷同相從，隨聲是非，抑此三學，以尚書為備，謂左氏為不傳春秋，豈不哀哉！（漢書楚元王傳，36:58）
22 夫象者，出意者也。言者，明象者也。盡意莫若象，盡象莫若言。言生於象，故可尋言以觀象；象生於意，故可尋象以觀意。意以象盡，象以言著。（王弼，周易略例，明象）
23 人希見生象也，而得死象之骨，案其圖以想其生也，故諸人之所以意想者皆謂之象也。（韓非子解老，20:24）
24 意不稱物，文不逮意。
25 鄭人有且置履者，先自度其足而置之其坐，至之市而忘操之，已得履，乃曰：「吾忘持度。」反歸取之，及反，市罷，遂不得履，人曰：「何不試之以足?」曰：「寧信度，無自信也。」（韓非子外儲左上32:48）
26 子路曰：「衛君待子而為政，子將奚先?」子曰：「必也正名乎！」（論語子路，13:3）
27 男子二十冠而字．．．女子許嫁笄而字。（禮記曲禮上，1:44）
28 幼名，冠字，五十以伯仲，死謚，周道也。（禮記檀弓上，3:62）
29 冠而字之，敬其名也。（禮記郊特牲，11:33）
30 以冠而字之，成人之道也。（禮記冠義43:2）
31 名不正，則言不順；言不順，則事不成；事不成，則禮樂不興；禮樂不興，則刑罰不中；刑罰不中，則民無所措手足。（論語子路，13:3）
32 人之所以為人者何已也?曰：以其有辨也。．．．辨莫大於分，分莫大於禮，禮莫大於聖王。（荀子非相，5:4）
33 不聞先王之遺言，不知學問之大也。（荀子勸學，1:2）
34 今以夫先王之道，仁義之統，以相群居，以相持養，以相藩飾，以相安固邪。（荀子榮辱，4:10）
35 凡言不合先王，不順禮義。（荀子非相，5:6）
36 是先王之道，忠臣孝子之極也。（荀子禮論，19:19.4b）

37 故王者之制名，名定而實辨，道行而志通，則慎率民而一焉。（荀子正名，22:1c）

38 Some scholars assert that appellation is arbitrary because the Confucian thinker Xúnzǐ in his book *Xúnzǐ* writes that '名無固宜，約以成命，約定俗成為之宜，異於約則為之不宜。' ('Names lack any intrinsic proper significance; they achieve their denominative power by virtue of users agreeing on it (i.e., on their significance or meaning). Once such an agreement has been established and a customary (meaning) has been achieved, we refer to that as (the name's) 'proper significance'. When (a usage) differs from the agreed upon (meaning), we refer to that as 'an improper significance' (Knoblock, 1994; cited in Boltz, 1999, p. 97). The above quotation suggests that giving names is conventional and based on common agreement. However, Xúnzǐ also claims that names are regulated and given by the former sage king (聖王) because only the sage king can understand and discover the nature and function of things. Overall, the sage king is esteemed as the source and criterion of appropriate appellation.

39 名生於真，非其真，弗以為名。（春秋繁露深察名號，35:4）

40 萬物載名而生，聖人因其象而命之。（春秋繁露天道施，82:2）

41 黃帝正名百物以明民共財。（禮記祭法，23:8）

42 名者，所以別物也。親者重，疏者輕，尊者文，卑者質，近者詳，遠者略，文辭不隱情，明情不遺文，人心從之而不逆，古今通貫而不亂，名之義也。男女猶道也。（春秋繁露天道施，82:2）

43 五百歲而聖人出 . . . 堯、舜、禹，君臣也而並；文、武、周公，父子也而處。湯、孔子數百歲而生。（法言八百，9:1）

44 權也、衡也、規也、矩也、准也。（管子揆度，78:2）

45 桓公曰：「事名二，正名五，而天下治。」「何謂事名二」?對曰：「天筴，陽也。壤筴，陰也，此謂事名二。」曰：「何謂正名五」。對曰：「權也、衡也、規也、矩也、准也，此謂正名五。其在色者，青黃白黑赤也。其在聲者，宮商角徵羽也。其在味者，醉辛鹹苦甘也。二五者，童山竭澤，人君以數制之人。味者，所以守民口也。聲者，所以守民耳也。色者，所以守民目也。人君失二五者，亡其國。大夫失二五者，亡其勢。民失二五者，亡其家，此國之至機也，謂之國機。」（管子揆度，78:2）

46 不正其名，不分其職，而數用刑罰，亂莫大焉。（呂氏春秋審分，93:4）(Lǚ Buwei, 291–235 BC).

47 蓋文字者，經藝之本，王政之始。前人所以垂後，後人所以識古。故曰：「本立而道生。」(說文解字卷一序1:13)

48 草木之生，華葉青葱，皆有曲折，象類文章，謂天為文字，復為華葉乎?(論衡，自然54:6)

49 子曰：「述而不作，信而好古，竊比於我老彭。」（論語述而，7:1）(The Master said, 'As a transmitter [narrator] and not a maker [writer], believing in and loving the ancients, I venture to compare myself with our old Peng'.) (*Analects, Shu Er,* 7:1; trans. Legge, 1861a)

50 聖人矢口而成言，肆筆而成書。言可聞而不可彈，書可觀而不可盡。（法言八百，9:18）

References

Bi, Wang. (1996). Elucidation of the image. In S. Owen (Ed. & trans.), *An anthology of Chinese literature: Beginnings to 1911* (pp. 63–64). New York, NY: W. W. Norton & Co.

Biesta, G. (2001). 'Preparing for the incalculable': Deconstruction, justice, and the question of education. In G. Biesta & D. Egéa-Kuehne (Eds.), *Derrida & education* (pp. 32–54), London, UK: Routledge.

Boltz, W. G. (1986). Early Chinese writing. *World Archaeology, 17*(3), 420–436.

Boltz, W. G. (1994). *The origin and early development of the Chinese writing system* (Vol. 78). New Haven, CT: American Oriental Society.

42   Chinese graphocentrism

Boltz, W. G. (1999). Language and writing. In M. Loewe & E. L. Shaughnessy (Eds.), *The Cambridge history of ancient China* (pp. 74–123). Cambridge, UK: Cambridge University Press.

Boltz, W. G. (2001). The invention of writing in China. *Oriens Extremis, 42*, 1–17.

Bottéro, F. (2002). Revisting the *wén* 文 and the *zì* 字: The great Chinese character hoax. *Bulletin of the Museum of Far Eastern Antiquities, 74*, 14–33.

Bottéro, F. (2006). Cang Jie and the invention of writing: Reflections on the elaboration of a legend. In C. Anderl & H. Eifring (Eds.), *Studies in Chinese language and culture* (pp. 135–155). Oslo, Norway: Hermes Academic Publishing.

Bullock, J. S. (Trans.). (2011). *Yang Xiong: Philosophy of the Fa yan*. Retrieved November 16, 2013, from D. Sturgeon (Ed.), *Chinese text project*. http://ctext.org/yangzi-fayan

Chang, Y-Y. 張彥遠 (n.d.). *A record of the famous paints of the history* 歷代名畫記. Retrieved March 29, 2019, from D. Sturgeon (Ed.), *Chinese text project*. Retrieved from http://ctext. org/wiki.pl?if=gb&chapter=129615

Chartier, R. (1994). *The order of books: Readers, authors, and librarians in Europe between the fourteenth and eighteenth centuries*. Cambridge: Polity Press.

Connery, C. L. (1998). *The empire of the text: Writing and authority in early imperial China*. Lanham, MD: Rowman & Littlefield Publishers.

Coulmas, F. (1989). *The writing system of the world*. Oxford, UK: Basil Blackwell.

Coulmas, F. (2003). *Writing system: An introduction to their linguistic analysis*. Cambridge, UK: Cambridge University Press.

Derrida, J. (1976). *Of grammatology*. Trans. G. C. Spivak. Baltimore, MD: John Hopkins University Press.

Derrida, J. (1978). *Writing and difference*. Chicago, IL: University of Chicago Press.

Derrida, J. (1979). Scribble (writing-power), *Yale French Studies, 58*, 117–147.

Derrida, J. (2016). *Of grammatology*. Trans. G. C. Spivak. Introduction by J. Butler. Baltimore, MD: John Hopkins University Press.

Dŏn, Z. S. (2011). *Chun Qiu Fán Lù* 春秋繁露. Retrieved November 10, 2016, from: D. Sturgeon (Ed.), *Chinese Text Project*. http://ctext.org/chun-qiu-fan-lu

Forke, A. (Trans.) (1907). *Lùnhéng*. London, UK: LUZAC & Co. Retrieved March 29, 2017, from https://archive.org/stream/lunheng01wang#page/n0/mode/2up

Gao, Y. 高誘 (1965). *Commentaries on Húinánzì* 淮南子注. Taipei: World Book Co. 臺北: 世界書局 Retrieved from http://ctext.org/huainanzi/zh

Geaney, J. (2010). Grounding language in the sense: What the eyes and ears reveal about *ming* 名 (names) in early Chinese texts. *Philosophy East & West, 60*(2), 251–293.

Hamilton, E., & Cairns, H. (Eds.). (1961). *Plato: The collected dialogues*. Princeton, NJ: Princeton University Press.

Hansen, C. (1983). *Language and logic in ancient China*. Ann Arbor: University of Michigan Press.

Kane, D. (2006). *The Chinese language: Its history and current usage*. North Clarendon, VT: Tuttle Publishing.

Kavanagh, D. (2004). Ocularcentrism and its others: A framework for metatheoretical analysis. *Organization Studies, 25*(3), 445–464.

Knoblock, J. H. (1994). *Xunzi: A translation and study of the complete works vol. III*. Stanford, CA: Stanford University Press.

Legge, J. (Trans.). (1861a). *Confucian analects. The Chinese classics, volume 1*. Retrieved November 10, 2013, D. Sturgeon (Ed.), *Chinese text project*. Retrieved from http://ctext.org/analects

Legge, J. (Trans.). (1885). *Sacred books of the east, volume 28, part 4: The Li Ki*. Retrieved November 19, 2013, from D. Sturgeon (Ed.), *Chinese text project*. Retrieved from http://ctext.org/liji

Legge, J. (Trans.). (1985). *The works of Mencius*, Clarendon. Retrieved August 27, 2015, from D. Sturgeon (Ed.), *Chinese text project*. Retrieved from http://ctext.org/mengzi

Leung, A. K. C. (1994). 'Societies for cherishing written characters' (*his-tzu hui*) in Ch'ing China. *New History*, 5(2), 83–115.

Levi-Strauss, C. (1974). *Tristes Tropiques*. Trans. J. Weightman and D. Weightman. New York, NY: Atheneum.

Lewis, M. E. (1999). *Writing and authority in early China*. New York, NY: State University of New York Press.

Liao, W. K. (Trans.). (1939). *The complete works of Han Fei Tzǔ with collected commentaries*. Retrieved September 10, 2013, from http://www2.iath.virginia.edu/saxon/servlet/Saxon Servlet?source=xwomen/texts/hanfei.xml&style=xwomen/xsl/dynaxml.xsl&doc. view=tocc&chunk.id=tpage&toc.depth=1&toc.id=0&doc.lang=bilingual

Liu, A. (2011). *Huainanzi*. Retrieved November 18, 2013, from D. Sturgeon (Ed.), *Chinese text project*. Retrieved from http://ctext.org/huainanzi

Liu, J. J. Y. (1988). *Language-paradox-poetics*. Princeton, NJ: Princeton University Press.

Liu, X. (Ed.). (2011). *Guangzi*. Retrieved November 18, 2013, from D. Sturgeon (Ed.), *Chinese text project*. Retrieved from http://ctext.org/guanzi

Lǔ, B. (2011). *Lǔshì Chunqiu*. Retrieved November 18, 2013, from D. Sturgeon (Ed.), *Chinese text project*. Retrieved from http://ctext.org/lv-shi-chun-qiu

Makeham, J. (1991). Names, actualities, and the emergence of essentialist theories of naming in classical Chinese thought. *Philosophy East & West*, 41(3), 341–363.

Marinelli, M. (2012). Word-images: Politics and visual culture in China. *PORTAL Journal of Multidisciplinary International Studies*, 9(3), 2–15.

Olson, H. A. (2002). *The power to name: Locating the limits of subject representation in libraries*. Dordrecht, The Netherlands: Kluwer Academic Pub.

Ong, W. (1967). *The presence of the word: Some prolegomena for cultural and religious history*. New Haven, CT: Yale University Press.

Ong, W. (1977). *Interfaces of the word: Studies in the evolution of consciousness and culture*. New York, NY: Cornell University Press.

Ong, W. (1982). *Orality and literacy: The technologizing of the word*. London: Routledge.

Plato. (1925). *Plato in twelve volumes* (Vol. 9). Trans. H. N. Fowler. Cambridge, MA: Harvard University Press.

Ssu-yǔ, T. (1968). *Family instructions for the Yen Clan by Yen Chih-t'ui*. Leiden: E. J. Brill.

Xu, G. Q. (2004). The use of eloquence: The Confucian perspective. In C. S. Lipson & R. A. Binkley (Eds.), *Rhetoric before and beyond the Greeks* (pp. 115–130). Albany, NY: State University of New York Press.

Xū, S.許慎(n.d.) *Shuowén Jiězì*.說文解字. Retrieved March 15, 2017, from D. Sturgeon (Ed.), *Chinese text project*. Retrieved from http://ctext.org/shuo-wen-jie-zi

Zha, P. (1992). Logocentrism and traditional Chinese poetics. *Canadian Review of Comparative Literature/Revue Canadienne de Littérature Comparée*, 19(3), 377–394.

Zhang, L. (1985). The *Tao* and the *Logos*: Notes on Derrida's critique of logocentrism. *Critical Inquiry*, 11, 385–398.

Chapter 3

Graphocentric education

The cultivation of the writing subject

The only phenomenon with which writing has always been concomitant is the creation of cities and empires, that is the integration of large numbers of individuals into a political system, and their grading into castes and classes . . . at the time when writing first emerges: it seems to have favoured the exploitation of human beings rather than their enlightenment . . . the primary function of written communication is to facilitate slavery.

—(Lévi-Strauss, *Tristes Tropiques*, 1974, p. 299)

於是一個長衫人物拿了一張紙，並一支筆送到阿Q的面前，要將筆塞在他手裡。阿Q這時很吃驚，幾乎「魂飛魄散」了：因為他的手和筆相關，這回是初次。他正不知怎樣拿；那人卻又指著一處地方教他畫花押。
「我……我……不認得字。」阿Q一把抓住了筆，惶恐而且慚愧的說。
「那麼，便宜你，畫一個圓圈！」
阿Q要畫圓圈了，那手捏著筆卻只是抖。於是那人替他將紙鋪在地上，阿Q伏下去，使盡了平生的力氣畫圓圈。他生怕被人笑話，立志要畫得圓，但這可惡的筆不但很沉重，並且不聽話，剛剛一抖一抖的幾乎要合縫，卻又向外一聳，畫成瓜子模樣了。

——（魯迅，阿Q正傳，第九章）[1]

We have seen that Chinese culture and philosophy tend to value writing over speaking. For this, I coin the term 'graphocentrism'. In contrast, Western phonocentrism values speech over writing. Lévi-Strauss's words are an example of how the written word has been seen as dangerous in Western culture. Graphocentrism tends to value things and objects that are physical, visible, tactile, verifiable, credible, and inalterable. This tendency is associated with credentialism – the belief that favours credentials and diplomas and that has been popular and influential in contemporary Chinese cultural societies. In Chinese tradition, an educational or academic degree greatly affects social status and promotion. A higher education degree leads to higher status and faster promotion. Writing provides a lens with which to penetrate education, as an educational degree or qualification is based on the development of literacy – the ability to read and write. Throughout literary history, the privileging of writing has been canonised by a series of complex measures of institutionalisation of education and politics. This chapter will explore how this process of canonisation cultivated a human person as the 'writing subject' with respect to graphocentrism.

By the term 'writing subject', I do not mean the authors of the written canonical works or the early sage kings, although they were privileged authors in the sense that their words were preserved and obeyed with caution and respect. By the 'writing subject', I mean the traditional Confucian literati, intellectuals, scholar-gentry, or scholar-officials. They had admirable writing skills, such as handwriting and composition skills. In ancient times, they were the elite of society. The ideal Confucian-educated man is called a junzǐ (君子), as described in the *Analects* and other Confucian classic texts. The most important meaning of the concept of junzǐ lies in its moral significance. A junzǐ is the exemplary moral role model in the Confucian tradition. The term 'rú' (儒) refers to the Confucian literati, while 'shìh' (士) refers to aristocrats holding offices or those born of good families. We may say that the word 'rú' carries cultural and academic implications, whereas 'shìh' has a sociopolitical meaning. In some historical periods of time, such as the later Han period (25–220 CE), the Three Kingdoms period (220–280 CE), or the Súi dynasty (581–618 CE), the class of 'shìh' may have been more recognisable for its 'subjective, idealist, indeterminate, "cultural" character' (Connery, 1998, p. 98). The terms 'aristocracy, bureaucracy, oligarchy, great families or simply elite' were used as tags (Connery, 1998, p. 98). Many figures of the 'shìh' at that time indeed held high Daoist values. While the meanings of 'junzǐ', 'rú', and 'shìh' are not identical, these terms usually refer to the same group of people – the aristocratic elite. We can make the following comparison between these three concepts: 'rú' is more suitable for describing cultural identity; 'shìh' is used to refer to official identity, and 'junzǐ', most important of all, refers to an exemplary moral role model. In the Confucian tradition, the junzǐ as an exemplary person is a model of refinement. The words 'rú' and 'shìh' are used to describe the condition of a person in relation to a cultural or official context. In contrast, the concept of junzǐ has a profound moral and ethical implication. The aristocratic elite were expected to be excellent, both culturally and morally. The curriculum, means, and institutionalisation of education in ancient China all focused on the cultivation of the morally and culturally qualified aristocratic elite.

In ancient Chinese society, it was very important for the literati to gain an office of the state. For the literati, holding an office in the imperial government was virtually the only path to career development. In order to acquire proper offices in the government, they had to acquire special knowledge and ability to pass imperial examinations. And to pass the imperial examinations, the literati had to be able to read and write with skill and proficiency and have extensively developed knowledge of the contents of the examinations, which mainly focused on canonised Confucian classics. In this view, writing played a decisive role in the complex and complicated process for one to become an official serving the government. A qualified aristocratic elite or scholar-officer, a 'rú' or 'shìh', had to be very skilful in writing. One had to know what to write and how to write well. The subject of writing thus encapsulated ideal personal identities in relation to culture, education, politics, society, and morality.

The cultivation of writing was the ultimate goal of traditional Chinese education. The objective of graphocentric education was to achieve ideal personhood, which entailed not only being a junzǐ but also being a writing subject. Three aspects of graphocentric education will be discussed: the discipline of writing calligraphy, the institutionalisation of writing through the imperial civil examination system, and, most importantly, the cultivation of the moral writing subject.

The discipline of writing calligraphy

The discipline of writing means the training of handwriting, the writing of Chinese calligraphy. Chinese calligraphy is, of all Chinese traditional art forms, the most fascinating and delicate. It involves writing, painting, and seal carving. In Chinese, calligraphy writing is called '書法' (shufǎ), meaning the method and rule of writing. In Japanese, it is called '書道' (shudào), the Dao of writing.

Chinese calligraphy is not easy. It must be practiced in accordance with strict rules. First, a calligrapher must be able to select the best instruments and use them in the most appropriate or skilful way. The four utensils of writing calligraphy – the brush, paper, inkstone, and ink stick – are called the 'Four Treasures of the Study' (文房四寶, wén fán szì baŏ) (Long, 1987). Second, a calligrapher needs to obey codes that impose restrictions upon the content and method of writing. Each Chinese character is composed of several strokes. To write characters correctly, one must follow the conventional order of brushstrokes from top to bottom and from left to right. The calligrapher also must be attentive and careful in order to give each character balance, force, and harmony. Handsome handwriting was one of the requisites for literate Chinese and was an emblem of the officials' sophistication (Kraus, 1991). In the long history of calligraphy, there has been a corpus of literature on the skills and method required. Ancient calligraphers advised apprentices about how to hold the brushes, how to keep the body balanced when writing, how to select the best instruments and materials, how to create artistic appreciation of past works, etc. Over the years, a system of rules was established regulating the selection and use of utensils, the writing content, and the process of writing. The rules concerning the didactic method and the restriction of writing comprise what I call the calligraphy code.

The calligraphy pedagogical code includes the restriction of writing, the didactics of writing, and the end of writing. The overall code structure is a set of procedures for regulating and domesticating the calligrapher's body and mind.

The restriction of writing

The restriction of writing concerned taboo words that were prohibited in certain circumstances. A taboo word in Chinese is called '諱' (huì). In ancient China, the names of emperors, respected sages, and, contrarily, even traitors and the like were considered taboo, so it was forbidden to pronounce or write their names or to name others with the same characters. The naming taboo as a cultural practice existed for thousands of years, beginning during the Zhou dynasty. It was written in *Zuǒ Zhuàn* (左傳), the Spring and War period (771–403 BCE) classic on narrative history, that 'the people of Zhou do not use the name which they bore in serving the Spirits of the dead; and the name is not mentioned after death' (*Chun Qiu Zuǒ Zhuàn, Book II, Duke Huán: Sixth Year*; trans. Legge, 1872).[2]

Tabooing (避諱, bì huì) included substitution, bracketing, intentional typographical errors, and modification of pronunciation (Chén, 1997). In substitution, the forbidden taboo word was replaced by synonyms or parasynonyms. In bracketing, the taboo word was simply removed from a text, and a space was left in its place. Intentional typographical errors can be traced back to the Táng dynasty. The taboo word was intentionally miswritten in such a way that one stroke of the character was omitted. Pronunciations of taboo words were also changed while speaking them.

The naming taboo practice was fundamentally concerned with showing respect for exalted persons. It was forbidden to speak or write the names of those honoured persons, which may have included rulers and their ancestors (the empire naming taboo, 國諱, gúo huì), former sages (the sages naming taboo, 聖諱, shèn huì), one's own ancestors (the family naming taboo, 家諱, jia huì, or the private naming taboo, 私諱, si huì), and chief magistrates (the magisterial naming taboo, 憲諱, xiàn huì) (Biàn, 2008; Huáng, 2000). The empire naming taboo had great influence because not only the name of the current ruler but also those of his ancestors were considered taboo. A record of the empire naming taboo can be found in writings of the Chín dynasty (221–206 BCE) – the first imperial dynasty in China. As written in the chapter *Annals of Chín Shi Huáng* (秦始皇, the first emperor of Chín) in *Shǐjì* (史記), the name of the place Chǔ (楚) was changed to Jin (荊), for Chín Shi Huáng's father was called Zǐ Chǔ (子楚). As for the sages naming taboo, under the tradition of Confucianism, the names of Duke Zhou, Confucius, Mencius, and Laozi were proscribed as taboo. This cultural practice became stricter in the Sòng dynasty.

Even homonyms of taboo words were forbidden. An official of the empire would be punished if he disobeyed the taboo by using the forbidden words in any report or document. The examiners and candidate students of the imperial examinations also needed to be very careful not to commit the offense, lest the face a serious penalty.

48 Education

The naming taboo was related to the 'literary persecution' or 'literary inquisition' (文字獄, wén zì yù) (Ku & Goodrich, 1938), a means to censor and control the writing of intellectuals in ancient China. Those who wrote the forbidden words were punished. In the Ming and Ching dynasties, the literary inquisition was conducted intensively and extensively. For example, the founder and the first emperor of the Ming dynasty, Zhu Yuánzhang (朱元璋), was notorious for putting subjects under strict censorship by means of the naming taboo and literary inquisition. Many people who disobeyed the naming taboo were put to death. Some death penalties were given because the offenders used the word '殊' (shu, meaning unique). However, the word '殊' is composed of two characters: '歹' (dǎi) and '朱' (zhu). The word '歹' (dǎi) means bad, inferior, or wicked, whereas '朱' (zhu) was the family name of the emperor. Thus, the emperor assumed that any writer who used the word '殊' was castigating him (Biàn, 2008; Huáng, 2000). The emperor Yungzhèng (雍正, 1678–1735 CE) was notorious for ferociously executing the literary inquisition and naming taboo during the Ching dynasty (1616–1912 CE). In 1726, Chá Sì Ting (查嗣庭, 1664–1727 CE) was the chief examiner in charge of assigning topics for the imperial examinations. He was accused of giving 維民所止 (wéi míng sūo zhǐ) as the topic of the essay test. The phrase '維民所止' (wéi míng sūo zhǐ) is cited in the ancient classic *Book of Poetry* of the Western Zhou:

> The royal domain of a thousand Li,
>> Is where the people rest;
>> But there commence the boundaries that reach to the four seas.
>>> (*Book of Poetry, Part of Sacrificial Odes of Shang,*
>>> *Chapter of Xúan Nīao*; trans. Legge, 1898)[3]

The above excerpt means that the emperor's territory is where people reside. However, as reported to the emperor Yungzhèng, the phrase '維民所止' refers to the beheading of the ruler because his appellation was 雍正 (Yungzhèng), and the words '維' (wéi) and '止' (zhǐ) mean 'the decapitated Yungzhèng'. It was determined that this topic showed treasonous intent by the chief examiner. Brutal punishment ensued, including death sentences, exile, imprisonment, and enslavement imposed upon more than a hundred of the examiner's close family members, relatives, and colleagues.

The naming taboo and the related literary inquisition proved effective for putting subjects under meticulous and rigorous censorship and control, especially for the 'writing subject'.

The didactics of writing

There are two essential methods for acquiring the skill of writing calligraphy: imitation and repeated practice. These two activities are interdependent and inseparable in the tradition of calligraphic education. Literature highlights the imitation of scripts by calligraphers such as Yántǐ (顏體) and the calligraphic style of Yán Zhenquin (顏真卿, 709–785 CE), Liǔtǐ (柳體), and Liě Gongquán (柳公權, 778–856 CE) (Yen, 2005). As the Southern Sòng (1127–1279 CE) poet Jiang Kwéi (姜夔, 1155–1211 CE) puts it, 'The apprentices of calligraphy do nothing but trace . . . the masterworks of the ancients' (Huá, 1997, p. 361; my translation).[4] The Míng dynasty (1368–1644 CE) painter and official scholar Xìe Jìn (解縉, 1369–1415 CE) writes in his *Whims in Spring Rain* (春雨雜述) that 'the way of learning calligraphy . . . depends most greatly on the imitation of the ancients' writing' (Huá, 1997, p. 461; my translation).[5] The Ching dynasty writer Ju Lyǔ Cheng (朱履真), in *The Key to Calligraphy* (書學捷要), also stresses the importance of imitation when learning to write calligraphy. Ju says, 'The main point of learning calligraphy consists in the imitation' (Huá, 1997, p. 561; my translation).[6] Ju systematically proposes six basic things for the mastery of calligraphy: temperament, natural endowment, the method of holding the brush, imitation, diligence, and connoisseurship. On the fourth point, Ju says:

> Fourth, imitate. It is necessary to gain exemplary copybooks. Start writing calligraphy by imitation to master the skills of using the brush. This is the legacy of achieving proficiency in calligraphy from the predecessors.
> (Huá, 1997, p. 461; my translation)[7]

Writing as imitation is modelling past masterpieces. A novice at the beginning stage of learning to write with brushes must try hard to make a careful copy of a masterpiece. The more similar the copy appears, the higher level the learner attains.

It seems contradictory that, on the one hand, calligraphy is believed to manifest one's specific moral characters and, on the other, learning calligraphy begins with imitation. This means sacrificing one's personal character in some sense. Although works of prestigious calligraphers are usually acknowledged to be expressions of personality, calligraphers must start their education with imitation. This contradiction may be solved by clarifying the traditional Chinese pedagogical technique – imitation (Reed, 1992).

The procedures of pedagogy are prescribed in the following order: 'starting with the individual strokes, moving through the simple characters toward the more complex, then working toward combing characters into an artistically rendered composition' (Reed, 1992, p. 75). Each step must be strictly obeyed and executed before moving to the next step. Imitating with precision and repetition is an attempt to internalise the patterns of a masterpiece and the values of tradition. As the student gains proficiency, the student is able to write or paint more freely. The Chinese pedagogical technique of imitation does not merely aim for the production of replicas.

In Chinese, at least three terms designate 'copying': 'mó' (摹), 'lín' (臨), and 'fǎn' (仿). These three terms have subtle nuances: *mó* (摹) means to trace and to exactly copy, *lín* (臨), to copy freehand, and *fǎn* (仿), to imitate in a freer manner. Mó is the first stage of imitation. Lín and fǎn comprise the second stage. In the beginning stages of learning to write with a brush, a student must faithfully model past masterworks in a very mechanical way. Many ancient critics and calligraphers emphasise the importance of method observance and constant exercise repetition in learning calligraphy. The training is almost entirely technical. It is all about producing strokes that look identical to the scripts written by the masters (Yen, 2005). More importantly, the goal is to incorporate the master's personhood and propensity by assimilating his techniques. Imitation fosters the acquisition of artistic techniques and moral qualities of past masters, which we will discuss more in a later section.

While the initial stage of learning calligraphy involves the imitation of masterworks, the ultimate goal is to create a personal style (Ho, 2005; Yen, 2005). During the process of imitation, one experiments with 'script, size, and overall composition' (Mullis, 2007). The exercises, after all, 'pave the way for the personal appropriation of the art' (Mullis, 2007, p. 102). As the student achieves better skills and excellence, he or she internalises and personalises the merits and goodness of past masterworks. At this point, one does not produce works blindly and mindlessly but instead works with the brush in a freer manner to create more personal art. Past masters began their study by copying to create their own calligraphic styles (Yen, 2005). Take the most prestigious calligraphy master of the Northern Sòng dynasty (960–1127 CE), Su Shì (蘇軾, 1037–1101 CE), as an example. His handwriting incorporated the styles of calligraphers Xú Hào (徐浩, 703–783 CE) and Wáng Sunqián (王僧虔, 425–485 CE) (Húa, 1997, p. 505). The process of imitation allows for the absorption of masterworks' characteristics and thus results in the creation of the later master's individual and unique style.

Not all students – even those capable of developing their own styles of artistic creation – become well-known and renowned artists. The aim of calligraphy education is not limited to cultivating masters; it also instils traditional values and passes them on to younger generations through the repetitive, labourious process of practice. The process of writing, according to Mullis (2007, p. 101), 'establishes a somatic relationship between artist and tradition'. More importantly, the procedures for writing calligraphy become a ritual and, therefore, 'through embodiment and ritualised action, students appropriate the tradition in an intimate way' (ibid., p. 101). Imitating established works and following convention are thus crucial elements in calligraphy education. This mirrors the graphocentric mindset of ancestor worship in Chinese tradition, in which former sages establish invincible and unsurpassable moral standards and ideal role models. Although there are distinguished calligraphers who possess unique and outstanding artistic styles when compared to others, individual style is interpreted restrictively within a moralistic boundary. The artist's moral character is considered part of the criteria for evaluating his works. Art, aesthetics, and morality are intrinsically interconnected in Chinese tradition. I will explore the intertwined aesthetics and morality of graphocentric ethics in a later section.

On this point, I may conclude that imitation as the initial pedagogical technique of writing has two pursuits: 1) downgrading one's own personal idiosyncrasies by copying and imitating and 2) elevating and consecrating past masters, whether they be rulers of states, sages, or family ancestors.

Repeated practice, a key activity for incorporating the brush as part of the body, is essential to mastering calligraphy. Calligraphy skills and artistic refinement can develop only after one spends much time repeating calligraphic practices. Practicing calligraphy is a process of development in personal artistic ability and, more importantly, in moral goodness. During the process of learning, one must commit oneself with all one's heart, mind, strength, body, and time. In Chinese tradition, practicing calligraphy is thought to cultivate aesthetic ability and morality. Repeated practice was essential for ancient Chinese literati to live good lives in terms of lifelong self-cultivation.

A master calligrapher must use the equipment with great proficiency and skill. As mentioned previously, four instruments known as the 'Four Treasures of the Study' (Long, 1987) are used to write Chinese calligraphy: the brush, the ink stick, the inkstone, and the paper. Using the four instruments properly is critical to mastering calligraphy. Among these four instruments, the brush is the instrument that takes the most effort to use skilfully. Holding the brush properly is not merely keeping the brush in hand. One must be attentive to the posture of the body, the method of controlling the fingers, and the skill of using the wrist. As the Míng dynasty calligrapher Fong Feng (豐坊, 1492–1563 CE) writes, one must stand up and keep the body in balance and the back straight when writing calligraphy. The elbows shall not be put on the desk. One should use the upper arm to write big words and the forearm for small words. One's hands or other parts of the body are not allowed to touch the paper when writing calligraphy (Huá, 1997). One must pose 'correctly' in every move of preparation and brush writing. Each assumed posture is 'rigid and muscle-training' (Yen, 2005, p. 109). Students must obey a series of procedures and lengthy preparations when practicing calligraphy.

Before holding the brush to make strokes on paper, one must prepare the ink by grinding an ink stick on an inkstone. Ink sticks are usually round or square sticks made of pine soot and other ingredients. Ink is produced by mixing the soot with water while the soot is extracted by the repeated, constant, and circular grinding actions of the stick. The circular and slow motion of grinding the hands is 'almost a sacred rite' (Yen, 2005). During the quiet process of grinding, one is calm, tranquil, and concentrated. The exquisiteness of this is revealed in Yen's (2005, p. 114) description: 'As one grinds the ink, the gaze normally focuses on the repetitive circular motion of the hand and the ink stick, slowly, sedately and hypnotically. The sound of the pine-soot ink stick rubbing on the stone fills the ears, smooth and unintrusive, pure and humming'. This stage of preparation is nearly a rite of serenity and purification, the effect of which is similar to meditation and works through all senses: 'the visual, the acoustic, the olfactory and the kinetic' (Yen, 2005, p. 114). Moreover, 'It is a process that

52 Education

purifies sight, smell, hearing and motion . . . All this preparation aims to purify thoughts' (Yen, 2005, pp. 114–115). The circular, repetitive, and lengthy grinding prepares the body of the calligrapher to be a writing subject via all senses. The body and the mind at this moment are one, focused and tranquil, concentrative and quiet.

After the ink and the calligrapher's mind and body are prepared, the calligrapher is finally ready to set down strokes. There are specific rules to obey. A calligrapher must make great efforts to model each stroke of the masterworks with precision and accuracy. He must pay attention to every bodily movement. Constant repeated practice is critical. As Su Shì (蘇軾, 1037–1101 CE), one of the Sòng dynasty's most renowned artists, poets, painters, and calligraphers, writes, only when a practitioner uses a pile of brushes and exhausts a pond of water does he become a master calligrapher like Wáng Xìzhi (王羲之, 303–361 CE) or his son, Wáng Xianzhi (王獻之, 344–386 CE) (Huá, 1997, p. 288).[8] What is more, Su adds that only if one wears out the brushes of 1,000 pens and uses more than 10,000 ink sticks can one accomplish the degree of masters like Chang Zhi (張芝, n.d.–192 CE) or Sŏ Jìn (索靖, 239–303 CE).[9] The extravagant numbers of brush pens and ink sticks indicates that persistent repetition and labourious practice are indispensable for learning. Ink-stained sleeves, mouth, and teeth are often used to describe hardworking practitioners.[10] Xìe Jìn (解縉, 1369–1415 CE) advances this point with examples:

> Chang Zhi kept learning calligraphy by the pond. [After a long time], the water of the pond turned into black. Minister Zhong practiced calligraphy in the Mountain Bàodó for ten years. [As a consequence], the woods and rocks on the mountain were all blackened. Zhào Mèngfŭ did not go downstairs for ten years [because he stayed in the room to practice calligraphy]. Kúi Zĭshan Píngzhong always practiced one thousand words after work before dinner. The emperor Tang Taizong studied [calligraphy] hard during the wartime. He woke up in the midnight to imitate *Lantingji* in the candlelight. Writing big words helps the calligrapher to comprehend the structure of characters. The former calligraphers continued to practice calligraphy with wet brooms on the ground or stairs. In the end the slates or the stairs were eroded.
>
> (Huá, 1997, pp. 461–462; my translation)[11]

As the passage reveals, a student must make great effort and spend much time practicing. Constant, repeated practice finally unite the calligrapher and the brush as one. The calligrapher incorporates the brush, and the brush is embodied as an extension of the calligrapher's body (Kraus, 1991). Practicing calligraphy is an exhausting and laborious enterprise. It requires considerable rote repetition and the entire devotion of one's heart and mind. Writing does not only rest upon the contact point of the brush and paper. It relies on whole body movement – the coordination of fingers, arms, legs, shoulders, head, and instruments, especially the brush. The brush becomes a part of the body, enabling the calligrapher to write with the fullest expressiveness. The other instruments – paper, inkstones, and ink sticks – are of great importance as well. A master calligrapher is always meticulous about the selection of the instruments and pays great attention to the process of preparing the ink through the shaving and grinding of the ink sticks and the mixture with water. It is essential for the calligrapher to be well acquainted with these instruments, making them his own and incorporating them into himself.

The end of writing

The end of the practice of calligraphy is cultivation of the moral self. Calligraphy is a discipline of personality because, by means of labouring the body, it strengthens the mind. In Chinese, the cultivation of the self is called 'xiu-shen'. 'Xiu' (修) means to mend, to repair, to polish, and to improve. 'Shen' (身) means the body. Literally, 'xiu-shen' (修身) refers to the 'cultivation of the body' or the 'shaping of the body'. As a bodily exercise, brush writing, therefore, 'as believed in this time-honoured tradition, is more than an artistic expression; it is also a form of spiritual cultivation, a practice that has the potential to instil positive character traits in the practitioner' (Ying, 2012, p. 33). In the Chinese literary tradition, practicing calligraphy is closely related to the cultivation of the self in the sense that the constant exercises and drills are not only training in writing skills but also in developing personal character traits such as patience, endurance, hard work, persistence, devotedness, and so on. Spiritual and moral cultivation channels the shaping of the body, and vice versa. Development of personal character traits is achieved by attuning the mind and the body. Gunn (2001) gives an interesting explanation about how calligraphy is related to the development of the body and mind:

> In the process of the self-development of the calligrapher, the body and mind are understood as one, such that the body has its own awareness, its own memory, its own intuitive responses and initiatives, its own way of knowing. These faculties are proprioceptive, kinesthetic and intuitive. They are developed by practice and constant attention, especially through attention to the breath and in meditation.
>
> (Gunn, 2001, p. 158)

As a process of mental and physical exertion, repeated practice improves not only one's writing skill as an artistic technique but also one's personal moral disposition. The process of practicing calligraphy is, at the same time, a process of refining taste and improving moral character. Writing calligraphy was held in esteem by traditional Chinese literati as a means of self-cultivation, lifting the spirit, elevating morality, and refining aesthetic ability.

The institutionalisation of writing through the imperial civil examination

The imperial examination system, which institutionalised writing in terms of correct graphic orthography and content, was the second pillar for supporting the regime of writing in premodern China. By 'graphic orthography', I mean the rules regulating the writing of characters in correct structures and appropriate forms. Graphic orthography can be viewed as a prerequisite for the imperial civil examination system.

For more than 1,000 years, the government of the ancient Chinese empire was supported by scholar-bureaucrats. The scholar-officials were recognised as the embodiment of the state (Balazs, 1964, p. 17; Connery, 1998, p. 103). The process and mechanism of their selection as bureaucrats played a critical role in maintaining the effective and efficient working of the government.

From the Suí dynasty (581–619 CE) until the end of the Ching dynasty (1616–1912 CE), the imperial civil examination system controlled the process of recruiting talent and rendering social mobility. The examination system distinguished the literate from the illiterate, the qualified literati from the unqualified, and writing masters from neophytes in terms of graphocentrism. Some scholars, such as Chíen Mu (1982), believe that the imperial examination played an important role in social mobility in ancient China. As François Quesnay (1946, p. 172; also quoted from Kracke, 1947) writes in the eighteenth century,

> There is no hereditary nobility in China; a man's merit and capacity alone mark the rank he is to take. Children of the prime minister of the empire have their fortune to make and enjoy no special consideration. If they are inclined toward idleness, or if they lack talent, they fall to the rank of the common people, and are often obliged to adopt the vilest occupations. However, a son inherits his father's property; but to succeed him in dignities and to enjoy his reputation, the son must elevate himself by the same steps; thus all of the son's hopes depend on study, as the only avenue to honours.
>
> (Kracke, 1947, pp. 103–104)

Whoever passed the examinations had an opportunity to serve in the government, whether born in an aristocratic family or a commoner. However, this view could exaggerate or overly romanticise the role of civil imperial examinations in improving social equity and mobility. Some scholars, such as Karl August Wittfogel (quoted in Kracke, 1947, p. 104), believe that the examinations did not bring huge changes to the social strata: 'Some "fresh blood" may have been absorbed from the lower strata of society by means of the examination system; but on the whole the ruling officialdom reproduced itself socially more or less from its own ranks'. Not many commoners could afford the long period of full-time education and preparation, and the examination was extremely difficult and competitive. The literacy of the lower class was 'too vernacular to master the classical frames of language and writing tested in the local licensing examinations' (Elman, 2000, p. xxx). In premodern China, a very limited number of common people received education in reading and writing. The imperial examination was, therefore, a useful means for the literati-gentry as writing subjects to strive for and secure their offices in the government and hold political powers. Since the imperial examination played the most critical role in selecting the government's literati-bureaucrats, the system served as the most effective mechanism of curbing and controlling the character and thought of literate elites by mandating the subject matter of the examination and thereby controlling the curriculum of all levels of schools. The candidates had to produce qualified writing in terms of orthography, structure, and content in order to pass the examination and get a position in the government.

Graphic orthography

Graphic orthography refers to writing characters correctly in terms of word structure, type, and form. For the scholar-official, it was important to write correct characters in public, official, and formal documents. It was a serious mistake to write incorrectly in official documents. When the first ancient Chinese imperial dynasty, Qín (221–206 BC), was founded, one of the controlling strategies was the standardisation of the writing system – the homogenisation of word types and forms. Nearly every dynasty in Chinese history authorised correct forms of written characters and institutionalised official posts for graphic orthography. Incorrect writing could be a serious offense in ancient times. As written in the *Shǐjì* (史記, *Scribe's Records*), an official in the Hàn dynasty made an error in writing the character for horse (馬). He was condemned to death (Tsai, 2009). However, the types and forms of characters did not quickly become uniform. Ancient Chinese governments implemented four methods to ensure correct graphic orthography: the regulation of laws, compilation textbooks on literacy education for beginners, building of inscribed stele, and the edition and publication of graphic orthography dictionaries (Tsai, 2009). In the mid-Táng (618–907 CE) dynasty, there was a trend of producing compilation dictionaries (Mar, 2014; Tsai, 2008). One of the most well-known dictionaries was edited by the Táng scholar Yán Yúansun (顏元孫, n.d.). The dictionary is entitled *Ganlu Zìshu* (干祿字書), or *Character Book Seeking for Official Emoluments*. This book provided guidelines on writing characters in the correct form and type for candidates taking imperial examinations. The candidates were advised to write faultless and readable regular scripts. The title of the book clearly indicates the purpose of facilitating students' attainment of wealth and promotion (Tsai, 2009; Yen, 2005). In the Táng dynasty, if there were too many candidates for the imperial civil examination, the second part of the examination would be omitted. Handwriting was then taken as the sole criterion for selection. Candidates with excellent handwriting could be granted

56 Education

official posts (Yen, 2005). Thus, proper handwriting was inseparable from the cultural-political mechanism of the governing regime.

Imperial civil examinations

Now let us focus on the imperial civil examinations. What kind of knowledge did a candidate need to serve the state?

The imperial examination system appeared during the Suí dynasty (581–619 CE). Prior to this period, the process of recruiting civil servants relied mainly on official recommendation or kinship relations (Chíen, 1982; Elman, 2000). In the Hàn dynasty (206 BCE–220 CE), civil service recruitment occurred based on 'district recommendation upon village selection' (hsiang-chü li-hsüan鄉舉里選), which included irregular and regular recommendations. Irregular recommendations occurred for different reasons – for example, when a new emperor ascended the throne, when a special mission needed to be fulfilled, or when there had been years of calamity due to great famine, floods, or plagues (Chíen, 1982). The regular selection system for officials was known as the recruitment of the Men of Filial Piety and Incorruptibility (Xiào-lien 孝廉) (Chíen, 1982). The Confucian virtue of filial piety has been regarded since ancient times. We will discuss filial piety (孝 xiào) later in this chapter.

In this recruitment system, the acquisition of state-controlled knowledge still played a crucial role in gaining a government position. The emperor Wŭ of Hàn (157–87 BCE) enforced a policy of revering no school of thought but Confucianism (dú zun rú shù 獨尊儒術), which afterwards had a massive and far-reaching effect upon Chinese political culture. The emperor Wŭ of Hàn and his successor, Jīng (188–141 BCE), created offices of erudite professors (pó-shìh 博士) of Five Classics, including Yìjing (易 Book of Changes), Shu (書 Book of Documents), Lĭjì (禮 Book of Rites), Shih (詩, Book of Poetry), and Chunqiu (春秋 Spring and Autumn Annals). The erudite professors served in the Imperial Academy (太學 Tàixúe) as specialists on one of the Five Classics. Disciples of the erudite professors would be appointed government positions after finishing their studies and completing oral examinations. Since the Five Classics were typically acknowledged Confucian texts, the mastery of Confucian doctrine was key to recruiting civil servants during the Hàn dynasty. During the Eastern Hàn period (25–220 CE), the recruitment system became 'a composite of four processes: education, administrative experience, recommendation, and examination' (Chíen, 1982, p. 17). However, the examination was different in form and in subject from the civil imperial examination of the medieval period (ninth to fourteenth centuries) and the late period (fifteenth to nineteenth centuries) of imperial China. In early times, the examination was not very strict in execution. The selected candidates went to the court and were asked face-to-face about urgent problems by means of a process called 'questioning by bamboo slips' (tsèwèn 策問) (Chíen, 1982). Questions would be written on bamboo slips in advance. During the examination, the candidate needed to answer the

Education   57

question picked up by the examiner. Nevertheless, a successful candidate's ideas and knowledge were supposed to fall in line with Confucianism.

During the time between the fall of the Hàn dynasty (202 BCE–220 CE) and the rise of the Súi dynasty (581–619 CE), China collapsed into several states ruled by different dominions that confronted each other. The recruitment of civil servants developed into the Nine Grade Referee system (九品中正制度), which was carried out during the periods of Wèi, Jín, and the Northern and Southern dynasties (265–589 CE). In this system, senior and junior referees of the court were sent to their duty commanderies to recruit officials by grading candidates from one to nine. The referees were supposed to make impartial and objective judgements so that the Ministry of the Personnel (吏部) could allocate offices to candidates based on the results of the grading (Elman, 2000; Lewis, 2009). However, it did not take long for the referees to give unjust and biased grades. Candidates of noble birth were often ranked high and assigned higher offices. In contrast, those from humble families were mostly ranked low and appointed inferior offices. This followed the credo, 'No one of humble birth be ranked high; no one of distinguished birth be ranked low' (*my translation*).[12] The Nine Grade Referee system was practiced for about three hundred years and was abrogated in the Súi dynasty in the late sixth century. The imperial civil examination system took the place of the Nine Grade Referee system in the recruitment of civil servants.

The civil imperial examinations were first implemented in the Súi dynasty but were developed further in the Táng dynasty (618–907 CE). The examinations underwent many significant changes over hundreds of years. In general, they included several levels of local, provincial, metropolitan, and palace examinations (Elman, 2000). The system included a three-tiered test taken at the local, provincial, and national levels. The national-level examination took place in the capital, with the emperor often serving as the premier examiner. Thus, the highest examination was called the palace examination (殿試 dièn shìh) or court examination (廷試 tíng shìh). The names of the examinations, candidates, and graduates varied in different time periods. Among these different levels of examinations, the Jìnshìh (進士) was the most honoured and had the longest history. Therefore, I use the Jìnshìh as a key for outlining the development and curriculum of the imperial civil examination system.

The Jìnshìh examination was first mandated by emperor Yáng of Súi (隋煬帝) in 605 CE. There were many different examinations in the Táng dynasty (618–907 CE), but the two most popular were the Jìnshìh and the Míng-jin (明經). The Míng-jin examination stressed the classics and policy questions, while the Jìnshìh focused on belles lettres and often included poetry, rhymed prose, and eulogies (Elman, 2000). As some scholars (Elman, 2000; Twitchett, 1974) note, the curriculum for the imperial examinations of the Táng dynasty was very diverse compared with those of late imperial China. Moreover, there was no rigid set of limits for classical scholarship in terms of content and style. Classical scholarship was never overlooked in the curriculum for imperial

58 Education

examinations of middle imperial China, yet the classics often included Confucian and Daoist texts. For example, the candidates were tested on the *Laozi* during the Táng dynasty (Elman, 2000).

The Jìnshìh was recognised as the more difficult and esteemed examination. The tales of *Táng Zhí Yán* (唐摭言) of the Táng dynasty has an interesting comparison between the people passing the Jìnshìh and those passing the Míng-jin: 'It is too old for a person in his thirties to acquire the Míng-jin degree. In contrast, it is too young for a person in his fifties to acquire the Jìnshìh degree' (*my translation*).[13] This shows that the Míng-jin examination is perceived as easier than the Jìnshìh examination. It can therefore be concluded that the examinations on the classical canon were much easier than those on the belles lettres during the Táng dynasty.

The prestigious mid-Táng literati Hán Yù (韓愈, 768–824 CE) strongly advocated for the Classical Prose Movement (kǔ wén movement, 古文運動). He rejected the popular ornate style of writing and advocated for the clear and clean, realistic and candid writing style of earlier times. More importantly, Hán Yù was a forerunner of Neo-Confucianism. He strongly criticised the popular Buddhist and Daoist doctrines, and he advocated for the teachings of Confucius and Mencius. Without directly making changes to the imperial examinations, Hán Yù's view pioneered the Neo-Confucianism of the Sòng and Míng dynasties, when the imperial examinations became more rigid about testing on the classical Confucian canon and the control of knowledge (Elman, 2000).

From the Táng dynasty to the Sòng dynasty, the civil imperial examinations underwent some changes. The first was related to the social status and background of the candidates. During the Táng dynasty, many candidates came from families of high social status, prestige, and power. Due to the decline of aristocratic families in the late Táng dynasty, candidates in the Sòng dynasty could come from humble families and villages.

The system became much stricter and more formalised during the Sòng dynasty. During the Táng dynasty, a candidate was permitted before taking examinations to make himself known to the public, to local officials, or to eminent scholar-officials who might be examiners because 'the selection of candidates was based on the opinions of eminent men in government and society – not merely on a single examination' (Chíen, 1982, p. 78). However, this open mentality was superseded by the request for rigor and fairness. To prevent personal favouritism and assure anonymity, several measures were employed during the Sòng dynasty, including locking of examination halls (Sǔoyùan 鎖院), covering names of examinees (Húmíng 糊名), and transcription (Ténglù 謄錄) (Chíen, 1982; Fang & Gong, 2015; Qu, 2003). The locking of examination halls was meant to keep examiners in the halls during examination time. The method of covering names entailed covering candidates' names on the examination papers (Chíen, 1982). Transcription entailed having the examination papers transcribed in order to make the handwriting uniform on all examination papers. These measures were established to prevent the examiners' contact with candidates or recognition of a candidate's personal traits on the examination papers. After the Sòng dynasty, fairness became a standard of utmost importance during civil imperial examinations. Later dynasties continued to use the abovementioned measures against cheating.

Subject matter was a third major difference between examinations in the Táng and the Sòng dynasties. The Míng-jin examination was cancelled during the reign of the emperor Shénzong of Sòng (1048–1085 CE), leaving only the Jìnshìh. In addition, the focus of the Jìnshìh examination was changed from poetry to classics. This reform was related to an archaic debate about whether belles lettres or policy questions based on the classics should take precedence on imperial examinations of the Jìnshìh degree. In the mid-eleventh century, as suggested by the poet, statesman, and historian Ouyáng Xiu (歐陽修 1007–1072 CE), the candidates would answer policy questions first and then be tested on their literary ability. Thus, the classical canon was used as a criterion to test candidates of the Jìnshìh degree (Elman, 2000). Furthermore, the *Analects* and the *Mencius* were required texts for examinations. Two influential Neo-Confucian philosophers of the Northern Sòng dynasty, Chéng Hào (程顥 1032–1085 CE) and Chéng Yí (程頤 1033–1107 CE), endeavoured to re-establish the traditions of Confucius and Mencius in terms of 'Dao-learning' (Dàoxúe 道學). The orthodoxy of Dao-learning was not completely established until Zhu Xi (朱熹 1130–1200 CE) of the Southern Sòng dynasty. As Elman (2000) remarks, poetry and rhymed prose still had an eminent place in the oeuvre of the Northern Sòng dynasty literati, such as Ouyáng Xiu (歐陽修 1007–1072 CE) and Wang Anshíh (王安石 1021–1086 CE). Chíen Mu (1982, p. 79) concludes that 'to change the subject matter of the examinations from poetry to classics . . . was also a fine idea since a mastery of poetry on the beauties of nature and romance could hardly serve as a suitable standard for selecting political talent'. However, the reform did not lead to the expected result:

> Yet, more was lost than gained by this, for it turned out that examining on the classics worked less well than examining on poetry. As Wang Anshíh lamented, the idea was to turn scholars into [*sic*] degree-holders but unexpectedly degree-holders were turned into pedants.
>
> (Chíen, 1982, p. 79)

The later Chinese Míng dynasty (1368–1644 CE) made some changes to the examination system, and the Ching dynasty (1644–1912 CE) basically followed the Míng dynasty system. While the changes during the Míng period were complicated, two of them had far-reaching influence: schools became part of the institution of civil imperial examinations, and the eight-legged essay (ba-gū wén 八股文) became the format of examination writing.

In the dynasties before the Míng dynasty, individual literati could apply for the civil examinations or be recommended by the local administration without educational qualifications. This policy ended at the start of the Míng dynasty.

60 Education

Tàzŭ (太祖 1328–1398 CE), the first emperor during this period, emphasised the importance of school education. During his reign, the empire's school system was combined with the examination system, a change that continued into the Ching dynasty. Only the 'tribute students' (kòngsheng, 貢生) of the state-supported Confucian Schools of the prefectures, subprefectures, and counties regularly were qualified to take examinations hosted by the Hànlin Academy (翰林院), which was the academic and administrative institution of the court (Chíen, 1982; Hucker, 1958). In traditional Chinese, following the prescribed order, step by step, in aspiring to educational degrees and careers in government was called the pursuit of Zhèngtú (正途, the correct track or path). Steps on this track included gaining a seat in the state-supported Confucian school, passing examinations, being admitted to the highest imperial educational institution, Gúozĭjian (國子監, Imperial Academy), completing education at the highest stage, and finally being appointed to an official post (Chíen, 1982; Elman, 2000; Hucker, 1958). However, the absorption of schools into the civil imperial examination system undeniably resulted in a shortcoming in Chinese culture – devaluing the function and meaning of school and education. Schooling was viewed as a path to a higher educational degree and, ultimately, an official post. In this view of Zhèngtú, education easily became a means or an instrument, and its intrinsic value was thus forgotten. It is worth noting that the wide credentialism of Eastern Asia has a historical root. In addition, the imperial school system limited what the Chinese elites learned. Hence, what these literati–elites acquired was state-controlled knowledge, which in the Míng and Ching dynasties was limited to the Confucian doctrines inherited from the Sòng dynasty – the Dàoxúe orthodoxy (道學, Dào-learning).

The introduction of the eight-legged essay may have caused greater damage to the free thinking and imagination of the literati during the Míng and Ching dynasties. This examination essay style appeared for the first time in the reign of the ninth emperor of the Míng dynasty, the Chénghùa Emperor (reign, 1464–1487 CE) (Elman, 2000). According this format, an examination essay had to be composed of eight sections. Each section comprised a few sentences. The length of the essay was strictly regulated – under five hundred words in the late Míng dynasty and around seven hundred words in the mid-Ching dynasty. When composing the eight-legged essay, a candidate had to be very careful about the balance and parallelism between sections, lines, and words. A mistake meant a failed examination (Elman, 2000). This rigid structure provided an easy, impartial, and objective standard for the examiners to grade. Nevertheless, the structure limited the ways in which candidates composed their essays, as the format, structure, topic, references, ideas, length, word selection, and handwriting style were all restricted. Chíen Mu (1982, p. 113) makes perceptive comments on the eight-legged essay, referring to it as 'a kind of stylistic formalised classicism'. More importantly, Chíen Mu notes that 'the works of men however public-spirited and well-intentioned may go awry and result in harm' (1982, p. 113). It is undeniable that this rigidly regulated format was largely responsible

Education 61

for restricting the free spirit and imaginative ability of the literati in late imperial China.

The cultivation of the moral writing subject

The calligraphy code and the imperial examinations were imposed upon the writing subject in order to cultivate a reliable, steadfast, and loyal part of the regime. Aside from these, the most important goal of practicing calligraphy was to perfect the moral self in the holistic sense that the calligrapher developed his mind and body harmoniously. The writing subject was expected to follow and corporate numerous ethical values and principles. The values and principles used to cultivate the moral writing subject were graphocentric ethics.

Graphocentric ethics included three parts. The first part focused on the intertwining of aesthetics and morality. It was widely accepted that calligraphy revealed not only artistic quality but the moral character of the calligrapher. Calligraphy thus embodied a connection between morality and aesthetics that implied a profound and uniquely graphocentric holism – the second part of graphocentric ethics. Graphocentric holism referred to the unity that surpasses the separation between the material and the spiritual, between the body and the mind, between nature and culture. The third and final part of graphocentric ethics related to the core virtues of Confucian humanistic education, which, with respect to graphocentrism, aimed to elevate the writing subject as a Confucian ideal human being. As discussed previously, practicing calligraphy takes great effort and is a work of patience. In a fundamental sense, writing calligraphy is performing a certain ritual, which is, in the Confucian tradition, essential in building social order and creating ideal personalities. This brings us to the notion of lǐ (禮), meaning ritual, rite, manners, etiquette, and so forth. From the graphocentric viewpoint, the process of cultivating the writing subject included performing or practicing the lǐ – rituals. The notion of lǐ was essential to Confucian virtue and morality. The three parts together comprised the mainstay of the ethics for cultivating the moral writing subject.

The intertwining of aesthetics and morality: aesthetic morality and moral aesthetics

In the Chinese tradition, one's moral level or quality was manifest in one's handwriting. Handsome handwriting was thus esteemed as a moral emblem of the calligrapher. It was a popular belief that 'one is what one writes, and vice versa' (人如其字). The belief that moral character and handwriting share and show similar traits was concerned not only with the content of a calligraphy work, but, more importantly, with the image. In terms of graphocentrism, whether the content was morally acceptable or philosophically justified was not the main point of the intertwining of morality and aesthetics. The main point was how the brush strokes were drawn and how the space between the strokes was arranged. Moral implications were manifested not merely in the general meanings of the words but also, and more significantly, in the artistic and aesthetic configuration of the words.

The belief that the aesthetic quality of a calligraphy work corresponds to the moral value of the calligrapher is rooted in Confucianism. As Confucius says, 'Aspire after the Dào. Be devoted to the dé (goodness). Comply with rén. Wander the arts' (*Analects, Shù Ér*, 7:6; *my translation*).[14] In Confucianism, a junzǐ needs to be engaged with and good at these four requirements. A junzǐ needs to be a good human being, morally and aesthetically.

The fourth requirement, 'wander the arts' (遊於藝, yóu yú yì), means 'playfully wander the arts'. The word 'yóu' refers to 'playfully wander', a state of freely moving and enjoying. 'Playfully wander the arts' means to play with arts freely and joyfully. Chan (1963, p. 31) translates '遊於藝' as 'find recreation in the arts', whereas Legge (1861a) translates it as 'let relaxation and enjoyment be found in the polite arts'. How can a junzǐ playfully and freely wander the arts? A junzǐ can playfully wander the arts because of two reasons. First, one must have mastery of the arts. Second, the mastery of the arts must be in accordance with the Dao.

In the first place, a junzǐ can take recreation in the arts by creating graceful arts and using artistic tools without difficulty. To use artistic tools effortlessly, one must have done many exercises — that is, one must have executed the relentless and repeated practices mentioned previously. The six arts, as addressed by the Confucian classic *Rites of Zhou* (周禮), are ritual, music, archery, riding, calligraphy, and mathematics. The six arts form the outline of the Confucian liberal education curriculum programme (Ni, 1999). Mastery of calligraphy is one of the necessary skills for cultivating a junzǐ — a decent, educated human being in terms of Confucianism. This leads to the second point — that writing calligraphy as practicing the arts must be in accordance with the Dào. This is the holistic key point that morality and aesthetics are consonant.

As Confucius states, the Dào, the dé (goodness, or virtue), rén, and the arts are four significant things for a junzǐ. As a fully educated human being, a junzǐ must be well advanced in the six arts and simultaneously good at following the Dao, the dé, and the virtue of rén. As Wáng Xizhi writes, the Daoist master advised him about writing: 'The chi (force) of the calligraphy must reach the Dao. It is identical with the order of the chaos' (Huá, 1997, p. 34; my translation).[15] In the ultimate state of writing, the calligrapher is both united with the Dao and achieves his morality. The integrity and decency of a junzǐ will be manifested in the junzǐ's artistic performances and his moral characteristics. The way one behaves relates to the way one practices the arts, including writing calligraphy, and vice versa. The characteristics of a junzǐ's aesthetic performances and those of his moral practice are common and consonant. Concepts such as uprightness, courteousness, wisdom, benevolence, trustworthiness, harmony, purity, mildness, moderation, peacefulness, firmness, balance, and excellence are generally used to refer to personal character and calligraphy (Ni, 1999). In this vein,

Confucian aesthetics and Confucian morality are understood as inseparable and intertwined.

Assessments of this view are spread throughout literature on the arts in Chinese history. Yáng Xióng (揚雄, 53 BC–18 AD) writes, 'Writing is the xin's pictures' (*Fǎnyán, Asking About Shen* 5:13; trans. by Bullock). The word 'xin' is the heart or the mind. Thus, writing (calligraphy) depicts what is in the heart or the mind (Kraus, 1991).

Likewise, Liú Xīzǎi (劉熙載, 1813–1881), a literary critic of the Ching Dynasty, says in his *Essays on Art* (藝概): 'Calligraphy is what it is; what one's knowledge is; what one's ability is; what one's aspiration is; in a word, what the person is' (Huá, 1997, p. 666; *my translation*).[16] Calligraphy shows the quality of one's achievement in the arts. More importantly, though, it also marks the level of one's moral development. As morality is viewed in Chinese culture as the core of the cultivation of the human subject, criticism of one's calligraphy usually concerns aesthetics as well as morality. The poet Su Shì (蘇軾, 1037–1101) makes a remarkable double comparison between a Confucian junzǐ and a xiǎorén and between exquisite writing and vulgar writing. In the Confucian tradition, a junzǐ refers to a morally decent and respectable role model, whereas a xiǎorén, literally translated as 'petty man' or 'little man', is a dishonourable and villainous person. Su Shì says: 'There is refined or vulgar calligraphy in as much as the heart of a junzǐ will not be confused with the heart of a xiǎorén' (Su Shì, *On Calligraphy*) (Huá, 1997, p. 288; my translation).[17]

The moral quality of a human being – whether a nobleman or a villain – can be exposed by handwriting. The Táng dynasty calligraphers Yán Zhenqing (顏真卿, 709–785) and Liǔ Gongquán (柳公權, 778–856) are esteemed examples whose moral integrity and achievements in calligraphy are highly respected. Yán and Liǔ were hardworking and loyal officials serving the emperors and the government (Ni, 1999). Liǔ says that if one's mind is decent, then so is one's writing (心正則筆正). This view had great impact upon later literati. Xiàng Mù (項穆, 1550–1600) further illustrates:

> If one is decent, then one's writing is graceful. The heart is the arbiter of the person. If the heart is decent, the person is decent. The brush pen is the extension of writing; if one's writing is graceful [by using the brush appropriately], one's conduct is decent. Decency of personality depends on the heart; gracefulness relies on using the brush appropriately.
>
> (Huá, 1997, p. 493; *my translation*)[18]

As Xiàng Mù puts it, there is an inextricable relationship between the inner heart and outer writing. Writing is seen as an expressive form of morality. It is not possible to have direct contact with the hearts of others. A tenable way to make moral judgements of others is to examine their writing.

The notion of intertwining morality and aesthetics has gained philosophical insights from the doctrines of Confucius and his followers. In Confucian

64 Education

philosophy, the mind or the heart-mind (xin) is the origin of morality. On the one hand, the practice of calligraphy elevates the mind by labouring, controlling, and exercising the body. On the other hand, the artistic quality of writing reveals the level to which the body and the mind have committed to the discipline and, therefore, indicates the morality of the calligrapher.

The notion that the mind is the origin of morality is clearly addressed in Mencius (7A1), who says, 'He who has exhausted all his mental constitution [mind] knows his nature. Knowing his nature, he knows Heaven. To preserve one's mental constitution [mind], and nourish one's nature, is the way to serve Heaven' (Legge, 1985).[19] The mind is the primary source for understanding the nature of the self and the transcendent (Heaven) and is therefore the basis for serving Heaven. Serving Heaven is no ordinary act and is morally good conduct. Therefore, the mind is crucial for cultivating morality. Apart from that, as Mencius (4B19) argues, very little distinguishes human beings from animals – the potential of pursuing rén (benevolence) and yì (righteousness). Human potential is called rén (humanity) as well. Morality is innate. Confucius is certain about this point: 'Heaven produced the virtue that is in me' (*Analects, Shù Ér*, 7:23; trans. by Legge, 1861a) (天生德於予) (述而, 7:23). Human beings are born with four heart-minds and four recipient tendencies – the feeling of commiseration, the feeling of shame, the feeling of modesty and complaisance, and the feeling of distinguishing right from wrong. Corresponding to these four recipient tendencies are four cardinal virtues: rén (benevolence), yì (righteousness), lǐ (propriety or politeness), and zhì (wit or knowledge) (*Mencius*, 2A6). The four recipient tendencies are innate in the human mind, but not everyone can develop them in their entirety. A junzǐ is a person who has developed the four cardinal virtues well and fully. At the time of Mencius, the Four Treasures of the scholar's studio had not been invented. The key to cultivating a junzǐ consists of the idea of lǐ, meaning propriety, rites, rituals, manners, etiquette, and so forth. The *Analects* (12:1) articulates the following on virtue:

> Yán Yuan asked about perfect virtue. The Master said, 'To subdue one's self and return to propriety, is perfect virtue. If a man can for one day subdue himself and return to propriety, all under heaven will ascribe perfect virtue to him. Is the practice of perfect virtue from a man himself, or is it from others?' Yan Yuan said, 'I beg to ask the steps of that process'. The Master replied, 'Look not at what is contrary to propriety; listen not to what is contrary to propriety; speak not what is contrary to propriety; make no movement which is contrary to propriety'.
>
> (*Analects, Yán Yuan*, 12:1; trans. by Legge, 1861a)[20]

In this passage, lǐ means propriety that is distinct in a series of prescriptive procedures. One practices lǐ to cultivate rén so that one might develop oneself as a junzǐ. A junzǐ beholds, gives ear to, utters, and does nothing improper. His deeds, words, and acts are undertaken in conformity with propriety, appropriateness,

Education   65

and etiquette. Since the utensils of calligraphy were invented, calligraphy codes have been interpreted as a version of lǐ for the cultivation of a junzǐ. The utensils of writing – especially the brush – are an extension of the calligrapher's body. Critics and artists often use terminology related to human body, such as 'bone', 'flesh', 'muscle', 'sinew', and 'tendon', to describe and evaluate calligraphy. Su Shì (蘇軾) states:

> Calligraphy must have five elements, including spirit, energy, bone, flesh, and blood. None of them is absent to carry out calligraphy (*On Calligraphy*).
> (Huá, 1997, p. 288; my translation)[21]

The use of metaphors and analogous language linking physiology and aesthetics is widely adopted in Chinese thought. On this point, morality and aesthetics are taken as homologous studies dealing with the same subject matter – human personality. Inasmuch as humanity manifests in personal physiological features, aesthetical values, and ethical characters, moral conduct and handsome writing can be evaluated on the same scale.

The belief in the intertwining of aesthetics and ethics held sway throughout Chinese literary history. Esteemed calligraphers such as Yán Zhenqing (顔真卿) and Liǔ Gongquán (柳公權) were moral role models. They had to have virtues that promoted individual and collective goodness from the perspective of Confucianism. Yán and Liǔ, for example, showed their unyielding faithfulness and piety to the emperors. The problem is this: What if one writes beautiful calligraphy but shows no moral excellence? Can't a villain produce stunning handwriting?

The thirteenth-century calligrapher Zhaò Mèngfǔ (趙孟頫, 1254–1322 CE) was one of China's most influential artists due to his extraordinary achievement in Chinese painting, poetry, seal carving, and calligraphy. His works were greatly appreciated by Emperor Rénzong of the Yúan dynasty. Yet Zhaò Mèngfǔ was castigated by many critics over hundreds of years. The Ming dynasty art collector Chan Chǒu (張丑, 1577–1643 CE) criticises Zhaò's calligraphy as 'too delicate, coquettish and flirtatious' to be 'decent and integrate'.[22] Another renowned calligrapher during the Ching dynasty, Fù Shan (傅山, 1607–1684 CE), also depreciates Zhaò's works as 'charming' but 'shallow', 'villainous', and 'boneless' (Fu, 2002). In contrast, Fù highly values the calligraphy of the artists of the Jìn dynasty (晉朝, 265–420 CE) and the Táng dynasty (唐朝, 618–907 CE) as decent and righteous (Fu, 2002).[23] As the Yúan dynasty was built by Mongol conquerors who were foreign to the Chinese, many Chinese loyalists insist that Zhaò's 'treachery and obsequiousness' could not be more conspicuous in his calligraphy (Kraus, 1991).

Strictly speaking, criticism of Zhaò's writing for its lack of decency and integrity was not appropriate as an aesthetic judgement but rather as a moral judgement. Zhao was a descendant of the royal family of the Sòng dynasty, but he served the emperor of the Yúan dynasty (1271–1368 CE). Zhaò was thus thought to be unfaithful to his own nation and, therefore, to be a xiǎorén. The bitter art criticisms of Zhaò's calligraphy were indeed projections of judgements about his moral character.

Moreover, Fù's criticism of Zhaò is associated with praise for past calligraphers, which exemplifies the spirit of valuing the past over the present in Chinese culture. Following and imitating the words and deeds of the earlier sage kings was encouraged and praised. Esteem for past sages was incorporated in the virtues of zhong (loyalty) and xiào (filial piety). The concretisation of the virtues of loyalty and filial piety is related to one practice of the discipline of writing – imitation – that has already been discussed.

I do agree that practicing calligraphy can improve personal character in aspects such as patience, temperament, diligence, calmness, and so on because writing is such a tiring and consuming task. Many researchers have argued that practicing calligraphy can help a person to be calm and peaceful (Fang, 2012; Zhang, 2010; Ni, 1999; Yen, 2005). Nonetheless, it is one thing to take the activity of writing as an exercise of tempering oneself and another to say that the outcome of writing represents one's ethical performance. A human being's moral integrity is complex. The patience or peacefulness enhanced by the activity of writing is not necessarily associated with the improvement of loyalty or filial piety or moral reasoning. Facing the 'pretty' handwriting of despised people like Zhaò, the ancient critics turned to Daoist aesthetics for judgement criteria. The Daoist values are simplicity, spontaneity, naturalness, and truthfulness. The Míng dynasty literati Fù acknowledges the charm of Zhaò's works but makes the following statement about good calligraphy: 'Rather be dull than be clever; rather be ugly than be charming; rather be broken than be slippery; rather be straightforward than be arranged' (Ni, 1999, p. 25).[24] Fù reluctantly admits that Zhaò's works are charming aesthetically but that his works cannot achieve the supreme moral value of the Dao because his handwriting is too pretty and too pandering.

Modern critics no longer take for granted the straightforward connection between artistic creativity and moral personhood. The credible judgements we can make about a calligrapher's writing is an artistic criticism, not a moral one. Yet, it is plausible that practicing calligraphy can help one to be calm and tranquil and can enhance one's diligence and patience. More interesting is the point that the Daoist insight eclipses the Confucian view, enriching the understanding of calligraphy as a practice.

Graphocentric holism underpinning the cultivation of the writing subject

Underpinning the pedagogical codes of calligraphy is a holistic worldview that sees unity in the spiritual and the material, the aesthetic and the moral, the body and the mind, and culture and nature. With respect to spiritual-material unity, origin legends about the invention of words involve the holistic view.

It is generally believed that Chinese characters were invented by a legendary figure, Cang Jéi, who is described as an official historian in the time of the Yellow Emperor. Cang Jéi invented characters by imitating the footprints of birds and figures and the postures of animals. More interesting is the description that ghosts lament their fear of the invention of words because their secrets can never be concealed (Gao, 1965). The footprints of birds and figures and the postures of animals represent nature. The invented words are thought to reveal and set down the mysteries of nature. That natural and supernatural mysteries are seen as unified indicates the idea of animism implied by the Chinese view. Through writing, human beings become capable of penetrating and controlling nature and its supernatural mysteries. The legend regarding the invention of words indicates the communicability and reciprocity between the material and spiritual worlds. As physical and visible objects, written words have the power of commanding the invisible and spiritual world. Moreover, written words as cultural products have the magical power to dominate the natural world. Having the ability to write makes one capable of comprehending and controlling nature.

Graphocentric holism is incorporated in holistic anthropology, which simultaneously includes the unity of mind and body and the intertwining of the moral and the aesthetic. Body-mind unity and moral-aesthetic intertwining are in concert with each other in relation to writing.

On the one hand, the process of writing includes a series of self-demanding acts, such as concentrating, keeping oneself in peace and tranquillity, keeping oneself from distracting thoughts, focusing one's attention on the inner self, the body, and the brush, etc. The complex and repeated exercises prepare one's mind and body in a mutually integrative way. On the other hand, calligraphy is an exterior manifestation of inner moral personality. Writing externalises and makes concrete the invisible interior mind. How is this externalisation possible? It is possible because the act of writing is executed by the command of the inner heart-mind. As viewed in Chinese philosophy, the heart-mind is the faculty in which moral personality develops. Artistic activity prompted by the heart-mind must be morally good. Improvement in artistic ability equals refinement of moral personality, and vice versa. The heart-mind prompts and gives insight into the work, whereas the body executes the activity. Therefore, in Chinese cultural tradition, the very activity of artistic expression, especially calligraphy, unifies the mind and the body. Based on this, physiological terminology, such as 'flesh', 'bone', 'sinew', 'tendon', 'blood', 'energy', 'spirit', 'vein', 'pulse', 'breath', and so forth, is used to describe and critique calligraphy. Likewise, terms referring to personal character traits are adopted to give accounts of calligraphy. As Eric Mullis (2007, p. 103) notes, 'The artist's corporeality determines the form of the characters he or she writes'. On this point, calligraphy connects the body and the mind, the arts and personality, aesthetics and morality.

Brushwork is also critiqued using phrases about the natural world. The emperor Táng Tàizong (唐太宗, 599–649) criticises the calligraphy of Xiao

68 Education

Zǐyún (蕭子云, 486–549) as follows: 'The strokes are like curving earthworms in the spring; the characters are like curling snakes in the autumn' (Su Shì, *On the Calligraphy of Xiao Zǐyún*) (Shǔi, 1999 p. 17; my translation).[25] Critic and calligrapher Chang Wháiguàn (張懷瓘, n.d.), who served in the government in the Kaiyuán era (713–741) of the Táng Dynasty (618–909), wrote several essays on calligraphy. In his *Judging Calligraphy* (*Shu Duàn*, 書斷) (Huá, 1997), Chang uses myriad images of the natural world to describe different scripts and evaluates the brushwork of various masters: 'flashing lightning and shooting stars', 'dissipating fog and dispersing mist', 'majestic dragons and dignified tigers', 'steep mountains and deep valleys', and so forth. Natural phenomena and creatures are used without hesitation to provide accounts of calligraphy. As Ying (2012, pp. 38–39) aptly points out, 'Inherent in this approach is the Chinese belief in the notion of a "unity between nature and man" (tian rén hé yi [天人合一]), which, when applied to calligraphy, indicates that nature, art, and artist are interconnected'.

For Chinese literati, the understanding of the body and the natural world is inextricable from the understanding of the mind, the cultural world, the arts, and morality. Dàoism has influenced thoughts on calligraphy. As mentioned previously, the master Wáng Xizhi writes, 'The chi (force) of the calligraphy must reach the Dao' (Huá, 1997, p. 34; my translation).[26] In addition, practicing calligraphy is a way of being in harmony with nature as well as with the principles of Dàoism. The literary critic Liú Xīzǎi (劉熙載, 1813–1881) says, 'Calligraphy is written out of nature' (Huá, 1997, p. 666; my translation).[27] Mullis (2007, p. 104) provides readers with an excellent observation: 'Confucians, however, hold that the organic form of calligraphy can both *acquaint* viewers with moral situations and *cultivate* their moral sensibilities, including fine perceptual discrimination, imagination, and moral reflection, in ways that do not depend on narrative'. There is an essential component that renders this organic process and the juxtaposition of the arts and moral characteristics, the human body and nature. This component is gestural communication (Mullis, 2007).

On the one hand, calligraphy in its various aspects embodies the gestures of nature, of the human body with writing instruments as a bodily extension, of personal characteristics, and of culture. On the other hand, calligraphy expresses nature, the personal temperaments of the calligrapher, and the delicacy of Chinese culture. Certain procedures for practicing calligraphy become a ritual that aims to clear and calm the mind and to follow and control the natural force – chì – by living through the unity of the body, the utensils, and nature. As mentioned previously, repeated practice and modelling – two key steps for learning calligraphy – are indispensable to the constitution of the calligraphy ritual. Therefore, practicing calligraphy is a way of performing a ritual – lǐ (禮). Practicing calligraphy according to the ritual helps to define the writing subject.

Education   69

The requisite virtues for perfecting the writing subject

I have discussed the intertwining of aesthetics and morality and holistic human-ism in relation to graphocentrism. The process of cultivating the writing subject in the Chinese tradition involves political, aesthetical, artistic, and moral characteristics. The writing subject is not an individual independent from cultural, historical, and traditional contexts but instead is a living body imbedded in networks associated with the past, society, heritage, and so on. One of the writing subject's obligations is internalising cultural legacy and transmitting it to the next generation. The techniques, skills, content, codes, and rituals of writing are the components of this cultural legacy. Writing according to the codes and rituals manifests the virtue of lǐ. In addition to performing lǐ, an ideal writing subject must possess other cardinal virtues, such as rén (仁 benevolence), yì (義 righteousness), zhì (智 wisdom), xiào (孝 filial piety), zhong (忠 loyalty), and so on. These moral virtues are interrelated, and, in theory, a morally virtuous junzǐ should be able to perform all of them. In practice, the manifestation of these virtues depends on the context of a situation. In this book, the virtues are viewed through the lens of graphocentrism, and therefore three virtues are of particular importance: lǐ, xiào, and rén. At the centre of these concepts is rén. Indeed, rén can be understood as the most important of all Confucian virtues. With respect to writing, lǐ, xiào, and rén are an indispensable trio of ideas at the heart of graphocentric ethics. These three concepts refer to each other. The rest of this section explores the relationship between this trio of virtues and the cultivation of the writing subject.

i   rén

As stated, three moral virtues anchor graphocentric ethics: lǐ, xiào, and rén. These virtues are also crucial to the cultivation of an ideal Confucian per-son – junzǐ – and therefore, they anchor graphocentric humanism. As shown, a well-educated writing subject writes in accordance with codes and rituals, which is the performance of lǐ. As discussed, Chinese culture has a powerful inclination towards ancestor worship. A direct reference to ancestor worship is children's parental filial piety – xiào. Rén refers to the ideal personality – that of the junzǐ – as well as to the cardinal virtues that a junzǐ should have. Confucius repeated many times that rén involves other virtues and that it lies at the centre of ethics.

In Chinese, the word for 'humanity' and the word for 'a human being' both are pronounced 'rén'. The character for 'human' is written as '人,' whereas the character for 'virtue' is a homonym written as '仁'. The concept of 仁 could indicate humanity (humanness), the essence defining what it is to be a human being. The meanings of the two words '人' and '仁' are interrelated and insepa-rable. According to *Shuowén*, when rén refers to humans (人), it means 'the

70 Education

being of the greatest value in heaven and earth' (*Shuowén*, vol. 9, radical: rén; 天地之性最貴者也, 說文解字, 卷九人部). From the perspective of traditional Chinese lexicography, the word '人' belongs to the category of pictograph. The character '人' (rén) symbolises the physical shape of a human being. It is used to indicate a human being, a person, or a race. The more important point is that humanness differentiates a human being from other beings. The difference is neither biological nor physiological, but ethical. This ethical characteristic distinguishes a human being from other creatures and distinguishes a noble person from a villainous and ignoble one. This ethical characteristic is the virtue of rén (仁). For Confucian philosophers, a noble person must strive to cultivate and refine the virtue of rén (仁); otherwise, he is no different from an ordinary or even rustic person.

The concept of rén (仁) originated in Confucianism. Confucius was the first philosopher to consider rén a general virtue (Chan, 1975). This word is composed of two parts: '人' (human) and '二' (two). Thus, '仁' indicates a loving or benevolent relationship between two or more persons. It is defined in the dictionary *Shuowén* as 'benevolence (love) between [*at least*] two people' (親也, 从人从二, 說文解字, 卷九人部; italics added). As the core virtue of Confucian ethics, rén is 'the perfect virtue' (Legge, 1861a), the meaning of which is more than benevolence and humanness; it is also altruism, humanness, and goodness (Muller, 1990).

Mentioned more than one hundred times in the *Analects* and more than seventy times in the *Menzi*, rén has different and complicated meanings that depend on the context of a conversation. On many occasions, Confucius gives different definitions of rén when replying to different disciples. For example, when Yán Yuan asks about the meaning of rén, the Master replies that self-restraint and the recovery of propriety is rén.[28] Yet Confucius provides a totally different answer when Zhòng Gong asks the same question:

> It is, when you go abroad, to behave to everyone as if you were receiving a great guest; to employ the people as if you were assisting at a great sacrifice; not to do to others as you would not wish done to yourself; to have no murmuring against you in the country, and none in the family.
> (*Analects, Yán Yuan, 12*:2; trans. by Legge, 1861a)[29]

On another occasion, Confucius gives a brief but significant reply to Fán Chí on the same question: 'It [rén] is to love all human beings' (*Analects, Yan Yuan,* 12:22). These different interpretations of rén indicate that the concept is complicated and complex. More importantly, the meanings of rén depend on situations and contexts.

As the centre and prime virtue, rén symbolises the quintessence of Confucian virtues. Because the practice of rén is situation dependent, Confucius gives different replies to disciples who ask about rén. Rén could play different roles in different situations, such as love, the golden rule, the cultivation of special relationships, and ethical wisdom (Lai, 2008). Rén is considered the most resilient and comprehensive virtue in association with other desirable characteristics in the Confucius doctrines. Deference, generosity, sincerity, earnestness, and kindness are five admirable attitudes that a person with rén will express (*Analects, Yán Hùo*, 17:6). It is, as the Master says, 'in retirement, to be sedately grave; in the management of business, to be reverently attentive; in intercourse with others, to be strictly sincere' (*Analects, Zǐ Lù*, 13:19, trans. Legge, 1861a).[30] Rén is the rendering of a good life in public, private, and social aspects. With respect to graphocentrism, rén is embodied in the virtue of reticence. Confucius makes the following assessments:

> Fine words and an insinuating appearance are seldom associated with true virtue.
>
> (*Analects, Xúe Ér*, 1:3; Legge, 1861a)[31]

> The man of perfect virtue is cautious and slow in his speech.
>
> (*Analects, Yán Yuan*, 12:3; Legge, 1861a)[32]

A person with the virtue of rén is very cautious and slow in his or her speech. The ideal person is a rén of rén (仁人), or a junzǐ. The decency of a virtuous person is shown in one's deeds, not in one's speech. This is a key point that distinguishes Chinese graphocentric humanism from Western phonocentrism.

In Chinese tradition, skills of oral expression are not necessary to cultivate an educated person. The moral excellence of a junzǐ relies not on what one speaks but on what one does. The Northern Sòng dynasty Neo-Confucian philosopher Chén Yí (程頤, 1033–1107 CE) says, 'Brief speech refines meaning, while speechification makes the sense foul' (my translation).[33] Unspoken words carry richer and deeper meaning than spoken words. We can find responses in Daoism, although Confucians and Daoists have different understandings of the Dao and different aesthetic judgements of calligraphy (Ni, 1999). In *Tao Te Ching*, Lǎo Tzǔ says, 'Those who know do not talk. Those who talk do not know' (§56).[34] As Legge (1891a) interprets, those who know are those who know the Dao. Spoken words in this sense do little to help in seeking the truth of life and the universe. Rather, they might obstruct following the Dao. Confucian thinkers and Daoists both agree to follow and pursue the Dao. On the path of pursuing the Dao, Confucians and the Daoists undertake similar practices, but to different extents. For Confucians, reticence – 'less doing' – suffices. For Daoists, 'not doing' – entire silence – is the way to let the Dao manifest itself naturally and spontaneously. With respect to seeking the truth in terms of speech, Confucian and Daoist views are nuanced but resonant in the sense that spoken words are devalued. The quality of 'wú yán' (no words, 無言) or 'gǔa yán' (few words, 寡言) is credited as a virtue. 'Wú yán', one of the wú practices, will be pursued in more detail in Chapter 6.

In contrast, there is a linguistic tradition in Western thought. Elenchus, a technique of investigation through dialogue, has been the main form of inquiry

72 Education

in the Western intellectual tradition since Socrates. Elenchus is defined thusly in *The Cambridge Dictionary of Philosophy*:

> A cross-examination or refutation. Typically in early Plato's dialogues, Socrates has a conversation with someone who claims to have some sort of knowledge, and Socrates refutes this claim by showing the interlocutor that what he thinks he knows is inconsistent with his other opinions. This refutation is called an elenchus. It is not entirely negative, for awareness of his own ignorance is supposed to spur the interlocutor to further inquiry, and the concepts and the assumption serve as the basis for positive Platonic treatments of the same topic.
>
> (Halper, 1999, p. 257)

In the Western tradition, speech between persons, be it in any form of interlocution, such as conversation, debate, discussion, or questioning and answering, plays an indispensable role in searching for the truth (Vlastos, 1982, 1994). Even when Socrates is silenced by authorities, he still imagines them speaking to him (Vlastos, 1994). As Vlastos (1994) notes, method is all. With respect to the Socratic method, the point is the process of speaking, not the end of speaking. Based on the Socratic method, Plato develops his own pedagogical method as a maieutic method by questioning and facilitating dialogue (Leigh, 2007). In Aristotle, human beings are distinguished from beasts by their capacity for rational speech (Rahe, 1994). In the Jewish and Christian traditions, the word of God is the transcendent grounding principle of order and reason. As Derrida asserts, Western philosophy has put its focus on the 'voice' for a long time, and thus the metaphysics that underpin logocentrism with a phonocentric centre were constructed (Hendricks, 2014). I will continue the comparison between Chinese graphocentrism and Western phonocentrism in coming chapters. As the virtue rén is the core of Chinese morality, reticence is important. In the Chinese tradition, speaking is seen as an obstacle to the accomplishment of full humanness. This point distinguishes Chinese humanism as well as humanistic education from the West.

Rén is the most fundamental of all virtues. Mencius states: 'Now, benevolence (rén) is the most honourable dignity conferred by Heaven, and the quiet home in which man should awell [*sic*]' (Mencius, 2A7; trans. Legge, 1985).[35] If one lacks rén, possessing virtues such as wisdom (zhì) and righteousness (yì) do not make one a good person. With rén, one is able to be a completely or fully 'genuine' human being. Everyone has the potential to develop innate rén. Nevertheless, the potential for the 'beginning of humanity' lies in four cardinal goods: the heart of compassion (怵惕惻隱之心), the heart of shame (羞惡之心), the heart of courtesy and modesty (辭讓之心), and the heart of right and wrong (是非之心) (*Mencius*, 2A6; Lau, 1979, p. 73). As Mencius puts it, the cultivation of these four cardinal goods can initiate the development of full humanity – rén. These four heart-minds are to the virtue of rén as four limbs

Education 73

are to a human torso. Led by the virtue of rén, the other virtues can be perfectly developed.

ii   xiào

Xiào – filial piety – is the second moral excellence related to cultivation of the ideal Confucian personality. In the Confucian tradition, rén and xiào are often mentioned together. The first appearance of the word xiào in the *Analects* is in the chapter of *Xúe Ér*.

> The philosopher Yǒu said, 'They are few who, being filial and fraternal, are fond of offending against their superiors. There have been none, who, not liking to offend against their superiors, have been fond of stirring up confusion. The superior man bends his attention to what is radical. That being established, all practical courses naturally grow up. Filial piety and fraternal submission! – are they not the root of all benevolent actions?'
> (*Analects, Xúe Ér*, 1:2, trans. by Legge, 1861a)[36]

Thus, filial piety (xiào, 孝) and fraternal obedience (tì, 弟) form the foundation of rén. Xiào as filial piety and tì as fraternal duty are thought to be associated with each another in Confucianism. Both of these concepts indicate that respect and obedience reflect family goodness. Xiào emphasises respect and obedience to parents, whereas tì stresses compliance to older brothers. In the Confucian doctrine, xiào is more important than tì in terms of morality because parents bring children into the world. No one can live and grow up in the world without parents. It is understood that respect and obedience to parents extends to respect and obedience to seniors and elders and thus turns to the concept of tì.

As Xǔ Shèn explains about the etymology of xiào in the *Shuowén* (Xǔ, n.d.), this word means 'to be good at serving parents' (善事父母). The Chinese character '孝' is composed of two elements: the upper half is '老' (lǎo), meaning 'the old or the elder people' – implying parents – and the lower half is '子' (zǐ), which means son. The combination of 'lǎo' and 'zǐ' demonstrates that the son carries the old (parents). Xiào means that the son serves parents in a most careful and respectful way. As for the word '弟' (tì), the production of the character models the shape of a bound belt and thus refers to the order of binding. The order of binding is associated with birth order. Thus, the word '弟' (tì) is understood to imply multiple meanings: younger brother and respect and obedience to seniors. Although the above quote from the *Analects* asserts that the concepts of xiào and tì are both foundations of rén, it is clear that tì is dependent upon xiào. These two concepts do not weigh equally on the scale of Confucian ethics. It is from xiào that tì develops its meaning.

Xiào can be said to be the virtue that receives the highest esteem in Chinese culture. According to Confucius, filial piety is loyal and faithful compliance

74 Education

with parents' orders – especially a father's instructions. Such compliance is demonstrated in a son's steadfast following of his father's ways of doing things. As Confucius says, 'If the son for three years does not alter from the way of his father, he may be called filial' (*Analects, Li Rén*, 4:20; trans. Legge, 1861a).[37] It is even more important for a ruler to be a respectful governor when he shows such moral excellence. This is why Confucius admires the ruler of Lŭ, Mèng Zhuáng (孟莊), for his 'not changing the ministers of his father, nor his father's mode of government' (*Analects, Zĭ Zhang*, 19:18; trans. Legge, 1861a). The new king is praised, for he continues the late ruler's policy and appoints the same ministers.

Within the traditional Confucian text *Thirteen Classics* is a short treatise called *Xiào Jing* (孝經), which is said to be written by Confucius's disciple Zeng Zĭ (505–426 BC). *Thirteen Classics* explicates and deliberates on the concept of xiào. As mentioned, the concept of xiào literally means submission and obedience to parents and then extends to submission to elder brothers, the leader or boss, and the ruler. *Xiào Jing* comprises 18 chapters. The overall contents focus on the meaning and the practice of the virtue of filial piety (Feng, 2008; Legge, 1861b). The practice of the virtue of xiào differs depending on the status, position, and background of the agent. Thus, there are chapters concerning the xiào of the king, the xiào of the princes of states, the xiào of the higher ministers and inferior officers, the xiào of common people, and xiào in relation to a wide range of subjects such as the government, sages, punishment, reproof and remonstrance, serving the ruler, and mourning the death of parents (Feng, 2008; Legge, 1861b).

The contents of the *Xiào Jing* demonstrate a firm faith in parental or paternal authority, which is also related to ancestor worship. In Confucianism, a solid connection can be found between obedience to parents and family seniors and compliance with superior officers and rulers. Filial piety generating from family kinship is interpreted as loyalty to the political authority. The Confucian doctrines always insist on the inseparable relation between self-cultivation, the serving of parents, and the serving of the ruler. In this sense, according to Confucianism, it is essential to embody the virtues of rén and xiào to be a full human being. Yet, it is also apparent that the link between rén and xiào demonstrates the paternalism implied in Confucian political and ethical thoughts. The first chapter of *Xiào Jing* states, 'Thus xiào starts with serving one's parents, progresses with serving one's lord, and ends with establishing oneself' (trans. by Feng, 2008).[38] It is clear that self-realisation or self-fulfilment depends on the service of parents and the ruler. Filial piety links practices across the fields of ethics, education, and politics. For me, a more important question for Confucian philosophers is how this person with perfect virtue faces the contradiction between self-cultivation, filial piety, and obedience to the lord, and how he makes the decision between them.

As noted, an ideal Confucian person – a junzĭ – is a person with the virtue of rén. The meaning of the virtue of rén is not simple. Its meanings are complicated, complex, resilient, and context dependent. In practice, rén is always connected with many other virtues, like lǐ (禮, rules of propriety), chung (忠, loyalty, faithfulness), gong (恭, courteousness), jìng (敬, respectfulness), kwan (寬, generosity), xìn (信, trustfulness), mǐng (敏, keenness), hùi (惠, kindness), yì (義, righteousness), etc. To be a perfect junzǐ – a person with the virtue of rén – one must have all these virtues. As I observe, lǐ is one of most indispensable moral qualities in cultivating the writing subject in relation to graphocentrism. Lǐ regulates and prescribes the way that a junzǐ should behave. In this sense, lǐ provides guidance for dealing with difficult situations.

iii   lǐ

Viewed from the lens of etymology, the character '禮' (lǐ) comprises two parts: 'shì' (示) and 'lǐ' (豊). 'Shì' (示) means to display, show, or manifest, whereas 'lǐ' (豊) indicates ritual utensils – or, more specifically, the ritual vase (Mullis, 2007). The word 'lǐ' refers to rites and implies propriety. It is noteworthy that the concept of lǐ is strongly graphocentric, for the performance of rituals reflects the characteristics of visibility and physicality, which in turn confirm the holistic view of the human being.

As Mullis (2007) notes, the character for lǐ shares the common element of '豊' with the character '體' (tǐ) – the body. The word '體' consists of two parts, '豊' (lǐ) and '骨' (gǔ). '骨' (gǔ) means skeleton or bone. The Chinese character '體' (tǐ) conveys a clear message to the viewer that the body plays a decisive role in performing rituals. Moreover, the precise and accurate execution of the rituals in accordance with the prescribed sequences demonstrates propriety, meaning appropriateness with the purpose of rituals. The gestures and movements of the body indicate whether the person has the virtue of lǐ, or how well one performs the ritualised action. The body that writes according to the codes is a body that performs the rituals, and, furthermore, is a body that practices the virtue of lǐ. This corresponds to the holistic approach to calligraphy education for the writing subject and the embodied ethics.

Lǐ is manifested not only in rituals but in etiquette. Etiquette reflects the social expectation of manners or behaviours within a society or a group (Post, 1922). It involves observable, discernible politeness and good manners, such as how to dress, speak, and behave in a graceful, elegant, and proper way. Whether one speaks or behaves in a way that meets the expectation of conventional norms determines whether he or she has the virtue of lǐ. Yet, this view implies a problem that the more gracefully, elegantly, and beautifully one behaves, the more virtuous one is.

Confucius might be aware of the difficulty when he says, 'If a man be without the virtues proper to humanity [rén], what has he to do with the rites of propriety? If a man be without the virtues proper to humanity [rén], what has he to do with music?' (*Analects*, *Ba Yì*, 3:3; trans. by Legge, 1861a).[39] The execution of rites and the playing of music are important for putting the virtue of lǐ

76 Education

into practice, but they are not essential. The fundamental is rén, which precedes lǐ in morality. A similar view can be found in the West. As Emily Post (1922) states, the best society is 'an association of gentle-folk, of which good form in speech, charm of manner, knowledge of social amenities, and instinctive consideration for the feelings of others, are the credentials by which society the world over recognises its chosen members' (p. 28). In spite of the externally observable features in speech, behaviours, and dress, Post mentions 'instinctive consideration for the feelings of others,' which has something in common with the Confucian rén. Both of these concepts imply goodwill – a desire to do good for other people. The problem is that goodwill cannot be seen from the outside. Performance is the only principle for evaluating moral character. The precision and delicacy of executing rituals and graceful, polite, and exquisite manners – clear indicators of excellent lǐ – inconspicuously displace rén in the Confucian tradition, and such is the inclination in the West. Confucius does not give a clear definition of lǐ, but he stresses the importance of lǐ in cultivating a person with the virtue of rén:

> Yán Yuan asked about perfect virtue. The Master said, 'To subdue one's self and return to propriety, is perfect virtue. If a man can for one day subdue himself and return to propriety, all under heaven will ascribe perfect virtue to him. Is the practice of perfect virtue from a man himself, or is it from others?' Yán Yuan said, 'I beg to ask the steps of that process'. The Master replied, 'Look not at what is contrary to propriety; listen not to what is contrary to propriety; speak not what is contrary to propriety; make no movement which is contrary to propriety'. Yán Yuan then said, 'Though I am deficient in intelligence and vigour, I will make it my business to practice this lesson'.
>
> (*Analects*, *Yán Yuan*, 12:1; trans. Legge, 1861a)[40]

Rén should be internal goodwill that initiates external proper actions. According to the above quote, rén is manifested in the proper ways of seeing, listening, speaking, and moving. How one behaves indicates one's degree of kindness or benevolence. How one behaves according to lǐ (i.e., etiquette), including courtesy manners, table manners, cultural norm manners, and so on, reflects one's degree of virtue. Here again, the graphocentric features of physicality and visibility produce a tendency to view the external lǐ as an indication of the internal rén.

Some sayings from Confucius may encourage this graphocentric inclination. For example: 'Without an acquaintance with the rules of Propriety, it is impossible for the character [personality] to be established' (*Analects*, *Yáo Yue*, 20:3; trans. Legge, 1861a).[41] Rigorously speaking, what Confucius means is that if one aims to develop character, one must master lǐ. The mastery of lǐ is one necessary condition, but it is not sufficient for the full development of character.

As Zhu Xi (2004) interprets, if one does not know about the rules of propriety, one does not know how to arrange one's ears, eyes, and limbs.[42] The arrangement of ears, eyes, and limbs means careful control of movement and behaviour. It is obvious that Zhu Xi's view of lǐ has a connection to what we have just discussed, i.e., manners and etiquette. Yet in another Confucian classic, *Li Ji*, the concept of lǐ is given much more importance than in the *Analects*:

> The course (of duty), virtue, benevolence [rén], and righteousness [yì] cannot be fully carried out without the rules of propriety; nor are training and oral lessons for the rectification of manners complete; nor can the clearing up of quarrels and discriminating in disputes be accomplished; nor can (the duties between) ruler and minister, high and low, father and son, elder brother and younger, be determined; nor can students for office and (other) learners, in serving their masters, have an attachment for them; nor can majesty and dignity be shown in assigning the different places at court, in the government of the armies, and in discharging the duties of office so as to secure the operation of the laws; nor can there be the (proper) sincerity and gravity in presenting the offerings to spiritual Beings on occasions of supplication, thanksgiving, and the various sacrifices. Therefore the superior man is respectful and reverent, assiduous in his duties and not going beyond them, retiring and yielding – thus illustrating (the principle of) propriety.
> (*Li Ji*, *Qu Li I*, 1A:8; Legge, 1885) (*Li Ji, Qu Li I*, 1a:8; trans. Legge, 1885)[43]

Following the rules of propriety indicates that one possesses moral virtues, including rén, which should be of prime significance. It is clear that the statuses of rén and lǐ are reversed. In the context of *Li Ji*, lǐ edges rén out of the prime position of Confucian virtue/ethics. In this vein, Confucianism could entail conservative traditionalism (Lai, 2008).

This distinction is clear in a comparison of *Li Ji* and the writings of Mencius – the most faithful follower of Confucius. According to Mencius, rén is highly regarded as the rare essence that differentiates humanity from animals:

> That whereby man differs from the lower animals is but small . . . benevolence [rén] and righteousness [yì].
> (*Mencius*, 4B19; trans. Legge, 1985)[44]

From this case we may perceive that the feeling of commiseration is essential to man, that the feeling of shame and dislike is essential to man, that the feeling of modesty and complaisance is essential to man, and that the feeling of approving and disapproving is essential to man. The feeling of commiseration is the principle of benevolence. The feeling of shame and dislike is the principle of righteousness. The feeling of modesty and complaisance

78 Education

is the principle of propriety. The feeling of approving and disapproving is the principle of knowledge.

(Mencius, 2A6; Legge, 1985)[45]

In contrast, as written in *Li Ji*, the difference between humankind and other creatures lies in lǐ – rules of propriety:

> The parrot can speak, and yet is nothing more than a bird; the ape can speak, and yet is nothing more than a beast. Here now is a man who observes no rules of propriety; is not his heart that of a beast? But if (men were as) beasts, and without (the principle of) propriety, father and son might have the same mate. Therefore, when the sages arose, they framed the rules of propriety in order to teach men, and cause them, by their possession of them, to make a distinction between themselves and brutes.
>
> *(Li Ji, Qu Li I*, 1A:9; trans. Legge, 1885)[46]

As *Li Ji* describes, the rules of propriety – lǐ – distinguishes humans from beasts. Yet, for Confucius and Mencius, it is rén that holds the key, with lǐ playing a supporting role. In this regard, the prime virtue in Confucian ethics varies between rén and lǐ. On the one hand, rén is humanness, denoting goodwill, benevolence, kindness, or the feeling of doing good for others. Rén is the source of morality. As an internal feeling, rén exists in the heart-mind and is not liable to be discerned by others. On the other hand, lǐ is the rule of propriety that regulates observable human behaviours. The division between the internal rén and the external lǐ does not necessary mean that they are in opposition to each other. In fact, Confucius and Mencius claim that both rén and lǐ are essential for cultivating a junzǐ. Rén, however, is more comprehensive, more encompassing. The problem is that the inner, good, and benevolent heart-mind of a rén- based act is not discernible, while an act based on lǐ is clearly visible. Through the lens of graphocentrism, the development of ethics is rooted more in lǐ than in rén.

iv the writing subject/automaton

Viewed through a graphocentric lens, the cultivation of the writing subject is the goal of education. The writing subject as the prototype of ideal personhood integrates images of the junzǐ suggested in early Confucianism and images of the literati or scholar-bureaucrats constructed throughout imperial Chinese history. The writing subject incorporates significant Confucian virtues and requisite merits for serving the king. These virtues and merits are the criteria for distinguishing the writing subject from those who cannot write or those who are not virtuous.

Traditional Confucian moralists argue that anyone devoid of rén cannot be viewed as a human being. As mentioned, Mencius castigates anyone devoid of any of the four cardinal heart-minds, declaring that such persons are not human at all. Everyone is born with the potential for these heart-minds and is therefore able to develop them to the full extent of being human. Whoever denies his or her ability to extract this potential self-impairs. In this sense, he or she is not a human being. Mencius (3B9; Lau, 1979, p. 141) thus condemns his contemporary philosophers Mozi and Yanzi, for they deny prioritising rulers and fathers in the hierarchy of ethics and politics:

> Yang advocates everyone for himself, which amounts to a denial of one's prince; Mo advocates love without discrimination, which amounts to a denial of one's father. To ignore one's father on the one hand, and one's prince on the other, is to be no different from the beasts.
>
> (*Mencius*, 3B9; Lau, 1979, pp. 141–143)[47]

This truly is a serious accusation. Mencius declares that the doctrines of Mozi and Yanzi are heresies that shall be banished without hesitation. Similarly, the *Odes* describes what the former king – the sage ruler, the Duke of Chou (周公) – did in old times:

> He smote the barbarians of the west and the north; He punished Jing and Shu; And no one dared to resist us.
>
> (*Mencius*, 3B14; trans. Legge, 1985)[48]

According to this passage, the barbarians and alien tribes of the west and north (Rón, Dí, Ching, and Shu) should have been attacked and punished because they were not human, not civilised. 'They' are the others, the aliens, whom we can attack without regret or hesitation. This is where the Confucian anthropological machine works. One who disobeys one's ruler or father can be seen as a non-human, e.g., a barbarian or a beast or an alien. In the Confucian sense, this non-human creature can legitimately be attacked. According to Lewis's (1999, p. 210) account of how human society is separated from the animal world in early Chinese culture, 'In earliest times men hadn't been naturally separated from animals, but that the work of this separation had been accomplished by the "former kings", superman sages who physically expelled the animals, invented the technologies necessary for civilised existence, and introduced the moral practices and social hierarchies that defined humanity'. The sage ruler employs political power and military force to separate the human from the non-human, the civilised from the savages. In this vein, approval of separation and exclusion in terms of the anthropological machine can be found in Confucianism (Agamben, 1998, 2004; Hung, 2012, 2015). The Confucian version of the anthropological machine produces humans – filial and loyal subjects – and non-humans – disobedient beasts. It is widely acknowledged that Confucianism is ethical humanism. One of Confucianism's biggest concerns is 'how to become a true human'. I cannot help but wonder if the Confucian 'true human

80 Education

being' is truly 'humane' or 'just' when he or she is on the side of attacking, punishing, and excluding barbarians. If the Confucian human being is part of the anthropological machine that works to attack, punish, divide, and exclude the other, this version of humanism must be questioned or deconstructed because it becomes a pretext for authoritarianism on a political level and foundationism on an ontological level.

In a sense, the relation of disloyalty, faithlessness, and lack of filial piety to non-humanity or beastliness contributes to the discrimination between us-humans and they-aliens (including barbarians and animals). I cannot help but cast doubt on the outcome of the institutionalising the writing regime: Is it possible for the writing subject to be an automaton that operates according to the programmes of social rules and orders?

The end of the writing subject as the end of humans?

The goal of cultivating the moral writing subject was achieved via the literary excellence of the rú and shìh and the moral qualities of the junzǐ. Nevertheless, the process and system of graphocentric education created differentiation and discrimination, inclusion and exclusion. First, most of the aristocratic elites who received institutional education and were thus able to pass the examinations were born into privileged families. Throughout history, the aristocratic elite have been closely linked to great families with wealth, land, and superior social status (Connery, 1998).

Over hundreds of years, taking and passing imperial examinations was the way for the rú (儒) or shìh (士) to acquire their offices. In this sense, the Confucian literati – those who were able to read and write – were followers of the canon. The main body of the Confucian classics can thus be understood as discourse focusing on the cultivation of the scholar-gentry. Writing as a part of literacy has always been described as a tool for liberation and enlightenment; however, it may have the opposite function. Echoing Lévi-Strauss, Derrida (1979) says that writing always partakes of power and is a part of it. Writing is situated within forms of control (Lewis, 1999). Social stratification and division is grounded in the power of writing. An inquiry into the construction of the 'writing subject' is, in terms of Derrida, an act of deconstruction that problematises the political-institutional codes inherited from politics and ethics (Derrida, 1992).

The population of literate people – those who could read and write – was quite limited in imperial China. As Lewis (1999, p. 3) observes, 'all written languages are a form of expertise'. Acquiring the skills and knowledge required for writing is a laborious and time-consuming task. Thus, the population of the educated literati was small. Those who were able to write in ancient times gained new abilities and powers. As Li Feng and Branner (2011) suggest, literacy can be classified into scribal literacy, elite literacy, craftsman's literacy, functional

Education 81

literacy, professional literacy, and mass literacy (which was never achieved in the ancient world).

Some ordinary people, including soldiers and their families and merchants, were functionally literate in the time of the Chín (221–207 BC) and Han (202 BC–220 AD) empires (Yates, 2011). Most lower-class people, such as peasants, were illiterate. The Chín empire united the Chinese states in 221 BC, and a centralised bureaucracy based on Legalist proposals has existed ever since. The centralised system continued in later dynasties, even though Confucianism in the Han played a central role in legitimating the ruling authority. The bureaucracy system was one of the pillars supporting the centralised imperial government. The bureaucrats and the members of the royalty and nobility were the literate minority who had the empire and the illiterate mass population under control. Household registration, legal procedures, military reports, and other inscriptions were imposed upon the mass population, yet the power to impose these measures was in the hands of a small number of literate people. Writing is extremely important for exerting political, economic, and cultural hegemony (Barbieri-Low, 2011). Moreover, after the Chín dynasty, China's territory was so vast that the subjects spoke many diverse dialects. The laws and governance of the huge empire were able to be carried out through writing. Kraus (1991) remarks on grapholiteracy, 'Speaking is superficial; in the writing lies the power'.

According to Connery (1998), writing in ancient China was canonised and codified to constitute grapholiteracy:

> Politically, small ruling groups used writing to classify, conscript, and exploit lower-ranking groups in society. Economically, writing was used to tax the labour and products [sic] of farmers, hoard and store commodities and luxury items, and facilitate the trade of raw materials and finished goods. Culturally, writing was used hegemonically by small groups of scribes, diviners and priests to maintain privileged access to divine wisdom through oracles, revealed texts, and liturgies.
>
> (Barbieri-Low, 2011. p. 398)

The bureaucracy system in ancient China worked on a basis of grapholiteracy and textual culture (Connery, 1998). The system was basically meritocratic, the notion of which can be understood in terms of the contemporary Western scholar Michael Young. According to Young (1994), merit is construed as ability plus effort (Daniel, 1978). Some common people who were literate and hardworking had the opportunity to become parts of the bureaucracy in imperial China. The imperial examination or civil service examination, used to select appropriate candidates to serve in the state bureaucracy, was established in 603 AD, during the Suí dynasty (隋朝, 581–618 AD). It was not abolished until 1905 AD, in the late Ching dynasty. Writing competency was a main part of the

82 Education

examination. In order to pass, one needed to have knowledge of at least nine thousand sinographs and mastery of six scripts (Connery, 1998). The ruling elite and the writing system collaborated with mutual support to uphold the Chinese state for over 1,000 years (Fairbank, 1986).

The writing system was highly pedagogical and highly political. Acquiring grapholiteracy involved the recognition of characters, skills in using writing instruments, and knowledge of regulations and codes about writing. The writing system still affects current education. It takes time and effort for anyone to master the knowledge and skills of writing. The cultivation of grapholiteracy developed loyalty and piety in subjects who protected the writing regime. As Derrida (1979) remarks, by serving the communication of laws and the order of society, 'a writing becomes the instrument of an abusive power, whether its own or that of special interests: the violence of a secretariat, a discriminating reserve, an effect of scribble and scrypt' (p. 124). Hence, the separation between the literate and the illiterate supported the privilege of the writing subject, and vice versa.

These discussions reveal the dynamic mechanism of power behind the graphocentric regime. The calligraphy code was used to control and develop one's body and mind and to inculcate discipline as one trained to become a writing subject. The taboos of writing imposed imperial authority upon a writing subject by keeping the writer cautious and vigilant about forbidden words. The writing subject had to be loyal to and comply with the emperors. The institutionalisation of writing was embodied in the imperial examination systems, which selected and recruited qualified scholar-officials for the government. The system distinguished the literate from the illiterate and separated qualified and unqualified scholar-officials among the literati. In addition to being acquainted with the calligraphy code, the taboos of writing, and the institutionalisation of writing through the examination system, an accomplished writing subject had to possess Confucian moral excellence. The regime of writing was constructed over hundreds of years on a complicated and complex system, and so were the authority and power related to it. This created the situation that the novelist Lu Xun (1990) describes about Ah Q in his story quoted at the beginning of this chapter. Ah Q is just a small potato, a little person, who does not even have a name. He is timid and is afraid to use a pen because he is illiterate. As the author depicts with deep irony, the first time Ah Q attempts to write, he approves his own death sentence.

One more point must be addressed. The element of graphocentrism aimed at establishing authority in relation to writing produced an even wider ethnocentric distinction between the subjects ruled by the writing regime and those who were outside the government, such as aliens, foreigners, the exotic, barbarians, beasts, and so on. As stated in *Mencius*, 'Now here is this shrike-tongued barbarian of the south, whose doctrines are not those of the ancient kings' (3A.4; Legge, 1985).[49] Knowing or not knowing about the word of the sage king was seen as the standard for distinguishing the civilised from the barbarians. It was

Education 83

assumed that people of nations outside China who could not recognise the word of the sage king were savages. The Chinese anti-barbarian attitude was widely accepted. Consider the words denoting foreign tribes – '蠻' (mán), '夷' (yí), '戎' (róng), and '狄' (dí). '蠻' denotes the tribes of the south, '夷' the east, '戎' the west, and '狄' the north. Etymologically, these words originate from words referring to animals or insects. In using them, the written Chinese language implies a deep ethnocentrism. The writing regime comprising methods, didactics, and ethical-political philosophy provided a solid ground of 'humanism' that divided humans from non-humans (e.g., beasts, barbarians, aliens, foreigners, etc.). Non-human beings could not write. They were out of the control of the writing regime and thus were to be attacked, tamed, and subjugated.

This exploration reveals the prejudice and danger hidden in Chinese education, thought, and culture. Longing for the cultivation of the perfect writing subject may carry ethnocentric bias and sociopolitical discrimination.

Notes

1 Then one of the longgowns presented him with a sheet of paper and a writing brush. When the said personage thrust the brush into the prisoner's hand, Ah Q was so terrified that it was almost a case of the heavenly part of the soul took to wing, and the earthly part to heel, for this was the first time in his whole life that any relationship had ever been established between his hand and a writing brush. Just as he was wondering how you were supposed to hold the thing, the longgown pointed to a place on the paper and told him to sign. Ah Q's fingers tightened around the brush. In a voice that echoed with fear and shame he confessed: 'Don't . . . don't know how to write'.
  'In that case we'll go easy on you. Just draw a circle'.
  Ah Q tried to compose himself enough to make the circle, but the hand that held the brush refused to stop trembling. The longgowns carefully spread the paper out flat on the floor before him. Ah Q leaned forward over it, and marshaling all the strength and concentration at his command, approached the task at hand. Dreadfully concerned lest someone laugh at him, he was determined to make that circle a nice round one, but that damned brush lay heavy in his hand and turned out to be disobedient as well. Tremble after tremble, he traced the circle around and was on the point of closing it up when suddenly the brush shrugged off to one side, producing something that looked more like a watermelon seed than a circle (Lu Xun, 1990, p. 166; trans. Lyell).
2 周人以諱事神, 名, 終將諱之。(左傳桓公六年).
3 邦畿千里、維民所止、肇域彼四海。(詩經•商頌•玄鳥)
4 唯初學者不得不摹 . . . 皆須是古人名筆 . . .(姜夔: 續書譜) (華正人, 1997. p. 361)
5 學書之法 . . . 大要須臨古人墨跡。(解縉: 春雨雜述) (華正人, 1997. p. 461)
6 臨摹用工, 是學書大要。(朱履貞: 書學捷要) (華正人, 1997, p. 561)
7 學書需求古帖墨跡, 模摹研究, 悉得其用筆之意, 則字有師承, 工夫易進。(華正人, 1997, p. 568)
8 筆成冢, 墨成池, 不及羲之即獻之。(蘇軾, 論書) (Huá, 1997, p. 288)
9 筆禿千管, 墨磨萬錠, 不作張芝作索靖。(蘇軾, 論書) (Huá, 1997, p. 288)
10 領袖如皂, 唇齒常黑。(趙壹, 非草書) (Huá, 1997, p. 2)
11 張芝臨池學書。池水盡墨。鍾丞相入抱犢山十年, 木石盡黑。趙子昂國公十年不下樓。嶷子山平章每日坐衙罷, 寫一千字才進膳。唐太宗皇帝簡板馬上字, 夜半起把燭學《蘭亭記》。大字須藏間架, 古人以箒濡水, 學書於砌, 或書於幾, 幾石皆陷。(解縉, 春雨雜述) (Huá, 1997, pp. 461–462)

84 Education

12 上品無寒門, 下品無世族。(劉毅, 資治通鑑, 卷81)

13 三十老明經, 五十少進士。(唐摭言, 卷一, 散序進士)

14 志於道, 據於德, 依於仁, 游於藝。(論語, 述而, 7:6)

15 書之氣, 必達乎道, 同混元之理。(王羲之, 記白雲先生書訣) (Huá, 1997, p. 34)

16 書者, 如也; 如其學, 如其才, 如其志, 總之曰如其人而已。(劉溪載, 藝概)(Huá, 1997, p. 666)

17 書有工拙, 而君子小人之心, 不可亂也。(蘇軾, 論書) (Huá, 1997, p. 288)

18 人正則書正。心為人之帥, 心正則人正矣。筆為書之充, 筆正則事正矣。人由心正, 書由筆正。(項穆, 書法雅言) (華正人, 1997, p. 493)

19 盡其心者, 知其性也。知其性, 則知天矣。存其心, 養其性, 所以事天也。(孟子盡心上, 7A1)

20 顏淵問仁。子曰：「克己復禮為仁。一日克己復禮, 天下歸仁焉。為仁由己, 而由人乎哉?」顏淵曰：「請問其目。」子曰：「非禮勿視, 非禮勿聽, 非禮勿言, 非禮勿動。」(顏淵, 12:1)

21 書必有神、氣、骨、肉、血, 五者闕一, 不為成書也。(論書) (華正人, 1997, p. 288)

22 明代張丑的《清河書畫舫》中云：「子昂書法, 溫潤閑雅, 遠接右軍正脈之傳; 第過妍媚纖柔, 殊乏大節不奪之氣, 似反不若文信國天祥書體清疏挺竦, 其傳世《六歌》等帖, 令人起敬起愛也耶！」

23 《霜紅龕集》, 卷四·五言古, (作字示兒孫)：「貧道二十歲左右, 於先世所傳晉唐楷書法, 無所不臨, 而不能晷肖。偶得趙子昂〈香山詩〉墨蹟, 愛其圓轉流麗, 遂臨之。不數過而遂欲亂真。此無他, 即如人學正人君子, 只覺觚稜難近, 降而與匪人遊, 情不覺其日親日密, 而無爾我者然也。行大薄其為人, 痛惡其書淺俗, 如徐偃王之無骨, 始復宗先人四五世所學之魯公而苦為之。然腕雜矣, 不能勁瘦挺拗如先人矣。比之匪人, 不亦傷乎！」

24 寧拙毋巧, 寧醜毋媚, 寧支離毋輕滑, 寧真率毋安排。(傅山, 霜紅龕集; 作字示兒孫)

25 「行行如紆春蚓, 字字若綰秋蛇。」(蘇軾. 題蕭子云書) (水采田, 1999, 宋代書論, p. 17)

26 書之氣, 必達乎道。(王羲之, 記白雲先生書訣) (Huá, 1997, p. 34)

27 書當造乎自然。(劉熙載, 藝概)(Huá, 1997, p. 666)

28 'Yán Yuan asked about perfect virtue. The Master said, "To subdue one's self and return to propriety, is perfect virtue. If a man can for one day subdue himself and return to propriety, all under heaven will ascribe perfect virtue to him. Is the practice of perfect virtue from a man himself, or is it from others?" Yán Yuan said, "I beg to ask the steps of that process". The Master replied, "Look not at what is contrary to propriety; listen not to what is contrary to propriety; speak not what is contrary to propriety; make no movement which is contrary to propriety". Yán Yuan then said, "Though I am deficient in intelligence and vigour, I will make it my business to practice this lesson"' (The *Analects*, *Yán Yuan*, 12:1; trans. by Legge, 1861a).

29 出門如見大賓, 使民如承大祭。己所不欲, 勿施於人。在邦無怨, 在家無怨。(顏淵12:2)

30 居處恭, 執事敬, 與人忠。(子路13:19)

31 巧言令色, 鮮矣仁。(學而1:3)

32 仁者其言也訒。(顏淵12:3)

33 欲言精微, 言多則愈粗。(河南程氏遺書卷第十五)

34 知者不言, 言者不知。(道德經56章)

35 夫仁, 天之尊爵也, 人之安宅也。(孟子公孫丑上, 2A7)

36 有子曰：「其為人也孝弟, 而好犯上者, 鮮矣; 不好犯上, 而好作亂者, 未之有也。君子務本, 本立而道生。孝弟也者, 其為仁之本與！」(論語學而1:2)

37 三年無改於父之道, 可謂孝矣。(倫語里仁, 4:20)

38 夫孝, 始於事親, 中於事君, 終於立身。(孝經)

39 人而不仁, 如禮何?人而不仁, 如樂何? (論語八佾, 3:3)

40 顏淵問仁。子曰：「克己復禮為仁。一日克己復禮, 天下歸仁焉。為仁由己, 而由人乎哉?」顏淵曰：「請問其目。」子曰：「非禮勿視, 非禮勿聽, 非禮勿言, 非禮勿動。」顏淵曰：「回雖不敏, 請事斯語矣。」 (論語顏淵12:1)

41 不知禮、無以立也。(論語堯曰, 20:3)
42 不知禮, 則耳目無所加, 手足無所措。(朱熹.四書集注.論語集注:堯曰第二十)
43 道德仁義, 非禮不成, 教訓正俗, 非禮不備。分爭辨訟, 非禮不決。君臣上下父子兄弟, 非禮不定。宦學事師, 非禮不親。班朝治軍, 蒞官行法, 非禮威嚴不行。禱祠祭祀, 供給鬼神, 非禮不誠不莊。是以君子恭敬撙節退讓以明禮。(禮記, 曲禮, 1A:8)
44 人之所以異於禽於獸者幾希...仁義。(孟子離婁下19)
45 由是觀之, 無惻隱之心, 非人也；無羞惡之心, 非人也；無辭讓之心, 非人也；無是非之心, 非人也。惻隱之心, 仁之端也；羞惡之心, 義之端也；辭讓之心, 禮之端也；是非之心, 智之端也。(孟子公孫丑上6)
46 鸚鵡能言, 不離飛鳥；猩猩能言, 不離禽獸。今人而無禮, 雖能言, 不亦禽獸之心乎？夫唯禽獸無禮, 故父子聚麀。是故聖人作, 為禮以教人。使人以有禮, 知自別於禽獸。(禮記, 曲禮, 1A:9)
47 楊氏為我, 是無君也；墨氏兼愛, 是無父也。無父無君, 是禽獸也。(孟子滕文公下, 3B9)
48 戎狄是膺, 荊舒是懲。(孟子滕文公下3B9)
49 今也南蠻鴃舌之人, 非先王之道。(孟子滕文公上, 3A.4)

References

Agamben, G. (1998). *Homo Sacer: Sovereign power and bare life*. Stanford, CA: Stanford University Press.

Agamben, G. (2004). *The open: Man and animal*. Stanford, CA: Stanford University Press.

Balazs, E. (1964). *Chinese civilisation and bureaucracy: Variations on theme*. New Haven, CT: Yale University Press.

Barbieri-Low, A. J. (2011). Craftsman's literacy: Uses of writing by male and female artisans in Qin and Han China. In L. Feng & D. P. Branner (Eds.), *Writing & literacy in early China* (pp. 370–400). Seattle & London: University of Washington Press.

Biàn, R. H. 卞仁海 (2008). Chinese characters and the ancient naming taboo漢字與古代避諱. *Journal of Language and Literature Studies*語文學刊, 7, 43–44.

Bullock, J. S. (Trans.). (2011). *Yang Xiong: Philosophy of the Fa yan*. Retrieved November 16, 2013, from D. Sturgeon (Ed.), *Chinese text project*. Retrieved from http://ctext.org/yangzi-fayan

Chan, W. (1963). *A source book in Chinese philosophy*. Princeton, NJ: Princeton University Press.

Chan, W. (1975). Chinese and Western interpretations of Jen (humanity). *Journal of Chinese philosophy*, *2*(2), 107–129.

Chén, Y. 陳垣 (1997). *Examples of taboos in history*史諱舉例. Shanghai: Xinhua (New China) Bookstore.上海:新華書局

Chíen, M. (1982). *Traditional government in imperial China: A critical analysis*. Trans. C. Hsüeh & G. O. Totten. Hong Kong: The Chinese University of Hong Kong.

Connery, C. L. (1998). *The empire of the text: Writing and authority in early imperial China*. Lanham, MD: Rowman & Littlefield Publishers.

Daniels, N. (1978). Merit and meritocracy. *Philosophy & Public Affairs*, *7*(3), 206–223.

Derrida, J. (1979). Scribble (writing-power). *Yale French Studies*, *58*, 117–147.

Derrida, J. (1992). Mochlos; or, the conflict of faculties. In R. Rand (Ed.), *Logomachia: The conflict of faculties* (pp. 1–34). Lincoln, NE: University of Nebraska Press.

Elman, B. A. (2000). *A cultural history of civil examination in late imperial China*. Berkeley, CA: University of California Press.

Fairbank, J. K. (1986). *The great Chinese revolution: 1800–1985*. New York, NY: Harper & Row.

Fang, F., & Gong, Y. 方芳、龔延明 (2015). The management of examination halls in the Song 宋代科場管理. *Zhejiang Academic Journal* 浙江學刊, *1*, 46–51.

Fang, Y. 方玉霞 (2012). *Action research on the effect of using the five-upright orthodox calligraphy instruction to cultivate pupils' virtue and calligraphy skill* 以五正書法教學培養小學生德行與書法能力之行動研究. Master dissertation. National Taipei University of Education. 國立臺北教育大學課程與教學研究所學位論文,1–263.

Feng, X-m. (Trans.). (2008). *Xiao Jing: The classic of Xiao*. Retrieved March 15, 2017, from www.tsoidug.org/Papers/Xiao_Jing_Comment.pdf

Fu, S. 傅山 (2002). *Shwang Hung Kan Ji* 霜紅龕集. Shanghai: Shanghai Old Texts. 上海:上海古籍出版

Gao, Y. 高誘 (1965). *Commentaries on Húinánzi* 淮南子注. Taipei: World Book Co. 臺北:世界書局 Retrieved March 15, 2017, from http://ctext.org/huainanzi/zh

Gunn, R. W. (2001). Intimacy, psyche, and spirit in the experience of Chinese and Japanese calligraphy. *Journal of Religion and Health*, *40*(1), 129–166.

Halper, E. C. (1999). Elenchus. In R. Audi (Ed.), *The Cambridge dictionary of philosophy* (p. 257). Cambridge, UK: Cambridge University Press.

Hendricks, G. P. (2014). A Darridarean critique of logocentrism as opposed to textcentrism in John 1v1. *Koers: Bulletin for Christian Scholarship*, *79*(1), 1–8.

Ho, W. P. (2005). The Chinese approach to learning: The paradigmatic case of Chinese calligraphy. In C. Ota & C. Erricker (Eds.), *Spiritual education: Literary, empirical and pedagogical approaches* (pp. 155–170). Brighten: Sussex Academic Press.

Hua, C-R. 華正人 (Ed.). (1997). *Selected essays on calligraphy over history* (Vols. 1–2) 歷代書法論文選上下冊. Taipei: Hua Cheng. 臺北: 華正書局.

Huang, W-C. (2000). A study on the namingtaboo under the Liao & Chin. *Journal of the Historical Studies*, *26*, 23–60. 黃緯中. (2000). 略論遼金的避諱, 史學彙刊, 26, 23–60.

Hucker, C. O. (1958). Governmental organisation of the Ming dynasty. *Harvard Journal of Asiatic Studies*, *21*, 1–66.

Hung, R. (2012). Being human or being a citizen? Rethinking human rights and citizenship education in the light of Agamben and Merleau-Ponty. *Cambridge Journal of Education*, *42*(1), 37–51.

Hung, R. (2015). To be *as* not to be: In search of an alternative humanism in the light of early Daoism and deconstruction. *Journal of Philosophy of Education*, *49*(3), 418–434.

Kracke, E. A. (1947). Family vs. merit in Chinese civil service examinations. *Harvard Journal of Asiatic Studies*, *10*, 103–123.

Kraus, R. C. (1991). *Brushes with power: Modern politics and the Chinese art of calligraphy*. Berkeley, CA: University of California Press.

Ku, C-K., & Goodrich, L. C. (1938). A study of literary persecution during the Ming. *Harvard Journal of Asiatic Studies*, *3*(3/4), 254–311.

Lai, K. K. (2008). *An introduction of Chinese philosophy*. New York, NY: Cambridge University Press.

Lau, D. C. (Trans.). (1979). *Mencius: A bilingual edition*. Middlesex: Penguin Books.

Legge, J. (Trans.). (1861a). *Confucian analects. The chinese classics, volume 1*. Retrieved November 10, 2013, D. Sturgeon (Ed.), *Chinese text project* from http://ctext.org/analects

Legge, J. (Trans.). (1861b). *Xìao Jing. Sacred book of the East, volume 3*. Retrieved September 20, 2016, from D. Sturgeon (Ed.), *Chinese text project*. http://ctext.org/xiao-jing

Legge, J. (Trans.). (1872). *The Ch'un Ts'ew with the Tso Chuen*. Retrieved March 21, 2015, from A. Kinney (Ed.), *Chunqiu Zuo zhuan*. http://www2.iath.virginia.edu/saxon/servlet/

SaxonServlet?source=xwomen/texts/chunqiu.xml&style=xwomen/xsl/dynaxml.
xsl&doc.view=divtoc&chunk.id=tpage&toc.depth=1&toc.id=0&doc.lang=bilingual

Legge, J. (Trans.). (1885). *Sacred books of the East, volume 28, part 4: The Li Ki*. Retrieved November 19, 2013, from D. Sturgeon (Ed.), *Chinese text project*. http://ctext.org/liji

Legge, J. (Trans.). (1891a). *The Tao Te Ching*. Retrieved October 10, 2015, from D. Sturgeon (Ed.), *Chinese text project*. http://ctext.org. http://ctext.org/dao-de-jing

Legge, J. (Trans.). (1898). *The book of poetry: The Chinese classics, volume 4*. Retrieved March 22, 2015, from D. Sturgeon (Ed.), *Chinese text project*. http://ctext.org. http://ctext.org/book-of-poetry

Legge, J. (Trans.). (1985). *The works of Mencius*, Clarendon. Retrieved August 27, 2015, from D. Sturgeon (Ed.), *Chinese text project*. http://ctext.org/mengzi

Leigh, F. (2007). Platonic dialogue, maieutic method and critical thinking. *Journal of philosophy of education, 41*(3), 309–323.

Levi-Strauss, C. (1974). *Tristes Tropiques*. Trans. J. Weightman & D. Weightman. New York, NY: Atheneum.

Lewis, M. E. (1999). *Writing and authority in early China*. New York, NY: State University of New York Press.

Lewis, M. E. (2009). *China between empires: The northern and southern dynasties* (Vol. 2). Cambridge, MA: Harvard University Press.

Li, F., & Branner, D. P. (2011). Introduction: Writing as a phenomenon of literacy. In L. Feng & D. P. Branner (Eds.), *Writing & literacy in early China* (pp. 339–369). Seattle, WA: University of Washington Press.

Long, J. (1987). *The art of Chinese calligraphy*. Poole: Blandford Press.

Lu, X. (1990). *Diary of a madman and other stories*. Trans. W. A. Lyell. Honolulu, HI: University of Hawaii Press.

Mar, W. 馬偉成 (2014). The nonstandard forms of characters in Tang Dynasty論唐代字書的俗字類型. *Annual of Tatung University General Education*大同大學通識教育年報, *10*, 1–28.

Muller, A. C. (1990). *The analects of Confucius* 論語. Retrieved March 15, 2017, from www.acmuller.net/con-dao/analects.html

Mullis, E. C. (2007). The ethics of Confucian artistry. *The Journal of Aesthetics and Art Criticism, 65*(1), 99–107.

Ni, P. (1999). Moral and philosophical implications of Chinese calligraphy. *Grand Valley Review, 20*(1), 18–31.

Post, E. (1922). *Etiquette*. New York, NY: Funk & Wagnalls Company.

Qu, C. 屈超立(2003). Civil imperial examinations and the Song bureaucracy科舉制度與宋代吏治. *Qilu Journal issue 齊魯學刊5*, 85–88.

Quesnay, F. (1946). *China, a model for Europe*. Trans. L. A. Maverick. San Antonio, TX: Paul Anderson Company.

Rahe, P. A. (1994). *Republics ancient and modern*. Chapel Hill, NC: University of North Carolina Press.

Reed, G. G. (1992). Modelling as a pedagogical technique in the art and life of China. *Journal of Aesthetic Education, 26*(3), 75–83.

Shǔi, C. 水采田(Ed.). (1999). *Calligraphy criticism of the Song Dynasty*宋代書論. Changsha: Hunan Art Press.長沙: 湖南美術出版社

Tsai, C. 蔡忠霖(2008). A study of the classification of words with different attributes in 'Record of Standard Form of Characters' ('Zhèng Míng Yào Lù') 《正名要錄》 之文字屬性歸類研究. *Journal of the Dunhuang Studies* 敦煌學輯刊, *1*, 21–38.

88 Education

Tsai, C. 蔡忠霖(2009). The study in norm of character forms and appearances of coexisted standard characters of Chinese characters – an instance for dictionaries in Tang Dynasty 論字書的字形規範及其「迚正」現象 – 以唐代字樣書為例. *Literature & Philosophy* 文與哲, *15*, 33–60.

Twitchett, D. C. (1974). *The birth of the Chinese meritocracy: Bureaucrats and examinations in T'ang China* (Lecture given to the China Society in London, 17 December, 1974). London, UK: China Society.

Vlastos, G. (1982). The Socratic elenchus. *The Journal of Philosophy*, *79*(11), 711–714.

Vlastos, G. (1994). *Socratic studies*. Cambridge, NY: Cambridge University Press.

Xǔ, S.許慎(n.d.). *Shuowén Jiězì*. 說文解字. Retrieved March 15, 2017, from D. Sturgeon (Ed.), *Chinese text project*. http://ctext.org/shuo-wen-jie-zi

Yates, R. D. S. (2011). Soldiers, scribes, and women: Literacy among the lower orders in early China. In L. Feng & D. P. Branner (Eds.), *Writing & literacy in early China* (pp. 339–369), Seattle, WA: University of Washington Press.

Yen, Y. (2005). *Calligraphy and power in contemporary Chinese society*. New York, NY: Routledge Curzon.

Ying, L-h. (2012). Negotiating with the past: The art of calligraphy in Post-Mao China. *ASIA Network Exchange*, *19*(2), 32–41.

Young, M. (1994). *The rise of meritocracy*. New Brunswick, NJ: Transaction Publishers.

Zhang, T.張韜 (2010). The cultural-philosophical essence of calligraphic creation: wisdom and morality. 書法創作的文化哲學思想內核：仁智與道德*Chinese Calligraphy*,中華書道*70*, 35–40.

Zhu, X. 朱熹(2004). *Notes on four books*.四書集注. Hunan:Yuelu Publisher. 湖南： 嶽麓書社。

Chapter 4

The paradox of graphocentrism
Dao-logocentrism

復與書銘, 自天子達於士, 其辭一也。

—(禮記喪服小記, 15:30)[1]

桓公讀書於堂上, 輪扁斲輪於堂下, 釋椎鑿而上, 問桓公曰：「敢問公之所讀者何言邪?」公曰：「聖人之言也。」曰：「聖人在乎?」公曰：「已死矣。」曰：「然則君之所讀者, 古人之糟魄已夫！」

—（莊子外篇天道篇）[2]

In this book, I claim that Chinese culture and thought are characterised by graphocentrism, which privileges writing over speech. In contrast, the underlying phonocentrism of Western thinking prioritises the spoken over the written. Having noted the difference between graphocentrism and phonocentrism, I hope in this chapter to clarify the similarities between these two traditions and, furthermore, between the Dao and logos. In doing so, I will make clear the logocentrism implied in graphocentrism. I will then argue that the meaning of the Dao is wider and more profound than that of logos. The Dao can be seen as coinciding with logos but also as opening and welcoming difference, as criticism, as deconstruction, as deviance.

Logos in writing and in speech: the Chinese prejudice

From the perspective of graphocentrism, the history of Chinese literature and education included a process of discipline and the institutionalisation of writing, both of which aimed to cultivate the writing subject. The institutional practice involved forms of violence with respect to the power of writing, which even now legitimises discrimination between those who can and cannot write, between those who are able and unable to write well, between those who understand the written word and those who do not. The violence suggests a common ethnocentrism in graphocentrism and phonocentrism. What makes

90 Paradox

these two traditions converge on ethnocentrism when they have different value hierarchies? Although the notion of presence assumed in graphocentrism varies from that in phonocentrism, is there any metaphysical similarity between these two notions? Here, let me return to Derrida and his 'Chinese prejudice'.

As Derrida (1976) posits, phonocentrism, logocentrism, and ethnocentrism formed an alliance that has dominated the Western history of metaphysics. Phonocentrism determines the meaning of being in general as presence, whereas logocentrism refers to metaphysics that takes 'thought, truth, reason, logic, the Word' as universal, existing in itself, and foundational (Culler, 2014, p. 92). Through the history of Western philosophy, the conspiracy of phonocentrism and logocentrism has formulated opposing groups of presence: meaning/form, soul/body, intuition/expression, literal/metaphorical, nature/culture, positive/negative, transcendental/empirical, serious/non-serious, etc. (Culler, 2014). In theory, the hierarchy is imposed in intellectual work to discriminate the true from the untrue, the dominating from the dominated, the privileged from the subjugated, and the centre from the marginal. In practice, the hierarchy is embodied in political or military campaigns and educational or cultural programmes (Brooker, 2003). Logocentrism secures the hierarchy of dualist ideas and the higher position of the presence of the first group. Logocentrism refers to the privilege of presence – that which is or that which appears – in the Western philosophical tradition. For Derrida, the metaphysics of presence has haunted the Western philosophical tradition for thousands of years. He defines the metaphysics of presence as follows:

> 1. The hierarchical axiology, the ethical-ontological distinctions which do not merely set up value-oppositions clustered around an ideal and unfindable limit, but moreover subordinate these values to each other (normal/abnormal, standard/parasite, fulfilled/void, serious/non-serious, literal/non-literal, briefly: positive/negative and ideal/non-ideal) . . . 2. The enterprise of returning 'strategically', ideally, to an origin or to a 'priority' held to be simple, intact, normal, pure, standard, self-identical, in order then to think in terms of derivation, complication, deterioration, accident, etc.
>
> (Derrida, 1988, p. 93)

Derrida continues:

> All metaphysicians, from Plato to Rousseau, Descartes to Husserl, have proceeded in this way, conceiving good to be before evil, the positive before the negative, the pure before the impure, the simple before the complex, the essential before the accidental, the imitated before the imitation, etc. And this not just one metaphysical gesture among others, it is the metaphysical exigency, that which has been the most constant, most profound and most potent.
>
> (1988, p. 93)

Logo-phonocentrism has a long history in the West. As Derrida discusses, this history has lasted for thousands of years. In Plato (1961), the debasement of writing in favour of phonocentrism is articulated in the *Phaedrus* within the Myth of Teuth, in the *Cratylus*, and in the *Seventh Letter* (Stewart, 1989). In the *Phaedrus*, the inventor of writing, Teuth, claims that writing 'provides a recipe of memory and wisdom' (276e). The king of Egypt, Thamus, disagrees for two reasons: first, writing does not promote memory but implants forgetfulness; second, writing does not reflect knowledge, only a resemblance of knowledge (Stewart, 1989). Writing is seen 'at once mnemotechnique and the power of forgetting' (Derrida, 2016, p. 26).

In Aristotle, we find a similar belittlement of writing, which involves a double hierarchy of speech and writing and of the inner and the outer. At the beginning of *On Interpretation* (trans. by Edghill, 2015; Derrida, 1976), Aristotle says, 'Spoken words are the symbols of mental experience and written words are the symbols of spoken words. Just as all men have not the same writing, so all men have not the same speech sounds, but the mental experiences, which these directly symbolize, are the same for all, as also are those things of which our experiences are the images'. The communication of thoughts relies first on spoken words, which can then be recorded by written words. Thus, writing is the second-order signifier. The hierarchy assumes the supreme independence of thought in language and the inferiority of writing. This first hierarchy leads to the second hierarchy, which creates a dichotomy between the inner and the outer. The inner denotes 'the possibility of a pure inside, uncontaminated, unpenetrated' (Standish, 2001, p. 83). In contrast, the outer can be understood to refer to the opposite, the possibility of the impure outside, the contaminated, and the penetrated. The strong devaluation of writing as the outer possibility of expression can also be found in Jean-Jacques Rousseau.

In the second part of *Of Grammatology*, Derrida discusses the writing of Rousseau. At the beginning of Part II, Derrida (1976, p. 105) references interesting quotations from Rousseau's *Emile* (1886, p. 109): 'We have an organ that corresponds to that of hearing, that is, the voice. Sight has nothing like this, for thought we can produce sounds, we cannot give off colours. We have therefore fuller means of cultivating hearing, by exercising active and passive organs upon one another'.[3] The passage shows the significance and superiority of speaking and hearing over seeing and writing in the Western tradition, or the phonocentric tradition. Practising the active and passive organs, one with the other, supplies an additional means of cultivating the ear. In his *Essay on the Origin of Language* (Rousseau & Herder, 1966), Rousseau makes a sharp and fundamental distinction between the inner (essential) and outer (accidental): movement and voice are the first means human beings use to communicate with each other. Gestures and spoken language, which are initiated first to express feelings and passions and then to express reason, are natural signs. In contrast, script is invented based on exteriority: 'The art of writing does not at all depend upon that of speaking. It derives from needs of a different kind which develop . . . according to circumstances entirely independent from the duration of the people' (Rousseau, 1966, p. 19). While the voice expresses feelings, writing transmits ideas. From Rousseau's viewpoint (1966, p. 21), there is no essential connection between writing and meaning because it 'changes not the words but the spirit, substituting exactitude for expressiveness'. Vocal expression does a better job than writing at conserving the truthfulness and genuineness of the inner self. Underlying Rousseau's *Essay* is phonocentrism – spoken language outweighs writing.

For Derrida, Hegel is another representative of Western phonocentrism. In Hegel's view, rational thinking/logical thinking is the essence of humanity, distinguishing humankind from beasts. Yet logical thinking must be communicated through logical language, which is phonetic language. Hegel thus criticises non-phonetic writing – Chinese – severely: 'It is only to the exegeticism of Chinese spiritual culture that their hieroglyphic writing is suited', 'the hieroglyphic reading is for itself a deaf reading and a dumb writing', and 'in the case of alphabetic script there is only *one* foundation, and in fact it stands in the correct relationship: the visible language is related to the audible only as a sign; the intelligence externalises itself immediately and unconditionally by speaking' (quoted in Derrida, 2016, p. 27).

Throughout Western intellectual history, logo-phonocentrism as a myth has been produced by 'exigent, powerful, systematic and irrepressible desire' (Derrida, 1976, p. 49). Logo-phonocentrism is due to people's powerful desire to believe that language can signify all non-linguistic entities, objects, intentions, or ideas (Novitz, 1985). In the West, logocentrism is 'the metaphysics of phonetic writing (for example, of the alphabet) which was fundamentally . . . nothing but the most original and powerful ethnocentrism, in the process of imposing itself upon the world' (Derrida, 1976, p. 3). In Derrida's view, the metaphysics of presence – logo-phonocentrism – has involved the deepest problem in intellectual history, which can be termed ethnocentrism and sometimes phallogocentrism. Accompanying ethnocentrism/phallogocentrism are various dubious ideologies, such as sexism and racism, out of which come exclusion, oppression, and discrimination. In order to deconstruct logo-phonocentric metaphysics, Derrida turns to non-phonetic forms of language: hieroglyphics, ideograms, algebraic notations, and non-linear writing. In this way, Chinese language can be seen as a 'deconstructed language' that may provide an antidote to the conspiracy of the Western trilogy of logo-phono-ethnocentrism (Graham, 1989; Hall & Ames, 1998).

In the Western intellectual history of phonocentrism, some have admired Chinese as a vision-oriented language. Countering Hegel (1894, 2001), Leibniz (1981, p. 290) praises Chinese characters for their strikingly immediate quality of 'speaking to the eyes'. The American art historian Ernest Fenollosa (Fenollosa & Pound, 1936, p. 8) comments that Chinese notation is much more than arbitrary symbols: 'It is based upon a vivid shorthand picture of the operations of nature'. Based on its immediacy, the Chinese language for Leibniz and his followers is a prototype for developing a universal language.

As Derrida (1976, p. 86) reveals, the 'Chinese prejudice' is paradoxical. On the one hand, phonocentrists like Hegel hold it in contempt. On the other, it garners hyperbolic admiration from those, like Leibniz, who are eager to find in Chinese a model for a universal script because it 'seems to have been "invented by a deaf man" (*New Essays*)' (Derrida, 2016, p. 85). The seemingly contradictory disdain and admiration are, indeed, both effects of ethnocentrism. Derrida (ibid., p. 87) notes the irony that the effort of reversing ethnocentrism 'silently hides behind all the spectacular effects to consolidate an inside and to draw from it some domestic benefit.' Seventeenth-century sinologist studies of Egyptian hieroglyphs or Chinese scripts imply mysticism, taking the scripts as sublime rather than using scientific deciphering. Such 'blindness' of the 'Chinese prejudice' or 'hieroglyphist prejudice' produces a 'hyperbolic admiration' that is no less ethnocentric than Hegelian scorn (pp. 86–87).

Although Derrida insists that logo-phonocentrism is a property of the West, we can observe similar ethnocentric practices, such as discrimination and exclusion, in Chinese graphocentric histories and societies. As Spivak (1976, p. lxviii) puts it, all kinds of centrism, be they logocentrism, phonocentrism, or graphocentrism, are about the human desire to believe in the first and last things – 'the Logos, the Word, the Divine Mind'. Logocentrism takes logos as the central principle for language and philosophy. As Derrida (1976, 1982) argues, logos is basic to the Western metaphysics that is fundamental to cultural practices and languages. 'Logos' is the Greek word for 'word', meaning that by which inward thought is expressed but also meaning 'speech' and 'reason' (logic) (Jeffery, 1992, pp. 459–461). Roger Crisp (1995, p. 518) summarises five senses of the word 'logos' in Western philosophy: rule, principle, and law; proposition, account, explanation, thesis, and argument; reason, reasoning, rational faculty, abstract theory, and discursive reasoning; measure, relation, proportion, and ratio; and value and worth. Essentially, the concept of logos refers to speaking words of reason.

In this respect, logos indeed reminds us of the Dào (道) in Chinese philosophy, especially the philosophy of the *Daodejing* (Zha, 1992; Zhang, 1988, 1992). For example: 'The Dao that can be trodden is not the enduring and unchanging Dao. The name that can be named is not the enduring and unchanging name' (*Daodejing*: 1; trans. by Legge, 1891a)[4]; 'The Dao, considered as unchanging, has no name' (*Daodejing*: 32; trans. by Legge, 1891a)[5]; and 'The Dao produced One; One produced Two; Two produced Three; Three produced All things' (*Daodejing*: 42; trans. by Legge, 1891a).[6] These tenets from the *Daodejing* converge on a central belief that the Dao is the foundational idea at the cosmo-ontological level.

The term 'Dào' in Chinese can be used as both a noun and as a verb. As a noun, the 'Dào' indicates 'the path', 'the way', 'the principle', 'the law', 'the doctrine', and 'the truth'. As a verb, it means 'to say', 'to speak', 'to express', and 'to address'. In the *Daodejing*, these two important meanings – thinking and speaking – of the Dào coexist (Zhang, 1992). The similarity between the Dào and logos is noticeable, implying a possible connection between logocentrism and graphocentrism. Although its communicative mediation is non-phonetic language, Chinese thought may have the same desire as Western metaphysics to pursue the ultimate reality, the truth, the end, the One, etc.

Logocentrism and graphocentrism

According to Derrida (1976, 2016), logo-phonocentrism embodies three facets to conduct powerful ethnocentric control and imposition:

1 *the concept of writing* in a world where the phoneticisation of writing must dissimulate its own history as it produces itself;
2 *the history of the metaphysics* which, in spite of all differences, not only from Plato to Hegel (even including Leibniz) but also, beyond their apparent limits, from the pre-Socratics to Heidegger, has always assigned the origin of truth in general to the logos: the history of truth, of the truth of truth, has always been, except for a metaphorical diversion that we shall have to consider, the debasement of writing, and its repression outside 'full' speech;
3 *the concept of science* or the scientificity of science – what has always been determined as *logic* – a concept that has always been a philosophical concept, even if the practice of science has constantly challenged the imperialism of the logos, by invoking, for example, always and ever increasingly, nonphonetic writing (Derrida, 2016, pp. 3–4).

This definition provides three threads for further investigating how Chinese thought relates to language. Regarding the first facet, the concept of writing, Derrida's explanation seems only to fit the Western context because Western languages use spelling, alphabetic, and phonetic linguistic systems, whereas the Chinese language does not. However, a careful examination of the invention of characters tells a different story: there is a deep connection between Chinese characters and sound. A genealogical examination defies the myth of Western phonocentrism by showing that the invention of characters was based on principles not limited to mere realistic depiction. A phonetic principle was taken into consideration. In this sense, Chinese linguistic philosophy involves a certain degree of phonocentric episteme.

An examination of the second facet reveals the inseparable relationship between speech and writing in Chinese through a lexical-etymological clarification of the meaning of the word 'word' (zì, 字). The relation between 'zì', 'míng' (name, 名), and 'wén' (line, stripe, 文) implies a sophisticated and subtle connection between spoken words and written words, as well as the similarity between graphocentrism and logocentrism. Therefore, questioning the relationship between the word 'zì' and its relatives illuminates the profound congruity between graphocentrism and phonocentrism.

The third aspect, with respect to metaphysics, uncovers the implied logocentrism in Chinese thought through a critical analysis of the ideas of xin (mind, 心), yì (idea, 意), the Dao, and logos. As many scholars (Chang, 1988; Gu, 2000; Hansen, 1993; Tong, 1993; Zhang, 1985, 1988, 1992) have shown, a paradoxical and fruitful relationship exists between the ideas of the Dao and logos, which inspires me to propose the existence of Chinese Dao-logocentrism.

The six graphs – Lìu shu

The first point concerning the relationship between graphocentrism and logophonocentrism is implied in the phonetic elements involved in traditional Chinese lexicography: the six graphs (lìu shu, 六書), meaning the six categories or six principles by which Chinese characters were invented and classified.

Chinese written words are not entirely graphic in composition. They include pictographs, ideographs, and logographs. The earliest Chinese written words were produced as pictographs and ideographs. They arose from 'the drawing of realistic depictions of things', which is similar to the rise of writing in other parts of the world – for example, in Egypt, Mesopotamia, and Mesoamerica (Boltz, 2001, p. 6). Chinese written words have increased in number and changed in composition over time. The principles of composing a character were not limited to the drawing of a pictorial sign to represent an object or a thing. Some pictographs or words were invested with phonetic or semantic values and became constituent parts for developing new words that would not be simple pictographs or ideographs. According to Boltz (1986, 1999), Chinese writing arose largely as pictographs. The primitive pictographs were then used in two derivative ways to develop new, complicated words. The first way was substituting an already invented pictograph for another homophonous or nearly homophonous word that stood for an abstract idea. This kind of creation is termed paronomastic. The second kind was parasemantic, which means that more than one graph was used to stand for 'semantically congruent but phonetically distinct words' (Boltz, 1986, p. 426). The development of the Chinese script then entered the determinative stage, during which many semantic and phonetic determinatives were added to compose new written words. The evolution of the Chinese script was, briefly, a linear process of three formative stages: pictographic, multivalent, and determinative (Boltz, 2001).

Instead of viewing the three formations as linearly continuous stages, it is also plausible to see them as different situations that coexisted to use and evolve different words. This view is possible because some words that were generated based on realistic depictions are still functioning: 人 (human, rén) and 口 (mouth, kǒu) are but two examples. Ancient Chinese philologists recognised that there were diverse and complicated rules for the evolution of graphs. In 100 AD, Xǔ Shèn (許慎) wrote one of the most important and most typographically complex Chinese texts, *Shuo wén jiě zì* (說文解字), which is often

96 Paradox

abbreviated as *Shuowén* (說文) (Cook, 2001; Bottéro, 2002, 2006; Bottéro & Harbsmeier, 2008). *Shuowén* could be the most well-known, but not the earliest, book for identifying the six graphs (lìu shu, 六書) as six principles of composing Chinese characters, or, in terms of Bottéro and Harbsmeier (2008, p. 252), 'Six Categories of Scribal Acts'. The six principles or six categories include:

1 Zhǐ shì (指事): 'Simple ideographs' are characters expressing an abstract idea through an iconic form, as in the characters 上 (shàng, up) and 下 (xià, under).
2 Xiàng xíng (象形): 'Pictographs' (or 'form imitation') are characters symbolising 'physical shape,' as in the characters 日 (rì, sun) and 月 (yuè, moon).
3 Xíng sheng (形聲): 'Phonetic-semantic compounds' are characters which indicate 'shape and sound,' as in the characters 江 (jiang, waterway) and 河 (hé, river).
4 Huì yì (會意): 'Compound ideographs' or 'associative compounds' are characters that associate ideas, as in the characters 武 (wu, military, powerful) and 信 (xìn, trust, genuine).
5 Zhuǎn zhù (轉注): 'Derivative cognates' are characters that express by reciprocation. Traditional examples include 考 (kǎo, old, elder, attest) and 老 (lǎo, old, elder). Different words belonging to this category mean that they have the same meaning and thereby are used to refer to each other.
6 Jiǎjiè (假借): 'Rebus characters' 'borrow [one graph for another],' as in the characters for lìng /lǐng (令) (command, order), cháng/zhǎng (長) (senior, long). A single character has different meanings. Those meanings might be generated in different times. The meaning produced later is communicated by means of the character that has an original and different meaning. This way of using word is called jiǎjiè (Bottéro & Harbsmeier, 2008; Sampson & Chen, 2013).

Joseph Wu (1969) notes three reasons that the ancient traditional classification is illogical and inaccurate: first, it confused the structure of the characters with the use of the characters; second, the definition of 'zhuǎn zhù' has been very vague and unclear and thereby has caused divergent interpretations; and third, the classification was essentially based on the written characters used in the Chíng dynasty (221–207 BC), which were not exactly the same as the original forms. Despite these flaws, throughout Chinese literary history, the six principles have been firmly believed to be the basis for the development of written characters; therefore, they reflect the Chinese mindset about written language. Because of the inaccuracy of the six principles, Wu (1969) suggests three ways of categorising Chinese characters: simple characters, complex characters, and compound characters. By 'simple character', Wu (1969, p. 424) means 'an unanalysable unit that is self-sufficient in expressing an image or concept, and . . . a building brick of other types of characters,' for example, the names of animals, natural objects, and corporeal objects, like 門 (gate, mén), 雨 (rain, yǔ), etc. Some characters in this category denote abstract concepts based on observation, such as 長 (long, cháng), 上 (up, shàng), 下 (under, xià), etc. A 'complex character' is 'a character that is composed of at least one simple character and some symbol which is not, itself, a character' (Wu, 1969, p. 425). For example, the character 果 (fruit, guǒ) is composed of the character 木 (tree, mù), which is a simple character, and 田. The character 田 could mean a field (tián), but here it is borrowed because of its shape. The third category is 'compound character', which means 'a character that is composed of two or more characters of either one (or both) of the former two types' (Wu, 1969, p. 425). For example, 閂 (door latch, shuan) is composed of the character 門 (door, mén) and a bar (一). Wu's classification is a brief introduction to the invention and organisation of Chinese characters.

If we take a wider look at the principles of the six graphs, we will find that Chinese written words developed according to a number of principles, including realistic depiction, polysemic use, polyphonic use, rebus use, and the production of phonetic compounds with ideographic radicals. The formation of Chinese script undoubtedly involved the element of phoneticisation. By receiving the phonetic element, Chinese script incorporated phonocentrism in its foundation. In addition to the classic explanation of the composition of Chinese words, contemporary linguistic research supports the view that Chinese characters had pictographic origins. Research also has found resources in rebus and polyphonic uses (Boltz, 2001).[7] Therefore, what underpins the invention of Chinese script is not only the graphic element but also the phonetic element. It is certain that the Chinese language system is more vision oriented than voice oriented. Yet this does not exclude the oral and aural aspects in the formation of Chinese script and its subsequent cultural development.

As Derrida (1976, p. 90) remarks, 'But we have known for a long time that largely nonphonetic scripts like Chinese and Japanese included phonetic elements very clearly. They remained structurally dominated by the ideogram or algebra'. The difference between Chinese script and Western languages is that Chinese characters do not refer to meaning only by means of recording sound. Phonetic scripts developed through oral signs, whereas Chinese characters developed, for the most part, through visual signs. Chinese script generated from visual signs, although it gained phonetic elements during its process of evolution. Chinese graphocentrism can be found in the visual dependency and visual sensibility of Chinese script. Yet this does not rule out the phonetic element of the Chinese language. Some characters stand for sounds, and some are phonetic compounds. Therefore, graphocentrism is not entirely opposite to or incompatible with phonocentrism.

The word – zì

There also is an inextricable internal relationship between speech and writing, between spoken words and written words, at the lexical-etymological level. The character for 'word' in modern Chinese is 字 (zì), which can refer to both

98 Paradox

the spoken word and the written word. Yet the term 'zì' in ordinary language refers more often to the written word than to the spoken word. The character 話 (huà) is instead used to refer to the spoken word. In their ancient use, the words 'zì' and 'míng' (名) both indicated name, appellation, or title. As stated in *Lǐjì*, 'The giving the *name* of maturity in connexion with the ceremony was to show the reverence due to that *name*' (*Lǐjì*, 11:33, trans. by Legge, 1885).[8] The words 'zì' (字) and 'míng' (名) are both translated as 'name'. In modern Chinese, these two words are usually combined into a two-character term, 'míng zì' (名字), which means 'name' as well. What is noticeable is the close relationship between the two words 'míng' and 'zì'. Both can be used to refer to 'name' separately and can also be combined to refer to the same idea. The Eastern Han dynasty scholar Zhèng Xuán (鄭玄, 127–200 CE) writes, 'In the past, they said *míng*, now we say *zì*' (古曰名今曰字). Moreover, he writes, '*Míng* is the written graph. Now we call it *zì*' (名書文也今謂之字) (quoted in Geaney, 2010, p. 279, n. 29). In this sense, 'míng' and 'zì' are synonyms. The importance is that the word 'míng' as it refers to 'name' is a linguistic unit used to convey the meaning by sound (Geaney, 2010).[9] As Geaney (2010) discovers, 'míng' is an aural word; it functions as meaningful sound. According to the first Chinese dictionary, *Shuōwén Jiězì* (說文解字), 'míng' (名) is explained as connecting with another word, 'mìng' (命, ordain, fate, command, to name), which has a very similar pronunciation. The etymology of 'míng' is described as follows:

> Míng means to name (命, mìng) oneself. The character for 'míng' (名) is a combination of the characters for 'mouth' (口, kǒu) and 'darkness' or 'evening' (夕, Xì). [People cannot see each other] in the 'dark' (冥, míng). [In order to be recognised], they say their own names (名, míng).
>
> (*Shuōwén Jiězì; my translation*)[10]

This explanation shows that the original meaning of 'míng' is aural and vocal. The word 'míng' is produced by saying the name. A similar expression can be found in *Zhuangzi*: 'Thus it is that what we look at and can see is (only) the outward form and colour, and what we listen to and can hear is (only) names (míng) and sound.' (*Zhuangzi*, 13:9; trans. by Legge, 1891b).[11] What is interesting is that 名 (míng) has many homonyms, including the abovementioned 冥 (míng, dark), 明 (míng, bright), and 鳴 (míng, animals' cry). For Boodberg (1957), the etymology of the word 'míng' (名) in *Shuōwén Jiězì* suggests a phonetic realisation of this word by connecting 'name-call' (名) with 'bird-call' (鳴) and 'the call of fate' (命). Different calls or sounds are connected with 'míng' (名). Moreover, having carefully examined the term 'míng' (名) in many other texts, Geaney (2010) concludes that 'míng' is the word associated with sound. Overall, as 'míng' (名) and 'zì' (字) are synonyms, the aurality or vocality of 'míng' (名) is insidiously encapsulated in the meaning 'name' referred to by 'míng' (名) and 'zì' (字).

A similar situation can be found in the relationship between 'zì' (字) and 'wén' (文). In the aforementioned passage, '*Míng* is the written graph. Now we call it *zì*', 文 (wén) is translated as the written graph. Like 'míng' (名), the word 'wén' has many meanings. When it is used to indicate the written word or graph, 'wén' (文) and 'zì' (字) are synonyms. Xǔ Shèn (許慎 58–147 CE) states the following:

> Tsang Chíeh at the beginning of the invention of *writing* depicts according to the natural figures and so the 'vein' or 'venation' (wén) is grasped. Then forms and sounds are added to the figures to make 'words' (字 zì). The vein is the basis of realistic depiction; the word (字 zì) is named as it is generated (孳 zi) [from proliferating veins or venation]. Writing on bamboos or silk is named 'script' (shu). 'Script' (shu) means [to script] whatever as it is.
>
> (*Shuowén jiězì*, preface 1:2; *my translation*)[12]

According to Xǔ Shèn, the invention of characters began with the realistic depiction of natural beings. The concept of the written sign in Chinese is 'wén' (文). A Chinese character is imitative drawing of figures or footprints of natural creatures produced by veins or venation. With the development and proliferation of written signs, more and more characters were invented. One of the principles of inventing characters was taking into consideration sound – phoneticisation – and form (形聲相益, form and sound are added to each other) (Bottéro, 2002). As Bottéro (2002) explains, the addition of sound to the form means assigning 'pronunciations to graphs' without 'adding explicit phonetic elements to every graph'. Characters invented based on the principle of phoneticisation are called 'zì' (字). In this view, 'wén' is the primal form of the written word in comparison with 'zì', but 'wén' and 'zì' represent the word from different perspectives. Thus, Bottéro (2002, p. 28) suggests translating '*zì* as character (or "written words") and *wén* as "graph"'. In particular, when words have been invented based on adding sound to form, they belong to the category of 'xín-sheng' (phonetic-semantic compounds, 形聲) in terms of lìu shu (六書). Afterwards, the word 'zì' gradually takes the main place of 'wén' to refer to the written word. Currently, 'wén' and 'zì' are often combined into the two-character term 'wénzi' (文字), indicating the written word (Liú, 2015a, 2015b).

This discussion shows an extremely important and complicated relationship between name (名, míng; 字, zì) and graph (文, wén; 字, zì), or between the spoken word and the written word. 'Míng' and 'zì' are synonyms in terms of 'name'; 'zì' and 'wén' are equivalents in terms of 'graph'. In the beginning, the character for 'míng' was used to mean 'name', and then it was replaced by 'zì'. Likewise, 'wén' indicated the original graph, but then 'zì' took the place of 'wén' and now represents the written word. The character for 'zì' itself was invented based on the principle of making phonetic-semantic compounds (xíng sheng, 形聲). The character 'zì' has deep implications of sound or speech. Although the term 'zì' is acknowledged as the sign presenting the written word, there is

100 Paradox

a sophisticated and deep interrelationship between writing and speaking conveyed by the lexicography of 'zì'. A vocal element is implied in Chinese writing and characters. However, the relationship between writing and speech is dialectical rather than oppositional. There is also an intriguing and subtle relatedness between the Chinese and Western views of writing and speaking, which means the possibility of bridging graphocentrism and phonocentrism. Nonetheless, the dialectics of Chinese words/sounds do not entirely correspond to the writing/speaking binaries in the Western phonocentric episteme.

The Dao as logos

Commonality also exists between the underlying metaphysics of phonocentrism and graphocentrism. The core to logocentrism is the firm belief in truth as logos, speech, and presence. Non-linguistic entities (which are fixed) and transcendental realities can be mirrored, reflected, and captured by language, for they are present to the speaker. Logocentrism is the belief 'that the first and the last things are the Logos, the Word, the Divine Mind, the infinite understanding of God, an infinitely creative subjectivity, and, closer to our time, the self-presence of full self-consciousness' (Spivak, 1976, p. lxviii). We can see a similar belief in the Dao in Chinese philosophy.

In Chinese philosophical tradition, the concept of the Dao is decisive and of the greatest importance. The Dao was recurrently discussed in many ancient classics, in Daoist as well as Confucian texts. Although the concept has complex meanings, it is used to refer to the universal truth, the root, the origin, the principle, the path, the word, nature, speech, etc. The Dao in the graphocentric context is very similar to logos in the context of logocentrism. The focus of logocentrism is on the origin of what to know and what to express. Logocentrism indicates the metaphysical binary and the hierarchy between the origin of truth and the means of expressing the truth, between presence and absence, between reality and appearance. We could find a similar binary opposition implied in Chinese tradition.

Zhang Longxi (1988, 1992), Qian Zhongshu and Zha (1992) assert that Western conceptual binaries like inner/outer, thought/speech, and signifier/signified are found not only in logos but in the Dao. Zhang makes interesting comparisons between Greek philosophy and Daoism. 'Logos' in Greek means both 'ratio' and 'oratio', reason and speech. 'Ratio' means 'the inward thought itself,' and 'oratio' means 'the word or that by which the inward thought is expressed' (Zhang, 1992, p. 26). These two meanings can be found in the concept of the Dao. The Dao in the first sentence of *Daodejing* or *Laozi* implies these two meanings: 'The way [dao] that can be spoken of [daoed] is not the constant way [dao]. The name [of dao] that can be named [dao] is not the constant name [of dao]' (Lau, 1963).[13] The Dao also cannot be fully explained in human languages or be properly named. The Dao is beyond human understanding and manmade languages. A similar opinion can be found in the Western Enlightenment.

In the eighteenth century, the first chair of the sinology department at the College de France, Jean-Pierre Abel-Rémusat, suggested that the Chinese word 'Tao' or 'Dao' can be translated into 'logos' (speech), which corresponds to 'nous' (reason) (Chang, 1988; Pohl, 2003). Abel-Rémusat, in his *Mémoire sur la ve et les ouvrages de Lao-tseu*, states that the 'Tao, like logos, conveys "the triple sense of Supreme Being, reason and word [la parole]"' (quoted in Hardy, 1998, p. 166).

Based on these assertions, Zha (1992) argues that the Dao can be understood in the same way as logos: 'the rational order of the universe, an immanent natural law, a life-giving force hidden within things, a power working from above on the sensible world' (Eliade, 1987, vol. 9, p. 9; quoted in Zha, 1992, p. 386). Zha takes chapter 25 of *Daodejing* or *Laozi* as an example to prove that the Dao is very similar to logos:

> There was something undefined and complete, coming into existence before Heaven and Earth. How still it was and formless, standing alone, and undergoing no change, reaching everywhere and in no danger (of being exhausted)! It may be regarded as the Mother of all things. I do not know its name, and I give it the designation of the dao (the Way or Course). Making an effort (further) to give it a name I call it The Great.
>
> (Daodejing: 25; trans. by Legge, 1891a)[14]

The word 'Dao' is used to refer to the unnameable, the formless, the omnipresent, the Great One. It looks very similar to the Western divine and almighty God. Zha (1992) thus suggests that Daocentrism represents Chinese logocentrism. In Zha's view as well as Zhang's, Chinese logocentrism has nothing to do with phonocentrism.[15] The Western inter/outer (ratio/oratio) binary corresponds to the Daoist classification of language and meaning, words and concepts. Moreover, Zhang uses Zhuangzi as an example. Zhuangzi states, 'It is for the fish that the trap exists; once you've got the fish, you forget the trap ... It is for the meaning that the word exists; once you've got the meaning, you forget the word' (quoted in Zhang, 1992, p. 30). Zhang argues that this Daoist allegory reveals a dualism between the signified and the signifier, between meaning and language, and that there is a debasement of writing that is also claimed by Westerners.

Similarities with Western logocentrism do not exist solely in early Daoism. We can hear an echo in later scholars of the Chinese tradition. Liú Hsiéh (劉勰), the Chinese literary theorist in the Southern and Northern dynasties (南北朝, AD 420–589), wrote the first work on Chinese literary criticism in the fifth century. *Carving the Literary Dragon* (文心雕龍, *Wénxin Diaolóng*) demonstrates a phonocentric view of speech and writing and a logocentric view of idea and icon. Liú Hsiéh writes:

> How great it is for the wén (vein or venation) to be virtuous [because it is naturally generated]. What else can be born with heaven and earth?

> The world [with dark sky and yellow ground] is varicoloured. The square [earth] and the circle [heaven] are full of miscellaneous bodies. The sun and the moon shine up as jade to show the image of the splendour of heaven. The mountains and the rivers display beauty and elegance to manifest the form of the earth. This is the wén of dao . . . Only the human is engaged. Three beings (heaven, earth and humans) are the core of nature and spirit. The glamour of five elements is the heart-mind of heaven and earth. When the heart-mind is working, speech is uttered. When speech is uttered, wén (vein or venation) is manifested. This is the Dao of nature.
>
> (*Wénxin Diaolóng*, 1:1; *my translation*)[16]

The concept of wén (vein or venation, 文) designates the writing dimension of the Chinese language. In Chinese, 'wénzì' (文字) is a two-character term, meaning 'word', especially the written word. There are subtle differences between the origins and usages of these two characters. The word 'wén' originally meant a line, pattern, or texture that appears to be a vein or venation. In nature, wén is observed in the patterns of landscapes, the ridgelines of mountains, rock textures, and so on. Tattoos on the human body are called 'wén shen' (紋身), meaning 'the wén (lines) on the body (shen)' (Liú, 2015). In Chinese, the word 'wén' can also refer to composition, such as an essay. As claimed in many classics, Chinese script was produced by imitating nature – for example, copying the traces and footprints left by animals. Thus, Chinese script is very vision-centred. Liú Hsíeh (*Wénxin Diaolóng*, 1:4) writes, 'Writing originated when drawing of bird trace replaced string knitting' (Coulmas, 2003, p. 4).[17] This view is very similar to Xŭ Shèn's idea.

Liú Hsíeh also mentions the aural dimension of Chinese script. He writes, 'Everything in the world, be it fauna or flora, is *wén* . . . thus the figure is achieved then the composition is established. The sound is uttered then *wén* is generated' (*Wénxin Diaolóng*, 1:4; my translation).[18] Here we observe that the word 'wén' has two meanings: the primordial form of the word (meaning 'vein' or 'venation') and the fully developed (written) word (meaning 'zì' or 'script'). In the view of Liú Hsíeh, sound is indispensable when producing writing.

The discrepancy is worth notice – one the one hand, Liú Hsíeh claims that the origin of 'wén' (文) is the mimetic depiction of plants or animals. Writing was produced by drawing distinctive features in nature. The production of 'wén' depended on the human visual ability to grasp the visible feature. On the other hand, Liú Hsíeh asserts that writing was generated from hearing sound. Thus, writing (wén) relies on speech (sound uttering). Liú Hsíeh's view on the hierarchy of writing and speech implies inconsistency.

In another paragraph, Liú Hsíeh writes, 'The *heart-mind* entrusts its voice in *speech*; the *speech* is embodied in the *word*' (*Wénxin Diaolóng*, *39*:4; *my translation*).[19] The heart-mind produces the inner voice. The inner voice is expressed by means of the written word. In other words, written language depends on spoken language. Spoken language depends on thought and ideas. This view of communication or signification can be found in Western linguistics – the 'theory of ideas' (Hansen, 1993). Liu's statement clearly shows a phonocentric hierarchy that is in tune with Western thinking.

The problem of Liú Hsíeh's inconsistency can be found in Confucian classics as well. A passage in the *Xìcí* (繫辭) (*Commentary*) of the classical text *Yìjing* (易經) (*The Book of Changes*) expresses a thought very similar to Liú Hsíeh's statement about writing and speech.[20] Confucius says:

> *Shu (books, writing)* cannot fully carry the *speech*. The *speech cannot fully transport the idea.* Yet is the sage's *idea* invisible?
>
> (*Xici* I:12; my translation)[21]

The word 書 (shu) can refer to books, that which is written (writing), or, sometimes, the classic *Shàng Shu* (尚書) (*The Book of Documents*). The word 言 (yán) means 'speech' or 'the spoken word'. There has been debate concerning the understanding and translation of the first two sentences of this quotation. Zhang Longxi (1985, p. 394) provides an interesting translation: 'Writing cannot fully convey the speech, and speech cannot fully convey the meaning'. According to Zhang, an idea or thought is wider and richer than what is expressed vocally. The meaning of speech is greater than what can be written down. The written word can only express a part of a thought. Therefore, the Western phonocentric debasement of writing can be discerned in the above passage. This reminds us of the previous discussion about the word of the sage.

The sage has been posited as the origin of truth in the Chinese tradition. The sage's thought is invisible because it is too great to reach and grasp. Its invisibility implies inexhaustibility and uncertainty. A book or writing is unable to include all the sage's thoughts. The Western Han dynasty (西漢, 206 BCE–8 CE) poet and philosopher Yán Xióng (揚雄, 53–18 BCE) has a resounding description: 'The sage casually opens his mouth and his words become maxims. He effortlessly wields his brush and his writing becomes a classic. His words can be heard but cannot be used up; his writings can be read but cannot be exhausted' (*Fǎ Yán* 9: 18; trans. by Bullock, 2011).[22] As mentioned in chapter two, in the Confucian tradition, the sage is assumed to serve the important and irreplaceable role of connecting the ordinary world and truth. Only the sage can understand the truth of the cosmos. If a book or writing cannot cover all the words and thoughts of the sage, how can a book or writing express the truth completely? The truth is far beyond the scope of human ability to completely understand and express, and so is the idea mediated by the sage. Language, be it in spoken or written form, is limited and finite. Thus, it is difficult to use language to perfectly express infinite and limitless truth. In most Chinese schools of thought, infinite truth is called 'Dao'. Most important of all, the concept of language is also called 'Dao' in Chinese. The paradox of language in Chinese philosophy is that the Dao as language cannot fully convey the meaning of the Dao as infinite truth (Liu, 1988). In this vein, the Dao does have something in common

104 Paradox

with logos in the Greco-Christian tradition – its equivalence with the divine. A similar description is found in the chapter 'The Way of Heaven' in *Zhuangzi*:

> What the world thinks the most valuable exhibition of the Dao is to be found in books. But books are only a collection of words. Words have what is valuable in them – what is valuable in words is the ideas they convey. But those ideas are a sequence of something else – and what that something else is cannot be conveyed by words. When the world, because of the value which it attaches to words, commits them to books, that for which it so values them may not deserve to be valued – because that which it values is not what is really valuable. Thus it is that what we look at and can see is (only) the outward form and colour, and what we listen to and can hear is (only) names and sounds.
>
> (*Zhuangzi*, 2.6.9; trans. Legge, 1891b)[23]

The above passage is extraordinarily interesting because it contains a paradox with respect to logo-phonocentrism and logo-graphocentrism. First, the passage recognises the Chinese culture's popular belief in the value of writing (books), which is graphocentrism. The passage then notes that speech (of the sage) provides the foundation of writing. Here we discover that deep in the Chinese graphocentric mentality is the phonocentrism that prioritises speech over writing. Furthermore, speech is grounded in ideas that indeed transcend the limits of spoken language. This is where we notice the work of logocentrism. The paradox of logo–phono–graphocentrism is found in Chinese thought.

The preceding examination makes clear the consonance between Western phonocentrism and Chinese graphocentrism. We may suggest that logocentrism is implied in the Chinese tradition. It has many similarities with its Western counterpart but is not identical. This finding begs us to dig deeper. Derrida, in *Of Grammatology*, suggests the non-phonetic Chinese tradition can break out of the enclosure of logo-phonocentrism. Nevertheless, the above discussion discerns the congruity between logos and the Dao, between phonocentrism and graphocentrism. Non-phonetic language does not escape from the trap of logos. As a consequence, language, be it Western phonetic language or Chinese ideographic language, is destined to snare humankind with logocentrism as long as humans are linguistic animals.

Notes

1 'In calling the dead back, and writing the inscription (to be exhibited over the coffin), the language was the same for all, from the son of Heaven to the ordinary officer' (*Lǐ Jì, Sang Fu Xiao Ji*, 15:30, trans. by Legge, 1885).

2 'Duke Huan, seated above in his hall, was (once) reading a book, and the wheelwright Bian was making a wheel below it. Laying aside his hammer and chisel, Bian went up the steps, and said, "I venture to ask your Grace what words you are reading?" The duke said, "The words of the sages". "Are those sages alive?" Bian continued. "They are dead",

Paradox 105

was the reply. "Then", said the other, "what you, my Ruler, are reading are only the dregs and sediments of those old men" (*Zhuangzi*, 2.6.9; trans. Legge, 1891b).

3 This quotation is not directly cited from *Of Grammatology*. The English translation here is cited from the translation of Eleanor Worthington (Rousseau, 1886) *Emile; or, concerning education*.

4 道可道, 非常道。名可名, 非常名。(老子: 1) I will make further elaboration on the meaning of the dao and chapter 1 of the *Daodejing* in the next chapter.

5 道常無名。(老子: 32)

6 道生一, 一生二, 二生三, 三生萬物。(老子: 42)

7 I agree with Boltz's notion in part, including concerning the origin of Chinese characters. Yet I disagree on the point that all languages in Chinese are phonetic. Boltz insists that Chinese characters had pictographs as origins but, to stand as words, they must have gone through a stage of phoneticisation. On this point, I have more agreement with Chad Hansen, whose detailed discussion about the relationship between words and ideographs in Chinese refutes the notion of prohibitionists such as Boltz. See Hansen, C. (1993). Chinese ideographs and Western ideas. *Journal of Asian Studies*, 52(2), 373–399.

8 冠而字之, 敬其名也。(禮記郊特牲, 11:33)

9 In addition to 'name', 'míng' has other meanings, like 'fame' and 'reputation'.

10 名: 自命也, 從口從夕。夕者, 冥也。冥不相見, 故以口自名。(說文解字)

11 故視而可見者, 形與色也; 聽而可聞者, 名與聲也。(莊子天道, 13:9)

12 倉頡之初作書, 蓋依類象形, 故謂之文。其後形聲相益, 即謂之字。文者, 物象之本; 字者, 言孳乳而寖多也。著於竹帛謂之書。書者, 如也。(說文解字卷一序1:2)

13 道可道, 非常道。名可名, 非常名。

14 有物混成, 先天地生。寂兮寥兮, 獨立不改, 周行而不殆, 可以為天下母。吾不知其名, 字之曰道, 強為之名曰大。(老子:25)'

15 The Romanisation of 道 includes 'Tao' and 'Dao', the latter of which is used in this book. Thus, the term 'Taocentrism' in Zha is changed to 'Daocentrism'.

16 文之為德也大矣, 與天地并生者何哉?夫玄黄色雜, 方圓體分, 日月疊璧, 以垂麗天之象; 山川煥綺, 以鋪理地之形: 此蓋道之文也。......惟人參之, 性靈所鍾, 是謂三才。為五行之秀, 實天地之心, 心生而言立, 言立而文明, 自然之道也。(文心雕龍原道, 1:1)

17 自鳥跡代繩, 文字始炳。(文心雕龍原道1:4)

18 旁及萬品, 動植皆文...故形立則章成矣, 聲發則文生矣。(文心雕龍原道1:4).

19 心既托聲於言, 言既寄形於字。(文心雕龍原道39:4).

20 *Yijing* is one of the oldest Chinese classics. The time of its origin is said to be dated back to third to second millennium BCE. According to *Shǐjì* (史記) (Records of the Grand Historians, written by Simǎ Qian, 145–86 BCE), Confucius is intrigued by *Yijing* and writes *Xicí* (繫辭) (Commentary).

21 書不盡言, 言不盡意。然則聖人之意, 其不可見乎。(繫辭上:12)

22 聖人矢口而成言, 肆筆而成書。言可聞而不可殫, 書可觀而不可盡。(法言八百, 9:18).

23 世之所貴道者, 書也, 書不過語, 語有貴也。語之所貴者, 意也, 意有所隨。意之所隨者, 不可以言傳也, 而世因貴言傳書。世雖貴之, 我猶不足貴也, 為其貴非其貴也。故視而可見者, 形與色也; 聽而可聞者, 名與聲也。(莊子外篇天道, 2.6.9)

References

Boltz, W. G. (1986). Early Chinese writing. *World Archaeology, 17*(3), 420–436.

Boltz, W. G. (1999). Language and writing. In M. Loewe & E. Shaughnessy (Eds.), *The Cambridge history of ancient China: From the origins of civilisation to 221 B.C* (pp. 74–123). Cambridge, UK: Cambridge University Press.

Boltz, W. G. (2001). The invention of writing in China. *Oriens Extremis, 42*, 1–17.

106 Paradox

Boodberg, P. A. (1957). Philological notes on Chapter One of the Lao Tzu. *Harvard Journal of Asiatic Studies*, *20*(3/4), 598–618.

Bottéro, F. (2002). Revisiting the Wén 文 and the Zi 字: The great Chinese character hoax. *Bulletin of the Museum of Far Eastern Antiquities*, *74*, 14–33.

Bottéro, F. (2006). Cang Jie and the invention of writing: Reflections on the elaboration of a legend. In C. Anderl & H. Eifring (Eds.), *Studies in Chinese language and culture* (pp. 135–155). Oslo: Hermes Academic Publishing.

Bottéro, F., & Harbsmeier, C. (2008). The *Shuowen Jiezi* dictionary and the human science in China. *Asia Major*, *21*(1), 249–271.

Brooker, P. (2003). *A glossary of cultural theory* (2nd ed.). London, UK: Arnold.

Bullock, J. S. (Trans.). (2011). *Yang Xiong: Philosophy of the Fa yan*. Retrieved November 16, 2013, from D. Sturgeon (Ed.), *Chinese text project*. http://ctext.org/yangzi-fayan

Chang, H. L. (1988). *Hallucinating the other: Derridean fantasies of Chinese script*. (Working Paper No. 4). Milwaukee, WI: The University of Wisconsin-Milwaukee.

Cook, R. S. (2001). The extreme of typographic complexity: Character set issues relating to computerization of the Eastern Han Lexicon 《說文解字》 *Shouwenjeizi*. Paper presented at the 18th International Unicode Conference, Hong Kong, April.

Coulmas, F. (2003). *Writing system: An introduction to their linguistic analysis*. Cambridge, UK: Cambridge University Press.

Crisp, R. (1995). Logos. In R. Audi (Ed.), *The Cambridge dictionary of philosophy* (p. 518). Cambridge, UK: Cambridge University Press.

Culler, J. (2014). *On deconstruction: Theory and criticism after structuralism*. Ithaca, NY: Cornell University Press.

Derrida, J. (1976). *Of grammatology*. Trans. G. C. Spivak. Baltimore, MD: John Hopkins University Press.

Derrida, J. (1982). *Margins of philosophy*. Chicago, IL: University of Chicago Press.

Derrida, J. (1988). *Limited Inc*. Evanston, IL: Northwestern University Press.

Derrida, J. (2016). *Of grammatology*. Trans. G. C. Spivak. Introduction by J. Butler. Baltimore, MD: John Hopkins University Press.

Edghill, E. M. (Trans.). (2015). *On interpretation*. eBooks@Adelaide. Retrieved July 13, 2016, from https://ebooks.adelaide.edu.au/a/aristotle/interpretation/

Eliade, M. (Ed.). (1987). *Encyclopedia of religion*. 16 vols. New York, NY: MacMillan.

Fenollosa, E., & Pound, E. (1936). *The Chinese written character as a medium for poetry*. San Francisco, CA: City Lights Books.

Geaney, J. (2010). Grounding language in the sense: What the eyes and ears reveal about *ming* 名 (names) in early Chinese texts. *Philosophy East & West*, *60*(2), 251–293.

Graham, A. C. (1989). *Disputers of the Tao*. La Selle, IL: Open Court.

Gu, M. D. (2000). Reconceptualising the linguistic divide: Chinese and Western theories of the written sign. *Comparative literature studies*, *37*(2), 101–124.

Hall, D., & Ames, R. (1998). *Thinking from the Han: Self, truth, and transcendence in Chinese and Western culture*. Albany, NY: SUNY Press.

Hansen, C. (1993). Chinese ideographs and Western ideas. *Journal of Asian Studies*, *52*(2), 373–399.

Hardy, J. M. (1998). Influential Western interpretations of *Tao-de-ching*. In L. Kohn & M. LaFargue (Eds.), *Lao-tzu and the Tao-de-ching* (pp. 165–188). Albany, NY: State University of New York Press.

Hegel, G. W. F. (1894). *Hegel's philosophy of mind: A revised version of the Wallace and Miller*. Oxford: Clarendon Press. Retrieved November 30, 2013, from ftp://64.26.104.132/pub/gutenberg/3/9/0/6/39064/39064-pdf.pdf

Hegel, G. W. F. (2001). *Science of logic*. www.blackmask.com Retrieved September 5, 2013, from http://chhmhen.hegel.net/en/pdf/Hegel-Scilogic.pdf

Jeffery, D. L. (1992). *A dictionary of biblical tradition in English literature*. Grand Rapids, MI: William B. Eerdmans Publishing Company.

Lau, D. C. (Trans.). (1963). *The Tao Te Ching*. Retrieved January 8, 2014, from http://terebess.hu/english/tao/lau.html

Legge, J. (Trans.). (1885). *Liji: Sacred books of the East, volume 28, part 4: The Li Ki*. Retrieved November 19, 2013, from D. Sturgeon (Ed.), *Chinese text project*. Retrieved from http://ctext.org/liji

Legge, J. (Trans.). (1891a). *Tao Te Ching*. Retrieved August 8, 2013, from www.sacred-texts.com/tao/taote.htm

Legge, J. (Trans.). (1891b). *The writing of Chuang Tzu*. Retrieved November 19, 2013, from D. Sturgeon (Ed.), *Chinese text project*. Retrieved from http://ctext.org/zhuangzi

Leibniz, G. W. (1981). *New essays on human understanding*. Ed. P. Remnant & J. Bennett. Cambridge, UK: Cambridge University Press.

Liu, J.-Y. (1988). *Language-paradox-poetics*. Princeton, NJ: Princeton University Press.

Liú, M-G.刘民钢 (2015a). Shuo wen jie zi: wén說文解字 – 文. *Shu Fǎ書法*, 11, 65.

Liú, M-G.刘民钢 (2015b). Shuo wen jie zi: zì說文解字 – 字. *Shu Fǎ書法*, 12, 157.

Novitz, D. (1985). Metaphor, Derrida, and Davison. *The Journal of Aesthetics and Art Criticism*, *44*(2), 101–114.

Plato. (1961). *Plato: The collected dialogues*. Eds. E. Hamilton & H. Cairns. Princeton, NJ: Princeton University Press.

Pohl, K. H. (2003). Play-thing of the times: Critical review of the reception of Daoism in the West. *Journal of Chinese Philosophy*, *30*(3–4), 469–486.

Qian, Z. (1979). *Guan Zhui bian*. 4 vol. 管錐編. Beijing: Zhonghua Bookstore. 北京:中華書局.

Rousseau, J-J. (1886). *Emile; or, concerning education*. Trans. E. Worthington. Boston, MA: D. C. Heath & Company.

Rousseau, J.-J. & Herder, J. G. (1966). *On the origin of language*. Trans. J. H. Moran & A. Gode. Chicago, IL: The University of Chicago Press.

Sampson, G., & Chen, Z. (2013). The reality of compound ideographs. *Journal of Chinese Linguistics*, *41*, 255–272.

Spivak, G. C. (1976). Translator's preface. In J. Derrida, *Of grammatology* (pp. ix–xc). Baltimore, MD: John Hopkins University Press.

Standish, P. (2001). The learning pharmacy. In G. Biesta & D. Egéa-Kuehne (Eds.), *Derrida & education* (pp. 77–97). London, UK: Routledge.

Stewart, R. S. (1989). The epistemological function of Platonic myth. *Philosophy & Rhetoric*, *22*(4), 260–280.

Tong, Q. S. (1993). Myths about the Chinese language. *Canadian Review of Comparative Literature*, *20*(1), 29–47.

Wu, J. S. (1969). Chinese language and Chinese thought. *Philosophy East and West*, *19*(4), 423–434.

Zha, P. (1992). Logocentrism and traditional Chinese poetics. *Canadian Review of Comparative Literature/Revue Canadienne de Littérature Comparée*, *19*(3), 377–394.

Zhang, L. (1985). The *Tao* and the *Logos*: Notes on Derrida's critique of logocentrism. *Critical Inquiry*, *11*, 385–398.

Zhang, L. (1988). The myth of the other: China in the eyes of the West. *Critical Inquiry*, *15*, 108–131.

Zhang, L. (1992). *The Tao and the logos, literary hermeneutics, East and West*. Durham & London: Duke University Press.

Chapter 5

Post-graphocentrism
Dao-deconstruction

大方無隅；大器晚成；大音希聲；大象無形；道隱無名。夫唯道, 善貸且成。

—(老子, 41)[1]

東郭子問於莊子曰：「所謂道, 惡乎在?」莊子曰：「無所不在。」東郭子曰：「期而後可。」莊子曰：「在螻蟻。」曰：「何其下邪?」曰：「在稊稗。」曰：「何其愈下邪?」曰：「在瓦甓。」曰：「何其愈甚邪?」曰：「在屎溺。」東郭子不應。

—(莊子外篇知北遊, 2.15.6)[2]

In the beginning part of the book, I discussed the 'wordaholic' syndrome in Chinese cultures and identified the underlying metaphysics as graphocentrism, which is opposite of Western phonocentrism. Nevertheless, we also discovered that Chinese graphocentrism and Western phonocentrism have a similar primary principle: in the West, it is Logos that underpins the order of the world and knowledge, whereas in China, it is the Dao. The Dao is the fundamental and most significant idea in most Chinese schools of thought. From Confucius to Laozi, from ancient to modern times, the Dao has been esteemed as the determining principle and the ultimate truth of human life in Chinese societies. The Dao masters everything and every being in the cosmos (*Daodejing*, 41) and provides the fundamental rules of sustaining social order and ethical life, such as 'the Dao of the Master' (夫子之道), 'the Dao of a Father' (父之道), 'the Dao of the junzǐ' (君子之道),[3] 'the Ancient Dao' (古之道), 'the Dao of the Heaven' (天道), 'the Dao of Yáo and Shùn' (堯舜之道), 'the Dao and the sage' (聖賢之道), 'the Dao of the former kings' (先王之道), and 'the Dao of the learned' (儒者之道), which are repeatedly emphasised in the *Analects* and other Confucian texts. The ultimate and fundamental Dao is the graphocentric Dao. The Dao is understood and taken for granted as the determining principle of the 'high' part of life and thought. By 'high', I mean 'important', 'decent', 'respectable', 'proper', and 'appropriate' with respect to morality and culture. The understanding and discussion of the Dao are supposed to be intellectually and morally valuable, such as the cultivation of a junzĭ. The practice of the Dao is educational and virtuous so that it is manifest in the words and deeds of respectable people and appropriate practices. Nevertheless, does the great Dao take care of trivial and insignificant matters? Most Confucian followers – or, I should say, the graphocentrists – might not take it into serious account because the matters that the Dao takes into account should be serious, or heavy. The Dao is not involved in frivolous and petty things. It is offensive to graphocentrists to hear Zhuangzi (2.15.6) say that the Dao is in the ant, the weed, the debris, or even the excrement.

I recall that in 1997, I wrote a review for the journal of *Book Review* on Milan Kundera's *The Unbearable Lightness of Being*. A few days after receiving my manuscript, the editor called me to make sure if I used the right word, which was 'stool'. This word appears in the paragraph that summarises Tereza's affair with an engineer. I was very certain about the 'correctness' of the word because I deliberately cited it from 'Part 4: Body and Soul' of the novel. However, the tone of hesitation and the uncertainty of the editor impressed me so much; she could not believe that an insignificant, worthless, and repugnant thing is used in a book review that should reflect a serious, or 'heavy', attitude. This is exactly the contrast between the heavy and the light, the serious and the frivolous, and the graphocentric Dao and the Zhuangzi's daos. The inherent contrast in the graphocentric thought echoes the divergence between the Logos and the Derridean deconstruction. Interestingly and profoundly, we have arrived at a similarity between the Logos and the Dao and thereby face a dilemma: originally, graphocentrism was suggested to counter the tyranny of the constellation of logo–phono–ethnocentrism in the light of Derrida. We found that even graphocentrism cannot escape the snare of the Dao as Logos. How can human beings be liberated from the endless desire for binary and hierarchical thinking that results from centrism?

Derrida (1982, p. 3) proposes deconstruction as a strategy to counter the belief of Logos as presence. To explicate the concept of deconstruction, Derrida coins 'neographism',[4] such as *trace, supplement, archié criture*, and, most importantly, *différance*. *Différance*, neither a word nor a concept, is provisionally proposed to make a 'lapse' to permit 'different threads and different lines of meanings – or of force – to go off again in different directions, just as it is always ready to tie itself up with others' (ibid., p. 3). He repeatedly emphasises that this new word *différance* is a graphical difference: 'it is read, or it is written, but it cannot be heard. It cannot be apprehended in speech' (Derrida, 1982, p. 3). Derrida coins this new word by intentionally replacing the 'e' with an 'a' in the middle of the word 'différence'. This change troubles readers, by preventing them from pronouncing it, challenging their vision and hearing, and creating a silence. *Différance* as a graphic difference is and is not difference; it is a 'differ()nce' that simultaneously is and is not 'what makes possible the presentation of the being-present, it is never presented as such. It is never offered to the present' (ibid., p. 6). This neographism expresses what cannot be expressed of thinking, by thinking, in thinking, or not to express what can be expressed. In other words, *différance* is used to present the absence and to make the presence absent. Furthermore, as Derrida explains, the verb *différer* has two distinct meanings: to defer and to differ. To defer is to put off in time, a suspension in time and in space. In Derrida's term, to defer is temporalisation; it includes 'the becoming-time of space and the becoming-space of time', and it is both temporalisation and spacing. Derrida calls the first sense of *différence* 'temporisation' as well as 'temporalisation' (ibid., p. 8). The second sense of *différence* is to differ. To differ is to alter, to vary, to be not identical, to be other, discernible, and so on. Two French derivative nouns are *différends* and *différents*. These words are pronounced the exact same way, but they have different meanings. *Les différents* indicates different things, whereas *les différends* refers to differing opinions. The word *différence* cannot convey the two differences, however (Derrida, 1982, p. 8, TN). Thus, Derrida (1982, p. 8) suggests the word *différance* to refer 'simultaneously to the entire configuration of its meanings'. As Derrida puts it, this concept is immediately and irreducibly polysemic:

> In its polysemia this word, of course, like any meaning, must defer to the discourse in which it occurs, its interpretive context; but in a way it defers itself, or at least does so more readily than any other word, the *a* immediately deriving from the present principle (*différant*), thereby bringing us close to the very action of the verb *différer*, before it has even produced an effect constituted as something different or as *différence* (with an *e*).
>
> (1982, p. 8)

To liberate the concept of *différence* (with an *e*) from linguistic bondage, Derrida coins the term *différance* (with an *a*). *Différance* shows that the meanings of words are in the process of differentiation and deferral, spacing and temporisation, diastem and postponement, and therefore reveals the unreliability of the system. With this neographism, we are able to conceive undecided possibilities. *Différance* as the deconstructive strategy shows the possible impossibility of language and reminds us of the concept of dao, which carries great potential and possibilities against the system. Yet we must remember that no name for this new vocabulary exists to signify or specify any signified entity; it is 'the unnameable . . . the play which makes possible nominal effects' (Derrida, 1982, p. 26).

In the first chapter of *Daodejing*, Laozi points out the impossibility of doing justice to expressing and naming dao. Of course, there is much to be discussed concerning this chapter because the terms are ambiguous but meaningful, equivocal but profound. Despite this case, we can see the untrustworthiness of language entrusted by Laozi. More than that is Zhuangzi, who reiterates the interdependence and indispensability of the opposites in contradictions such as being versus non-being, word versus non-word and nothingness versus nonothingness. The dao expresses the limitedness and inexpressibility of language.

In this vein, we find that in the West, Derrida perceptively discovers the problems of logo-phonocentrism and proposes deconstruction as a breakthrough

Post-graphocentrism   111

strategy. The concept of deconstruction is used to unpack the dichotomy and hierarchy assumed and hidden in language. In the East, the Daoist philosophers are also aware of the predicament of thought and suggest the dao as a way of surpassing this predicament. The dao implies not only the consonance of the Logos but also the dissonance, which shows the paradoxical ambiguity of dao and the possibility of overcoming the problems of graphocentrism or post-graphocentrism. Overall, the notion of dao is equivocal. On the one hand, it is associated with the Logos that limits language. The related practices involve the aforementioned canonisation of the spoken word of the sage kings, the sanctification of the written word and the institutionalisation of writing disciplines. On the other hand, the notion of dao implies profound inspirations for thinking otherwise to break the confinement of logo-graphocentrism. In what follows, I explore the richness of dao as non-Logos in two steps of deconstruction. In the words of Derrida, to deconstruct is to 'put into practice a reversal of the classical opposition and a general displacement of the system' (1977, p. 21). Deconstruction is practiced through a double gesture; this is what I will do in the following sections. First, I explore the meaning of dao with respect to deconstruction by reading the notion of dao in alternate ways. Second, I explore the inspiration of dao as non-Logos for us to rethink and re-examine, encounter, and criticise the recognised meaning of humanity and the established institution of cultivating human beings.

The dao

To deconstruct the dao is to reverse the hierarchy of classical reading of dao and thereby to unmask the dao as non-Logos. How can we reverse the classical hierarchy? We must find alternative ways of reading the texts. Let us start from the most widely read and mostly admired chapter of Daoist classics. The first chapter of Laozi, which has aroused debate for thousands of years, implies great ambiguity and potential and is open to numerous interpretations. The first two sentences are as follows:

道(dao)可(can be)道(dao-ed),非(is not)常道(chángdao)。名(míng)可名,非常名。

Dao, that can be daoed, is not chángdao. Míng, that can be mínged, is not chángmíng.

The first dao is a noun. As discussed, dao may mean the principle, the universal law, the truth, the path, the way, the road, or the speech. The second dao is a verb, meaning to speak, to say, to walk, or to step. The first míng, a noun, designates the name, whereas the second, a verb, means 'to name'. An interesting word is 'cháng'. According to the *Shuowén Jěizì*, 常 originally means the skirt, dress, or robe. Its meaning is used metaphorically to designate the state of being in fashion or popular. In addition, the meaning of this word widens and varies to include the state of being constant, regular, unchanging, normal, ordinary,

112 Post-graphocentrism

general, or universal. When 常 is in the term 恆常 (héncháng), it means the state of being constant, unchanging, universal, and everlasting. It can also be used in the term 平常 (pingcháng), which means the condition of being ordinary, unexceptional, and undistinguished. When it is associated with the term 經常 (jingcháng), it means the state of being frequent. In Chinese, however, cháng can be used as an abbreviation to inform the three preceding terms with somewhat different meanings. The meaning of the word is often judged according to the context. The interesting point is that in the first chapter of *Daodejing*, the three situations mentioned above are workable. Therefore, the beginning sentences of *Daodejing* can be translated in the following ways:

1 Dao, that can be daoed, is not the constant dao. Míng, that can be mínged, is not constant míng.

    1.1 The way, that can be trodden, is not the constant way. The name, that can be named, is not the constant name.

    1.2 The truth, that can be spoken, is not the constant truth. The name, that can be named, is not the constant name.

2 Dao, that can be daoed, is not ordinary dao. Míng, that can be mínged, is not an ordinary míng.

    2.1 The way, that can be trodden, is not the ordinary way. The name, that can be named, is not an ordinary name.

    2.2 The truth, that can be spoken, is not ordinary truth. The name, that can be named, is not an ordinary name.

3 Dao, that can be daoed, is not the frequent dao. Míng, that can be mínged, is not a frequent míng.

    3.1 The way, that can be trodden, is not the frequent(ly trodden) way. The name, that can be named, is not the frequent(ly used) name.

    3.2 The truth, that can be spoken, is not the frequent(ly spoken) truth. The name, that can be named, is not a frequent(ly used) name.

Let us examine the first translation, which is accepted by most scholars. For example, the translation of Zhang Longxi (1992, p. 27) is as follows:

> The *tao* that can be *tao-ed* ['spoken of']
> Is not the constant *tao;*
> The name that can be named
> Is not the constant name.

James Legge's (1891b) translation is as follows:

> The Dao that can be trodden is not the enduring and unchanging Dao.
> The name that can be named is not the enduring and unchanging name.

The translation provided by Philip Ivanhoe (2002, p. 2) is

A Way that can be followed is not a constant Way.
A name that can be named is not a constant name.

This passage is translated by Edmund Ryden (2008, p. 5) as follows:

Of ways you may speak,
But not the Perennial Way;
By names you name,
But not the Perennial Name.

Stephen Addiss and Stanley Lombardo's (1993, p. 1) translation is

Tao called Tao is not Tao.
Names can name no lasting name.

Patrick Bryan (2002) provides his translation as follows:

The Tao that can be spoken of is not the enduring Tao,
Nor the name that comes by naming, the eternal name. (p. 13)

With respect to the word 道, most scholars use the transliteration of 'Dao' or 'Tao'. Some translate the word 'dao' as the way (or the Way). At the beginning of the chapter, either the way or the truth as the translation makes sense. The transliteration of 道 as dao retains more than one possible reference and keeps the interpretation open. The word 'cháng' is translated by most as 'constant', 'enduring', 'unchanging', and 'perennial'. In this view, it makes better sense to translate 'cháng dao' as the 'unchanging, everlasting, or constant way' – the way that lasts forever, can be followed eternally, and is the everlasting truth. Nevertheless, when dao is understood as the everlasting and unchanging Truth, it is the ever-present presence, the Logos of the ultimate presence. That is why we find most authors write the Tao or the Way with its first letter capitalised. Translated and understood in this vein, Dao is similar to the Logos conceived in the West. According to Qian Zhongshu (Zhang, 1992), Laozi's dao and Plato's idea are much alike. Laozi's dao is constant and invariable; it is nameless because no concrete name can do justice to constancy. Plato (1961), in his *Seventh Letter*, argues that language cannot represent the thing itself. He writes,

Names, I maintain, are in no case stable. Nothing prevents the things that are now called round from being called straight and straight round, and those who have transposed the names and use them in the opposite way will find them no less stable than they are now.

(343b)

On the basis of this passage, language as an artificial tool is arbitrary and conventional. Language cannot convey the truth – the extralinguistic reality – precisely and fully. Qian comments that Plato's words are likely to annotate the *Daodejing* (Zhang, 1992). I advance this point further. As constant and unchanging truth, the dao is 'the way the universe works' (Waley, 1934, p. 30), 'something very like God' (Waley, 1934, p. 30), 'a completely independent entity, and replaces heaven in all its functions' (Lau, 1982, preface, p. xx), and 'a mystical reality' (Schwartz, 1985, p. 194) (Tanaka, 2004). Dao understood as the constant and unchanging reality is similar to the Platonic idea and may contribute to mysticism. Daoist mysticism is associated with Daoism as religion – the so-called Dàojiào (道教). The doctrine of Dàojiào greatly influences Chinese folk culture and society. The primal ideas of Dàojiào in the early second century are referred to as the Huang-Lao traditions. As Zhongjian Wong (2016) illustrates, four newly excavated Huang-Lao materials exist, namely, *The Way's Origin* (*Dao Yuan*, 道原), *The Great One Birthed Water* (*Tàiyishengshuǐ*, 太一生水), *Primordial Constant* (*Héngxian*, 恆先), and *All Things Are Forms in Flux* (*Fánwùliúxíng*, 凡物流形). The core terms to these texts are, respectively, the Dao, the Primordial, the Great One, and the One (Wong, 2016). The meanings of these core concepts are not identical: one text focuses on ontology, while the other three focus on cosmology. However, all are influenced by Laozi's Dao to different degrees. The connotations of these core terms are exchangeable in some sense. The concept of Dao as the central notion of the Daoist religion is the foundation of the ultimate, unalterable, and nameless reality. The Dao is the Great Grand Dao. With respect to onto-cosmology, Dao has commonality with the Logos in the Western context of onto-theology and supports Chinese logo-graphocentrism.

Moreover, the Great Grand Dao in the Confucian school of philosophy takes a central position. There is orthodoxy of the Dao in Confucianism. In the *Analects*, the concept of Dao is mentioned and deliberated over many times. The Dao is the principle and the truth of the universe. The universal Dao sustains the natural and the human worlds. Complying with the Dao makes the universe, the human world and all beings exist harmoniously. Confucius and his disciples have numerous discussions about how the Dao accomplishes the human being and the state in different contexts wherein the Dao can be called 'the Dao of a Father' (父之道) (Xúe Ér, 1:11; Lǐ Rén, 4:20), 'the Dao of the former king' (先王之道) (Xúe Ér, 1:12), 'the Dao of the junzǐ' (君子之道) (Xúe Ér, 1:14; Gong Yě Cháng, 5:16; Xiàn Wèn, 14:28), 'the Ancient Dao' (古之道) (Ba Yì, 3:16), 'the Dao of the Master' (夫子之道) (Lǐ Rén, 4:15), 'the Dao of the Heaven' (天道) (Gong Yě Cháng, 5:13), and 'the Dao of the good person' (善人之道) (Xian Jìn, 11:20). With respect to the *Mencius*, there are numerous discussions on the Dao in general, 'the Dao of the king' (王道) (Liang Hui Wang I, 1B:3), 'the Ancient Dao' (古之道) (Gong Sun Chiu II, 2B:23), 'the Dao of the learned' (儒者之道) (Teng Wen Gong I, 3A:5), 'the Dao of the former king' (先王之道) (Teng Wen Gong II, 3B:9; Li Lou I, 4A:1), 'the Dao of the junzǐ' (君子之道) (Teng Wen Gong II, 3B:9), 'the Dao of Yáo and Shùn' (堯舜之道) (Teng

Wen Gong II, 3B:14; Li Lou I, 4A:1), 'the Dao and the sage' (聖人之道) (Teng Wen Gong II, 3B:14), and so on. The world is an organic whole, underpinning which is the Great Grand Dao. The Dao is one unity, whether it is called the Dao of the Heaven, the Dao of the Master, the Dao of the king, the Dao of the learned, or others. These terms are just used to designate how the universal and eternal Dao is spread and specified in different contexts and appropriated by different roles. That is why Confucius says, 'My Dao is One that pervades all.' (*Analects, Lǐ Rén*, 4:15; my translation).[5] There is no conflict or contradiction between the Dao of the Heaven and the Dao of the Master, or between the Dao of the king and the Dao of the learned Furthermore, or whatsoever because the Confucian Dao is One.

It is claimed that the Dao is embodied in different characters and contexts to make a perfect world, which means that these different characters comply with the congenic order and obey homologous rules. These different characters – e.g., the former king, the sage, the good person, the learned people, the junzǐ, or the father – play roles that collaborate with each other and compose an orderly society. On this basis, in the perfect Confucian state, everyone has a role to play. The duties and obligations are already commanded by the Dao. A good subject of the kingdom must observe and comply with the Dao with respect to one's own particular position. The Dao pervades all beings and every aspect of life. For anyone who may have multiple roles to play, e.g., son, brother, father, minister, or friend, comprehension of the Dao starts from the most personal and private realm and gradually extends to the public sphere. The progress of comprehending the Dao from the private realm to the public sphere is the process of self-cultivation. In the end, one may become a junzǐ. This process comprises a series of orderly successive tasks including 'studying the physical world, attaining knowledge, having the mind of sincerity, keeping the heart of integrity, self-control, managing the family, governing the nation, and bringing peace and justice to the world' (*Lǐjì, DàXúe*, 42:2; my translation).[6] The world is regulated by the Dao. When everyone as a part of the world fulfils his or her duty regulated and mandated by the Dao, then the ideal world is ready to be built.

The Confucian utopia somehow arouses my suspicion in that it leaves no room for otherness, deviance, weirdness, mutation or *différance*. Every person has a particular role to play. The understanding and practising of the duty associated with the particular role mandated by the Dao is a lifelong undertaking that is educational and ethical, political and moral, personal and communal, private and public. A literati elite in premodern China spent his whole life pursuing being a junzǐ morally and an official scholar politically. The cultivation process of a junzǐ – the Confucian ideal human person – or the writing subject included playing the roles of a son of filial piety, a respectable husband and father, a trustworthy friend, a humble student, a loyal subject of the kingdom, and a faithful disciple of Confucianism. From the junzǐ point of view, it is obligatory to comprehend and practice 'the Dao of the father' (父之道),

'the Dao of the friend'(朋友之道), 'the Dao of ruler and minister' (君臣之道) and 'the Dao of the minister-subject' (人臣之道). A junzǐ is able to play these different roles perfectly. For the roles that a junzǐ cannot play, he must ensure the functioning and the fulfilment of the pertinent duties of those roles. For example, it is not expected that a junzǐ plays the role of a mother or a wife. However, the duty of a junzǐ includes striving for the realisation of the Dao of other roles and the implying obligations, e.g., 'the Dao of women' (婦道). As noted by Mencius, 'At the marrying away of a young woman, her mother admonishes her, accompanying her to the door on her leaving, and cautioning her with these words, "You are going to your home. You must be respectful; you must be careful. Do not disobey your husband". Thus, to look upon compliance as their correct course is the rule for women' (*Mencius, Teng Wen Gong II*, 3B:7; trans. Legge, 1985).[7] It is assumed that a woman will play the role of a dependent, a subordinate or even a vassal with respect to man because she follows the Dao. In this view, the great grand Dao presented in Confucianism grounds the natural and human world within which every part or every member perfectly assembles with others. The Confucian worldview is like a jigsaw puzzle: all pieces together make a complete picture, while a single piece makes no sense.

Nevertheless, given that the great grand Dao provides a good explanation of the organic, complete and holistic worldview, there is something left, lost, and missed. If the world is like a jigsaw puzzle, there are pieces that cannot be parts of the whole picture. They are the 'useless' pieces. They may be deformed or broken. How then does the utopia deal with the ill-matched pieces? What if a woman does not want to play the role of a submissive wife, or a person refuses to be an obedient servant? This is a real challenge in modern times. I do not mean to discard the doctrines of the Dao by simply claiming that it is outdated. The problem of justice and fairness is what we encounter in the territory governed by the Dao as well as the Logos. The re-examination of the meaning of dao opens up new possibilities.

Myriad daos

The chángdao can be understood not only as the constant and eternal Dao, but also as the ordinary dao or the frequent dao – the petit dao. It also makes sense to see dao in these two approaches, although fewer scholars do so. If we understand the dao as an ordinary or frequent dao or daos, then the dao or daos can be perceived as diverse, miscellaneous, dynamic, and various in a post-structural way; this is how we apply the deconstructive strategy to the understanding of dao. As Derrida suggests, deconstruction is to question the normalisation of the Logos. In the context of classical Chinese philosophy, the normalisation of the Logos is the Dao, viz., the Ultimate Reality, the Heaven, or the Truth. Hence, when we shift the focus from the capital One Dao to the small miscellaneous daos, we are deconstructively rethinking and re-examining our assumption of the Dao. In recent years, the concept of dao as diverse and particular seems to have received increasing attention. In my view, the translation of Roger T. Ames and David L. Hall (2003, p. 77) is open to such a possibility, although claiming their translation as poststructuralist could be over-exaggerated. Below is their translation.

> Way-making (*dao*) that can be put into words is not really way-making,
>   And naming (*ming*) that can assign fixed reference to things is not really naming.

Three interesting points should be noted concerning these two sentences. First, Ames and Hall (2003) carefully translate dao as the activity of way-making. In this view, the dao is not an object but a process. Second, they use the lowercase 'way-making' rather than capitalising 'Way-making'. This nuance sophisticatedly prevents defining dao as the ultimate and absolute truth. Finally, the second sentence, 'Míng, that can be mínged, is not chángmíng', is attentively translated as 'And naming (*ming*) that can assign fixed reference to things is not really naming'. In this translation or interpretation, the possibility of the changeableness of the relationship between names and the named things, between signs and significations, is suggested. With this inspiration, can we conceive of the dao as many, diverse, changing, miscellaneous, uncertain, and developing, different from the Dao that has been traditionally conceived as the One, the Great One, the Way, the Primordial, and the Ultimate Reality?

The notion of dao in Laozi is open to many different interpretations. As Jiyuan Yu (2015) notes, in the *Daodejing*, the expressions of dao are various, including 'the dao of Heaven', the entity that exists before heaven and earth, the dao that gives birth to and nurtures the myriad things, the dao as the essence of things that makes all thing what they are, the dao that cannot be named and said and is thus beyond language, the dao that is undivided and cannot be expressed by name, the dao that concentrates on the weak side of the conventional-value dichotomy, and the dao as the balance of the opposites. It has been taken for granted to pay notice to the Dao but not to the dao or daos. For me, the recognition and interrogation of all other senses of dao can create meanings and widen imagination. That is why Daoist philosophers, including Laozi and Zhuangzi, reiterate the impossibility of exhausting the meaning of dao.

Both Laozi and Zhuangzi address the impossibility of speaking out on the meanings of dao. This impossibility is not only because the Dao is too great, vast, high, and massive to be communicated in words but also because myriads, countless daos and innumerable ways of articulating and disputing daos can be revealed from the proliferating dynamics of the lifeworld.

Myriad daos exist in various forms – present or absent, living or non-living, visible or invisible, in the ant, the weed, the debris, or in the excrement. The dao or daos can be understood as non-Logos. The term 'dao' in Confucian and Daoist philosophies has many different meanings. Yet in the Confucian school, dao understood as the Dao (as well as the Logos) predominates.

118 Post-graphocentrism

As Cheng Chung-ying (2003) notes, dao can be understood as the ultimate reality, truth, method, and essences of things on the one hand and as the human aspect on the other hand. The objective and subjective meanings are significant to our understanding of the dao. More importantly, the dao is both a metaphysical and a commonplace concept. The concept of dao is not solely a key term to Laozi and Zhuangzi but also to all Chinese thinkers who belong to different schools of thought. Cheng (2003, p. 203) suggests five characteristics of the dao as follows:

> 1. *Dao* is the whole of nature and the whole universe, as shown in our experience of natural things. *Dao* develops nature as a whole and produces nature as a whole. 2. *Dao* is thus the process in which the whole of nature manifests itself and the process in which and by which things are created or procreated and nature is manifested. The process is the way, and the way is the process. 3. *Dao* is the origin and source of the process of change and the creation of things. This origin and source is regarded as infinite, and its generative power as inexhaustible. Hence, *dao* is a creative power that creates by sustaining and sustains by creating. 4. Because the *dao* embodies the way things are created and the way events change, it can represent laws, limitations, or destiny – which things must obey and follow. 5. Although it transcends time and place, the *dao* remains a concrete presence in things as a whole. It is as dynamic as any actual event or object. And things and events – in order to function as things and events – must not be separate from the *dao*.

In addition to the five characteristics, the concept of dao can be explored from different perspectives. The dao is not only the key concept in Daoist philosophy but also the decisive idea prevalent in all traditional Chinese thought. Chad Hansen (1992) proposes to understand the concept of dao as a social practice with respect to language. Many different kinds of social practices exist. Thus, the dao has diverse meanings. Any one of the interpretations refers to performing the dao in a particular way to achieve a specific social goal. Hansen (1992) identifies four progressive stages in classical doctrines about language and mind: 1) the positive dao period or the Confucian-Mohist period; 2) the anti-language period; 3) the analytical period; and 4) the authoritarian period. The discourses about the dao and its role in each stage are different from each other. As Hansen (1992) suggests, the representatives of the first stage are Confucius and Mozi; the second stage is represented by Mencius and Laozi; the third stage is represented by Zhuangzi and the later Mohist thinkers; and the final stage is represented by Xúnzi and Héifezi. In each stage, dao as interpreted from a different approach manifests itself in different functions and has a different meaning. The dao in the Chinese philosophical context has diverse and various meanings; that is, the dao should be understood not only as the universal constant principle – the Dao – but also as miscellaneous daos. The daos that encounter and deconstruct the

Logos and the Dao can be seen as the *différance*, the trace, the supplement, the transformation, the continuity, and the discontinuity of the Dao. In this regard, daos are still evolving and working. In the postmodern era, Chinese culture is not a self-sustained and self-contained entity isolated and secluded from other cultures. The daos as the pulses of Chinese culture are receiving and responding to the different cultural entities and carried on in human life.

I suggest elucidating the meaning of dao as non-Logos from four viewpoints: the commonplace as the context where daos are perceived, the defect as an alternative way of addressing daos, the de-subjectification as the focus of the Daoist *wú*-practices, and daos as chaos/nature. These ways of understanding dao can be seen as subverting the conventional conception of the Dao. The meaning of the daos is disclosed by the dialectics of ancient wits and modern thinkers.

Commonplace

The understanding of dao in the commonplace means that dao is conceived in ordinary people, banal things, or insignificant trivialities. It is not solely in the Divine or Great Being, like the sage or Heaven, that daos can be learnt. The commonplace dao or daos are, as Zhuangzi articulates, 'everywhere'. Dong-guozi asked about where to find the dao. Zhuangzi said that dao was everywhere. When Dong-guozi asked for further details, Zhuangzi replied that dao was in the ant, in the panic grass, in the earthenware tile, and in the excrement (Legge, 1891b).[8] It is not only the waste or the excrement that provide occasions to comprehend dao but also different kinds of beings and things – the so-called 'wànwù' (萬物, thousands of things) or 'zhòngsheng' (眾生, vast creatures). Numerous beings and things – tigers and wolves, sparrows and hawks, turtles and rats, cicadas and crickets, fish and butterflies, winds and clouds, mountains and rivers, farmers and gardeners, carpenters and passersby, chefs and wheelwrights, kings and dukes, officers and soldiers, and so on – are mentioned in the *Zhuangzi* and *Daodejing*.

Defect

A defect is a shortcoming, imperfection, or fault. It is the deficiency, the deficit, or the failure that makes one living being or thing incomplete, unfinished, abnormal, or malfunctioning. It is found in the impaired and the defective. The problem is, is any defect an absolute defect? Is there anything that is a sheer, independent, and pure imperfection or failure? Having taken careful consideration, we find that the so-called defect is understood with the implicit understanding of the opposite – the state of being perfect, complete, accomplished, or successful – and vice versa. The dualities of perfection and imperfection, completeness and incompleteness, and success and failure depend on each other. This concept is what Laozi and Zhuangzi enlightened for us: the paradox of dichotomy, e.g., the useless versus the useful, the vulgar versus the noble, the

120 Post-graphocentrism

poor versus the wealthy, the ill versus the sound, the worthless versus the valuable, and so on. Zhuangzi often tell stories about deformed people and disfigured beings to illuminate that the deformed, the disfigured, or the ill are not valueless or miserable. On the contrary, handicapped people or detested creatures indeed embody or practise daos because they metaphorically and existentially demonstrate the relatedness and interdependence of worldly beings and human languages. The concept of defect accords with the Daoist value of wú, meaning 'non-', 'de-', or 'anti-'.

De-subjectification

By 'de-subjectification', I mean the deconstruction and questioning of subjectivity, which in my view is of the utmost importance in Daoist philosophy. Yet to achieve the end, Daoist philosophers suggest wú-practices as the methods (or anti-methods) of thinking, doing, and living. The Daoist wú-practices are non-practices that mainly include 'wúwéi' (無為), 'wúyù' (無欲), and 'wúzhi' (無知). 'Wúwéi' literally means no action, not doing anything, or doing nothing. Wúyù means 'nodesire', and wúzhi means 'noknowledge'. These three types of wú-practices are concerned with countering, transgressing, and deconstructing the process of subjectification – the formation and building of subjects – in three interrelated aspects: onto-cosmology, ethics, and epistemology. The realisation of wú-practices aims to reach the state of 'wúwǔo' (無我), meaning no-I or non-I.

The concept of 'wú-' could be of greatest importance in Laozi. According to Laozi, 'The sage deals with things by doing nothing and teaches by saying nothing' (*Daodejing*, 2; my translation).[9] The sage is highly regarded because he comprehends the dao or daos, acts by no-action, and speaks by saying no-word. The most well-known saying of Laozi is 'Doing nothing (no-action) is to do everything' (無為而無不為). Who does nothing to have everything done? Sometimes, it is described as the sage; sometimes, the dao, the Heaven, or nature. Zhuangzi also says, 'Dao has its states and its signs but is without action and form' (*Zhuangzi*, 1.6.3; my translation).[10] For whom and for what do Laozi and Zhuangzi describe the state of no-action of the sage or of the dao? Somehow, the audience or readers are the assumed subjects to learn after the sage or the dao. To do everything by doing nothing seems contradictory and paradoxical. However, the series of wú-practices should be put in the context of subjectification for further and wider understanding.

Actions, desires, knowledge, and speeches must be undertaken or possessed by a subject who has an ego or a selfhood. More actions, desires, knowledge, and speeches strengthen the ego or the selfhood of the subjectivity. Desires drive one to pursue what one likes and despise what one dislikes. People and objects are thus evaluated, judged, and discriminated. The discrimination, exclusion, and pursuit of satisfaction of desires result in conflicts, disturbance, and manipulation: 'Five colours blind the eyes. Five sounds deafen the ears. Five flavours

Post-graphocentrism   121

please the palate. Gallop hunting maddens one. Rare goods corrupt one. Therefore, the sage seeks to fill the stomach but not cater the appetite. He prefers the latter to the former' (*Daodejing*, 12; my translation).[11] The five colours, five sounds, five flavours, and gallop hunting are apparently metaphors to stimulate the senses and thereby incite the desires for more sensational satisfaction and pleasure. The pursuit is endless. One who is trapped in the endless pursuit of sensational stimuli will have a lost and miserable life.

Chasing external excitement can be sensational as well as intellectual. The object that satisfies the intellectual desire is knowledge – wúzhi – or no knowledge. That is why Laozi renounces wit (棄智) and Zhuangzi discards knowledge (棄知). With respect to wúzhi, we can summarise two points from the Daoist philosophers: First, knowledge may support the pursuit of satisfaction of desire and the resulting discrimination and calculation, exclusion, and inclusion. More knowledge equips people with more crafty strategies and cunning tricks to pursue satisfaction of desires. In turn, more knowledge creates more curiosity and desire. Thus, desire and knowledge mutually reinforce each other. Second, the communication of knowledge relies on language, but language is limited. This concept reminds us of Ludwig Wittgenstein, who writes in the preface of his *Tractatus Logico-Philosophicus*, 'What can be said at all can be said clearly, and what we cannot talk about we must pass over in silence' (Wittgenstein, 1961). Wittgenstein's statement beautifully coincides with the following Daoist descriptions:

> But those ideas are a sequence of something else – and what that something else is cannot be conveyed by words.
>
> (*Zhuangzi*, 2.6.9; trans. Legge, 1891b)[12]

> Words are employed to convey ideas; but when the ideas are apprehended, men forget the words.
>
> (*Zhuangzi*, 3.4.13; trans. Legge, 1891b)[13]

Words cannot convey everything. Sometimes, silence is needed. From the Daoist viewpoint, language always has limits, but we cannot be certain when, where, and how to encounter the limits of language. Language conveys meanings and ideas about the world where we are situated. Yet the world becomes more and more complex and complicated when we interact with and interrelate to each other. Daos are created at the moments of interactions and interrelations among wànwù, which are infinite. This is exactly why Zhuangzi laments the limit of life and knowledge: 'There is a limit to our life, but to knowledge there is no limit. With what is limited to pursue after what is unlimited is a perilous thing; and when, knowing this, we still seek the increase of our knowledge, the peril cannot be averted' (*Zhuangzi*, 1.3.1; trans. Legge, 1891b).[14]

The difficulty of using language is related to the paradox of daos. On the one hand, as the Dao, it transcends human language. We must be silent because

122   Post-graphocentrism

we cannot express the meaning of the Dao in a thorough and exhaustive way. On the other hand, daos are embodied in myriad beings and relations. We must keep silent as well because the interactions and interrelations between each of us are increasing, and thus, daos emerge and generate. Zhuangzi writes about the inexhaustibility of the meaning of the Dao and daos:

> There is no thing that is not 'that', and there is no thing that is not 'this'. If I look at something from 'that', I do not see it; only if I look at it from knowing do I know it. Hence it is said, 'That view comes from this; and this view is a consequence of that ' – which is the theory that that view and this (the opposite views) produce each the other.
>
> (*Zhuangzi*, 1.2.5; trans. Legge, 1891b)[15]

The above passage shows how the Daoist deconstructive strategy works to overturn, empty, and evacuate opposing dichotomies by reversing and questioning them. When Zhuangzi says that it is neither to be nor not to be, we are reminded of Derrida's *différance*:

> Henceforth, in order better to mark this interval ... it has been necessary to analyse, to set to work, *within* the text of the history of philosophy, as well as *within* the so-called literary text ... certain marks, shall we say ... that *by analogy* ... I have called undecidables, that is, unities of simulacrum, 'false' verbal properties (nominal or semantic) that can no longer be included within philosophical (binary) opposition, but which, however, inhabit philosophical opposition, resisting and disorganising it ...
>
> (Derrida, 1981, pp. 42–43)

Chaotic natures and natural chaos

The no-action or non-action of the onto-cosmology is to let beings and things be without interruption, disruption, and intervention. An interesting dialogue occurs in the chapter *Letting Be, and Exercising Forbearance*. Zhuangzi writes, 'Do you only take the position of doing nothing, and things will of themselves become transformed' (*Zhuangzi*, 2.4.4; trans. Legge, 1891b).[16] Accordingly, things will transform and change by themselves. Zhuangzi continues to say, 'Of all the multitude of things every one returns to its root. Every one returns to its root, and does not know (that it is doing so). They all are as in the state of chaos, and during all their existence they do not leave it. If they knew (that they were returning to their root), they would be (consciously) leaving it. They do not ask its name; they do not seek to spy out their nature; and thus it is that things come to life of themselves' (*Zhuangzi*, 2.4.4; trans. Legge, 1891b).[17] It can be observed that Zhuangzi endorses the nature as the justification of non-action and no-knowledge from the above passage. The state of chaos and the root seem to suggest the essence of being or thing. Thus, letting every being be is to let one thing be itself, one person be herself or himself. Is 'selfhood' a particular essence, the innate, inborn nature? The interesting point is that, on the one hand, every being or everything has its own nature, and on the other hand, nature is chaos. How is it possible for anything to have an essence or essences of chaos? An essence (or essences) is the attributes that make one what it is. An essence involves necessity. Nevertheless, chaos is a state of confusion or disorder. It is formless and without necessity. It seems entirely contradictory for anything to have an essence of chaos.

In the chapter "The Normal Course for Rulers and Kings", Zhuangzi provides an intriguing and thought-provoking anecdote.

> The Ruler of the Southern Ocean was Shu, the Ruler of the Northern Ocean was Hu, and the Ruler of the Centre was Chaos. Shu and Hu were continually meeting in the land of Chaos, who treated them very well. They consulted together how they might repay his kindness, and said, 'Men all have seven orifices for the purpose of seeing, hearing, eating, and breathing, while this (poor) Ruler alone has not one. Let us try and make them for him'. Accordingly they dug one orifice in him every day; and at the end of seven days Chaos died.
>
> (*Zhuangzi*, 1.7.7; trans. Legge, 1891b)[18]

Chaos died because he was given seven openings in his body: two eyes, two nostrils, a mouth, and two ears. In Chinese ordinary language, the 'seven openings' or 'seven holes' is a term used to refer to the bodily senses. A child who has learned something successfully or someone who has an idea, especially to solve a problem, will be described as 'having holes open' (開竅, kaiqiào). Nevertheless, Zhuangzi says that having holes open does not mean enlightenment but, rather, death. The seven holes signify the ability to acquire knowledge, from which knowledge, understanding and epistemology are derived. To open the seven holes improves the ability to know and broadens and deepens the sphere of knowledge. Yet, paradoxically, to know results in the demise of the knowing subject and highlights the temporality and unreliability of knowledge. Is Zhuangzi saying that the presence of truth legitimised by the refined reasoning ability indeed rings the bell of its own death?

This paradox is, from my viewpoint, the very insight that the Daoist philosophy aims to offer. For Daoists, every being, be it living or non-living, has its own nature or natures that are working of their own accord and are, at the same time, chaotic, formless, disordered, and beyond reason and measurement. Every being in its own natural state has its own way of generation, becoming, transformation, and demise. The process of the being proceeds, regardless of whether the natural course has been studied, made known, or understood to the being itself or to others.

The post-graphocentric thrust

This chapter has made inquiry into the concept of dao (referring to the Dao and daos) as the dao hinges most Chinese schools of philosophy. I have argued that there are two approaches to the understanding of the dao: the great grand Dao and the myriad petit daos. The great grand Dao is believed to be the ultimate truth and fundamental principle in the universe and the human world. The great grand Dao nearly dominates canonical Chinese traditions with respect to philosophical theories, cultural practices and educational institution. It is the Dao perceived from graphocentrism. Thus there is a delicate concurrence between phonocentrism and graphocentrism, and between Logocentrism and Daocentrism. As noted, Western phonocentrism means the view of prioritising speech over writing whereas the Eastern graphocentrism has a completely opposite perspective. In a certain sense, it is suggested that graphocentrism implies potential of breaking through the boundaries constructed by phonocentrism. Nevertheless, these two views are consonant with each other to produce particular forms of ethnocentrism and discriminations that are respectively embodied in culturally dependent contexts. More importantly, the metaphysical idea underpinning these two traditions are very much alike: the Logos and the Dao, in the sense that both are inscribed in language and determine the meaning and presence of reality.

The second approach to the understanding of dao, like deconstruction, provides the possibilities of seeing the world beyond the limit of canonical traditions. The petit and myriad daos are proposed in the sense that they are other than what is provided by graphocentrism. The great grand Dao is believed to be manifest in the serious, the noble, the important, the valuable, the grave, the everlasting, the pure, the heavy, etc. In contrast, the petit daos can be perceived in the unimportant, the frivolous, the trifling, the trivial, the foul, the whimsical, the weird, or the light. As a matter of fact, the daos as the 'insignificant' have been posed in ancient Daoist texts. I thus discussed the meaning of daos from four aspects: commonplace, defect, de-subjectification, and chaotic natures and natural chaos. Other possible ways of elaborating and articulating the daos are welcome and invited.

Notes

1 'The greatest square has no corners; the best utensil is the latest made; the strongest voice has no sound; the grandest image has no form. The Dao is hidden, and has no name; but it is the Dao which masters in provision and fulfilment' (*Daodejing*, 41; my translation).
2 Dong-guozi asked Zhuangzi, saying, 'Where is what you call the Dao to be found?' Zhuangzi replied, 'Everywhere'. The other said, 'Specify an instance of it. That will be more satisfactory'. 'It is here in this ant'. 'Give a lower instance'. 'It is in this panic grass'. 'Give me a still lower instance'. 'It is in this earthenware tile'. 'Surely that is the lowest instance?' 'It is in that excrement'. To this Dong-guozi gave no reply (*Zhuangzi*, 2.15.6; trans. Legge, 1891b).

3 The term junzǐ (君子) in Chinese philosophy means a noble person. It originally refers to a prince or an aristocratic man. As Confucius uses the term of junzǐ to refer to a noble person with ethical virtues, the junzǐ is generally recognised as the exemplary and ideal man.

4 Derrida purposefully uses 'neographism' rather than 'neologism', because 'neologism' seems to suppose the logos, which he intends to keep away from.

5 吾道一以貫之。(論語里仁, 4:15)

6 It is written in the Chapter of Da Xue of the *Book of Rites:* 'Things being investigated, knowledge became complete. Their knowledge being complete, their thoughts were sincere. Their thoughts being sincere, their hearts were then rectified. Their hearts being rectified, their persons were cultivated. Their persons being cultivated, their families were regulated. Their families being regulated, their states were rightly governed. Their states being rightly governed, the whole kingdom was made tranquil and happy' (*Lǐjì, DàXúe*, 42:2; trans. Legge, 1885). The original text is物格而後知至, 知至而後意誠, 意誠而後心正, 心正而後身修, 身修而後家齊, 家齊而後國治, 國治而後天下平。(禮記大學) To put it simply, the main ideas are格物、致知、誠意、正心、修身、齊家、治國、平天下。

7 女子之嫁也, 母命之, 往送之門, 戒之曰： 「往之女家, 必敬必戒, 無違夫子！」以順為正者, 妾婦之道也。(孟子滕文公下, 3B:7)

8 東郭子問於莊子曰： 「所謂道, 惡乎在?」莊子曰： 「無所不在。」東郭子曰： 「期而後可。」莊子曰： 「在螻蟻。」曰： 「何其下邪?」曰： 「在稊稗。」曰： 「何其愈下邪?」曰： 「在瓦甓。」曰： 「何其愈甚邪?」曰： 「在屎溺。」東郭子不應。(莊子外篇知北遊, 2.15.6)

9 聖人處無為之事, 行不言之教。(道德經, 2)

10 夫道, 有情有信, 無為無形。(莊子內篇大宗師.1.6.6)

11 五色令人目盲；五音令人耳聾；五味令人口爽；馳騁田獵, 令人心發狂；難得之貨, 令人行妨。是以聖人為腹不為目, 故去彼取此。(道德經, 12)

12 意之所隨者, 不可以言傳也。(莊子外篇天道, 2.6.9)

13 言者所以在意, 得意而忘言。(莊子雜篇外物, 3.4.13)

14 吾生也有涯, 而知也无涯。以有涯隨无涯, 殆已；已而為知者, 殆而已矣。(莊子內篇養生主, 1.3.1)

15 物無非彼, 物無非是。自彼則不見, 自知則知之。故曰：彼出於是, 是亦因彼。彼是, 方生之說也。

16 意！心養。汝徒處無為, 而物自化。(莊子外篇在宥, 2.4.4)

17 萬物云云, 各復其根, 各復其根而不知。渾渾沌沌, 終身不離；若彼知之, 乃是離之。無問其名, 無闚其情, 物故自生。(莊子外篇在宥, 2.4.4)

18 南海之帝為儵, 北海之帝為忽, 中央之帝為渾沌。儵與忽時相與遇於渾沌之地, 渾沌待之甚善。儵與忽謀報渾沌之德, 曰： 「人皆有七竅, 以視聽食息, 此獨無有, 嘗試鑿之。」日鑿一竅, 七日而渾沌死。(莊子內篇應帝王, 1.7.7)

References

Addiss, S., & Lombardo, S. (1993). *Tao Te Ching: Laozi*. Indianapolis, IN: Hackett Publishing Company.

Ames, T. R., & Hall, L. D. (2003). *Daodejing: Making this life significant*. New York, NY: Ballantine.

Bryan, P. M. (2002). *Tao Te Ching: The way of virtue*. Garden City Park, NY: Square One Publishers.

Cheng, C. (2003). Dao (Tao): The way. In A. S. Cua (Ed.), *Encyclopedia of Chinese philosophy* (pp. 202–206). New York, NY: Routledge.

Derrida, J. (1977). *Limited Inc.* Evanston, IL: Northwestern University Press.

Derrida, J. (1981). *Positions.* Chicago, IL: University of Chicago Press.

Derrida, J. (1982). *Margins of philosophy.* Chicago, IL: University of Chicago Press.

Hansen, C. (1992). *A Daoist theory of Chinese thought: A philosophical interpretation.* New York, NY: Oxford University Press.

Ivanhoe, P. J. (2002). *The Daodejing of Laozi.* Indianapolis, IN: Hackett Publishing Company.

Lau, D. C. (Trans.) (1982). *Chinese classics: Tao Te Ching.* Hong Kong: The Chinese University Press.

Legge, J. (Trans.). (1885). *Sacred books of the East, volume 28, part 4: The Li Ki.* Retrieved November 19, 2013, from D. Sturgeon (Ed.), *Chinese text project.* http://ctext.org/liji

Legge, J. (Trans.). (1891b). *The writings of Chuang Tzu.* Retrieved July 16, 2016, from http://ctext.org/zhuangzi

Legge, J. (Trans.). (1985). *The works of Mencius,* Clarendon. Retrieved April 5, 2017, from D. Sturgeon (Ed.), *Chinese text project.* http://ctext.org/mengzi

Plato. (1961). *Plato: The collected dialogues.* Eds. E. Hamilton & H. Cairns. Princeton, NJ: Princeton University Press.

Ryden, E. (2008). *Laozi: Daodejing.* Oxford, NY: Oxford University Press.

Schwartz, B. I. (1985). *The world of thought in ancient China.* Cambridge, MA: Harvard University Press.

Tanaka, K. (2004). The limit of language in Daoism. *Asian Philosophy, 14*(2), 191–205.

Waley, A. (Trans.). (1934). *The way and its power.* London, UK: George Allen & Unwin.

Wittgenstein, L. (1961). *Tractatus logico-philosophicus.* Trans. D. F. Pears & B. F. McGinnes. London, UK: Routeledge & Kegan Paul.

Wong, Z. (2016). *Order in early Chinese excavated texts: Natural, supernatural, and legal approaches.* London, UK: Palgrave Macmillan.

Yu, J. (2015). Logos and Dao: Conceptions of reality in Heraclitus and Laozi. In C. Li & F. Perkins (Eds.), *Chinese metaphysics and its problems* (pp. 105–119). Cambridge, UK: Cambridge University Press.

Zhang, L. (1992). *The Tao and the logos, literary hermeneutics, East and West.* Durham, UK: Duke University Press.

Chapter 6

Post-graphocentric education

結廬在人境, 而無車馬喧。
問君何能爾, 心遠地自偏。
采菊東籬下, 悠然見南山。
山氣日夕佳, 飛鳥相與還。
此中有真意, 欲辯已忘言。

—（陶潛, 396–427 CE, 飲酒）

In the mundane world is my hut, free from noise of horse and cart;
By what may thou be like this? I reply, detached set by detached mind;
Picking up daisies by the eastern hedge, I gaze the South Mountain in the distance;
When the mountain mist at dusk, birds fly back together;
Therein a true meaning is uttered with forgotten words.
—(Táo Qían 365–427 CE, *On Drinking*; my translation)

Graphocentrism, which I argued as the pillar of Chinese thoughts and culture, is grounded on the metaphysics of Dao, or Daocentrism. Concerning education, under the influence of graphocentrism, Chinese-speaking societies view 'the writing subject' as the ideal. The cultivation of the writing subject takes the centre of the system of education theoretically and practically. An ideal writing subject is a morally and intellectually admirable person – a junzǐ – one who complies with the Dao. In the old times, it included the scholar-bureaucrat (literati). In the present, it may be called an intellectual. In the old times, the writing subject was expected to pass the imperial examination to gain a position in the imperial academy and an office in government. The current educational system still strives to produce the writing subject. Higher education and civil service examinations are active mechanisms for selecting candidates for universities and governments. The content of examinations changes, but the form holds sway. The cultivation of the writing subject as subjectification is transformatively absorbed in modern schooling system and mentality. That being said, graphocentrism based on the Dao always faces occasions of being escaped, twisted, deviated, changed, or differing and deferring. Just like the Eastern Jìn dynasty (317–420 CE) poet Táo Qían (陶潛), or Táo Yuanmíng (陶淵明), who exemplifies the Dao and daos. Táo was born and brought up in a noble family. Like most literati in premodern China, he was educated to serve as an official in the imperial court. In this sense, Táo exemplifies the graphocentric writing subject. In 405 CE, he resigned from a position of a country magistrate and went home to live a country life of arcadian contentment. The epigraphic poem, *On Drinking*, reflects the spirit of simplicity and daos. Táo has been considered as one of the greatest poets not only for what he wrote but also for how he lived. Táo is thus called the 'Recluse Poet'. As a poet and a human person, Táo incorporates daos through his daoful poetry and lifestyle. The written word with the characteristics of visibility (physicality), inalterability, and verifiability, and the associating system of institutionalisation are challenged and discredited. This is the momentum of post-graphocentric thrust with functioning of unexpected and unpredictable daos.

In what follows, I will discuss the meaning of education in the light of post-graphocentrism. The post-graphocentric education can be termed 'daoful' because the underpinning forces are daos. The elucidation of the moves to be daoful comprises two parts: first, the critique and deconstruction of the established – the wú-practices – and second, the creation and innovation to be otherwise – the becoming of daofully otherwise. The two moves of being daoful can be understood as four phases of différance: deferring, differentiating, production and unfolding. The daoful moves resound with the four tones of différance in a dialectic – not a synchronic – way. Either of the two daoful moves embraces the three elements of différance. Derrida's three steps of différance are as follows. First, deferring consists of a varied but related, both active and passive movement of 'delay, delegation, reprieve, referral, detour, postponement, reserving' (Derrida, 1981a, p. 8). Second, differentiating is to produce different things, to create divergent things. Différance is 'the common root of all the oppositional concepts, such as, to take only a few examples, sensible/intelligible, intuition/signification, nature/culture, etc. As a common root, différance is also the element of the same (to be distinguished from the identical) in which these oppositions are announced' (ibid., p. 9). The third step of différance is the production of differences. Fourth, différance would name provisionally the unfolding of difference. It is 'a *différance* that is no longer determined' (ibid., p. 10). The discussion of the daoful moves will enfold the sophisticated consonances between the details of daoful moves and deconstruction/différances and help to envision the education crossing boundaries.

Wú-practices

Wú-practices are practices based on the Daoist conception of 'wú'. 'Wú' (無) means 'to be without', 'to be void', 'nothingness', or 'emptiness'. Wú-practices literally mean 'no action' or 'non-action', 'no doing' or 'non-doing'. In Daoist tradition, the most important elements of wú-practices are 'wúwéi' (無為), 'wúyù' (無欲), and 'wúzhi' (無知). Wúwéi literally means no-action, not doing anything, or doing nothing. Wúyù means no-desire, and wúzhi, no-knowledge. These three types of wú-practices are concerned with countering, transgressing, and deconstructing the process of subjectification – the formation and building of subjects. Wú-practices aim to attain the state of 'wúwǔo' (無我), meaning no-I or non-I, 'wúsi' (無私), or 'wújǐ'(無己), both meaning no self. Other derivative activities of wú-practices include 'júeshèn' (絕聖) (abstaining from sageness or sagehood), 'chìzhì'(棄智) (renouncing wit), 'chìzhi' (棄知) (discarding knowledge), forgetting the self (忘我, 忘己), fasting of the heartmind (心齋), sitting and forgetting (坐忘), xu (虛, emptiness or emptying), jìng (靜, stillness or tranquillity), etc.

Wú-practices, like the différance phase of deferring, include both active and passive movements. With respect to passivity, wú-practices are about keeping silence, reservation, suspension, pausing, refraining, and so on. With respect to activity, they are related to making peace, creating lapse, evacuating, giving up, renouncing, disavowing, and so on. The active and passive sides are correlated. Forgetting is to recollect nothing. It transgresses the border between the active and passive aspects. Wú-practices highlight the dichotomy in the first step and then overturn the difference and hierarchy by suspension, reversal, and erasure. There are numerous dichotomies, such as the useful and the useless, the valuable and the worthless, the mean and the noble, the permanent truth and the idle talk, etc. Because 'the hierarchy of dual oppositions always reestablishes itself' (Derrida, 1981a, p. 42), it is significant to be careful about the hierarchy in order to have it overturned and deconstructed. This is what we can discover in the Daoists texts.

In Chapter 11 of the *Daodejing*, Laozi gives three examples to demonstrate that what is present depends on what is absent, and that what is useful depends on what is useless:

> The thirty spokes unite in the one nave; but it is on the empty space (for the axle), that the use of the wheel depends. Clay is fashioned into vessels; but it is on their empty hollowness, that their use depends. The door and windows are cut out (from the walls) to form an apartment; but it is on the empty space (within), that its use depends. Therefore, what has a (positive) existence serves for profitable adaptation, and what has not that for (actual) usefulness.
>
> (trans. Legge, 1891)[1]

Laozi's text suggests that the 'imperfection' or the 'deficiency' is the key that makes possible and useful the entity or the reality. The invisible renders the visible and so does the sensible the insensible. In general, the useful, the visible, and the sensible are taken as more valuable and real than the useless, the invisible, and the insensible. However, it is the very uselessness that adds value to

130 Post-graphocentric education

the useful, and likewise with the invisible and insensible. A similar view can be found in the passage from *Zhuangzi*:

> Where there is acceptability there must be unacceptability; where there is unacceptability there must be acceptability. Where there is recognition of right there must be recognition of wrong; where there is recognition of wrong there must be recognition right. Therefore, the sage does not proceed in such a way, but illuminates all in the light of Heaven.
>
> (*Zhuangzi* 1.2:5; trans. Watson, 1970, pp. 39–40)[2]

It is not only the paradoxical feature of language that Zhuangzi attempts to shows us, but also the point that the forgetting of language itself approaches deeper and higher understanding: 'Words exist because of meaning; once you've gotten the meaning, you can forget the words' (Watson, 1970, p. 302). Meaning is conveyed – but not bound by – the words. More importantly, meaning in abundance cannot be accessed merely on a literal level.

In addition to the metaphysical and linguistic aspects, ethical means for reversing dichotomy may be of more concern to early Daoists. The ethical-political significance of the concept of wú is deeply related to subjectification – the formation and building of the human subject with his or her ego, selfhood, or identity. How one relates oneself to the world is the primary concern of Chinese thinkers. The self is focal, relational, and dependent on other selves within the context of society (Hall & Ames, 1998). Yet, as argued, the institution of subjectification through history has resulted in discrimination, oppression, and exclusion. For example, Confucius in the *Analects* describes a harmonious society wherein the king is to be a king; the subject, a subject; the father, a father; the son, a son (*Analects*, 12: 11; my translation).[3] Everyone must hold a specific role and position in society and act, behave, speak, perform, and even dress properly so that societal order is well maintained. Social order is grounded in social hierarchy. To maintain the order of society, it is critical to safeguard the hierarchy by binding each person to a specific, unchangeable position and status. I cast doubt on the outcome of the process of the writing regime or, in Agamben's term, the anthropological machine. Is the outcome, the writing subject, a self with free soul or an automaton who operates based on the programme of social rules and orders?

In this vein, Laozi and Zhuangzi reverse the hierarchy and erase the distinction between the human and the non-human or inhuman, between the human and the object, between the sage and the common people, the beautiful and the ugly, the noble and the mean, the strong and the weak, the sane and the insane, and so on. Laozi and Zhuangzi unfasten the ties between the signifiers and the signified on the linguistic level and further liberate the value attached to these concepts with respect to ethical-political concerns. Thinking, speaking, and judging are suspended through wú-practices. However, this suspension does not mean to nullify or to invalidate the function of signification of wú-concepts but to wait for and invite more potential and possibilities. Language is the means of communicating and expressing, rather than a means to set limits on, reify, or standardise actions or ways of living. All language is useful and appropriate in a particular way, within a particular context. 'Appropriate language is language aware of its own provisionality' (Burik, 2010, p. 511). Language, as it is limited, carries and transmits limited knowledge. In order not to be bound to limited knowledge, Laozi uses the term 'wú' (無) to show ways in which living, acting, and speaking could surpass conventionality. 'Wú' is generally translated as 'non-' or 'in-' or 'un-'. It is not a simple negation or mere nihilism. Rather, it denotes a non-coercive, open, receptive, and responsive way of doing, speaking, acting, and thinking. Laozi suggests 'wúwéi' (無為), which is aptly translated by Ames and Hall (2003) as 'non-coercive action'; 'wúyù' (無欲) as 'achievement of deferential desire'; and 'wúzhi' (無知) as 'unprincipled knowing'. 'Wúzhi' does not mean the mindset of embracing ignorance or stupidity (Nelson, 2009), but the mindset of 'facing' conventionality without force, resistance, and presupposition. Here, 'facing' means neither passive and submissive acceptance nor inane idiocy, but not taking conventionality for granted. This does not occur in a state of fighting or conflict but instead takes place in a state of peace and 'nature' (zìran). In the natural state, one faces the other as a non-self. This is tremendously important for the education of self-cultivation as self-deconstruction.

As Nelson (2009) points out, both early Daoist views and the ancient Confucian rú (儒) tradition care about self-cultivation, but through different approaches. In the Confucian rú tradition, self-cultivation is generally construed as 'the hierarchically organised social education, moulding, and shaping of a pre-established and inborn nature, whether good or bad', whereas early Daoist view 'does not require the constancy of an internal nature or essence' (Nelson, 2009, p. 298). In early Daoist views, 'self-cultivation is an unforced turning toward the unfolding naturalness of the world and of oneself as a responsive, unforced, spontaneous attunement with it' (Nelson, 2009, p. 298). This resonates with 'wú' in many aspects, such as 'wúwei', 'wúzhi', 'wúyù', and, more importantly, 'wúwŭo' – 'non-I', or 'non-self'.

'Wúwŭo' is deconstruction of self. This self-deconstruction is not meant to negate the self, however. Far from being pessimistic or nihilistic because of self-negation, the Daoist self-deconstruction aims to open and empty one's mind and heart to others. It is self-humbleness in mind and intriguingly practised (or 'unpractised') in 'doing nothing' or non-action – 'wúwéi'. Moreover, 'wúwéi' can be translated as 'non-coercive action' (Ames & Hall, 2003). A coercive action is purposeful, deliberative, and calculated. Performing coercive actions or intending to do so shackles or even enslaves people. It is interesting to grasp the spirit of the practices of wúwŭo and wúwéi in Táo Qían's poem *On Drinking*. This poem portrays a vignette of the poet's ordinary life. It gives an impression of a moment the poet takes in his yard. It is in an ordinary day. The poet does nothing on purpose. As usual, he just rambles around, picks up flowers and rests his gaze on mountains at a stretch. In the scene depicted in this poem,

132 Post-graphocentric education

the human subject, action, utterance, or intention is hardly discernible. This is a world of nature but 'I'.

Within the Daoist context, 'mind-fasting' (心齋, xinzhai) and 'sitting and forgetting' (坐忘, zùowàng) are ways to put wú-practices into action. I take 'mind-fasting' and 'sitting and forgetting' as similar exercises. Although these two terms appear in different chapters of *Zhuangzi*, the concept of wú is of primary importance for both.

With respect to mind-fasting, Zhuangzi writes that Yán Húi, Confucius's favourite disciple, asked advice from Confucius about serving in State Wei. Yán Húi said that he would try as many ways as possible to be a good councillor to the Governor of State Wei. Confucius replied, 'Goodness, how could that do? You have too many policies and plans and you haven't seen what is needed. You will probably get off without incurring any blame, yes. But that will be as far as it goes. How do you think you actually convert him? You are still making the mind your teacher' (*Zhuangzi*, 1.4.1; trans. Watson, 1968, p. 52).[4] Yán Húi asked for further suggestions. Confucius answered with 'fasting of the mind':

> Make your will one! Don't listen with your ears, listen with your mind. No, don't listen with your mind, but listen with your spirit. Listening stops with the ears, the mind stops with recognition, but spirit is empty and waits on all things. The Way [Dao] gathers in emptiness alone. Emptiness is the fasting of the mind.
>
> (*Zhuangzi*, 1.4.2; trans. Watson, 1968, p. 54)[5]

In this passage, Confucius tells Yán Húi to sense the world not through his faculties, but with his empty mind. This seemingly contradictory advice deconstructs what it means to gain knowledge through the senses and recasts the relationship between the body and the external sensible world. In this story, Yán Húi plays the role of the hard-working moraliser who is eager to pursue the good by giving opinions. However, the meaning of the 'good' relies on conventional views. The value itself and the criteria are accepted and followed. Since there has been a conventionally approved definition of the good, there must be a recognised definition of the bad as contrast. The dichotomy is assumed when Yán Húi articulates his judgement. Moreover, Yán Húi demonstrates his own selfhood by giving voice to words. It is the voice of the speaker who prevails by giving advice, who commands. In contrast, the Daoist pedagogue does not impose his or her views on others. Rather, he or she opens and empties him- or herself. The 'fasting of the mind' is to deconstruct the subjectivity of the speaker as well as the listener, to create the horizon of wú to welcome every interlocutor.

The concept of sitting and forgetting appears in another exciting dialogue between Confucius and Yán Húi again. Their exchange is extremely insightful:

> Yán Húi said, 'I am making progress'. Zhongni replied, 'What do you mean?' 'I have ceased to think of benevolence (rén) and righteousness (yì)',

was the reply. 'Very well; but that is not enough'. Another day, Húi again saw Zhongni, and said, 'I am making progress'. 'What do you mean?' 'I have lost all thought of ceremonies (lǐ) and music (yùe)'. 'Very well, but that is not enough'.

A third day, Húi again saw (the Master), and said, 'I am making progress'. 'What do you mean?' 'I sit and forget everything'. Zhongni changed countenance, and said, 'What do you mean by saying that you sit and forget (everything)?' Yán Hui replied, 'My connexion with the body and limb dissolved; my perceptive organs are discarded. Thus leaving my material form, and bidding farewell to my knowledge, I am become one with the Great Pervasion. This I call sitting and forgetting all things'. Zhongni said, 'One (with that Pervasion), you are free from all likings; so transformed, you are become impermanent. You have, indeed, become superior to me! I must ask leave to follow in your steps'.

(*Zhuangzi*, 1.6.9; trans. Legge, 1891; my modification)[6]

Again, the meanings of the concepts – benevolence (rén) and righteousness (yì), ceremonies (lǐ) and music (yùe), which have been recognised as the most important elements, means, and goals for Chinese traditional education – are questioned. The value system, the effective hierarchy, and the underlying metaphysics are suspended. In this tradition, benevolence (rén) and righteousness (yì), ceremonies (lǐ) and music (yùe) are essential for cultivating a junzǐ or a ruler and educating common people. These notions are of moral and political significance. As Mencius says to king Hùi of Liáng, with respect to ruling a state, it is insignificant to think about benefits. Rather, what matters is 'benevolence (rén) and righteousness (yì)', and that is enough (*Mencius*, 1A.1; trans. Legge, 1985).[7] Concerning ceremonies or rituals (lǐ) and music (yùe), Confucius mentions that they are indispensable for becoming a complete human person (*Analects*, 14.12; trans. Legge, 1861a).[8] Nevertheless, Zhuangzi's story overturns the meanings of these notions. It is more radical to overturn the status and the hierarchy of master and student, as demonstrated when Confucius is willing to learn from his student. In the Confucian tradition, as honoured and respected, the teacher is juxtaposed with the king. Both are ordained by Heaven: 'Heaven having produced the inferior people, made for them rulers and teachers' (*Mencius*, 1B.10; trans. Legge, 1985).[9] On the one hand, Zhuangzi reverses the established hierarchy by Confucius the Supreme Master. The reversal implies the subtle and sophisticated deconstruction of the social hierarchy, which in the ancient times was difficult to challenge. On the other, the significance of education is shown in the attitude of being committed and devoted to the process of learning, but not to an authority who dictates the official writing in the East (or speaking in the West). Such an authority fosters hierarchy to reinforce his or her power.

The dao in the Daoist philosophers is in harmony with the deconstruction in Derrida in many respects, such as challenging the established dichotomy, critiquing authority, questioning the limits of language and thought, doubting social and individual identity, etc. As Derrida comments on the last phase of différance, as to 'name' provisionally, Daoist philosophers suggest 'wúmíng' (no name or no fame, nameless or fameless 無名), a thought-provoking notion.

In the first chapter, *Free and Easy Wondering*, Zhuangzi states: 'The perfect one has no self; the spirit-like one has no merit; the sage has no name' (Zhuangzi, 1.1.3; my translation).[10] In this short conclusion, Zhuangzi proposes three forms of wú: 'wújǐ' (no self, 無己), 'wúgong' (no merit or achievement, 無功), and 'wúmíng' (no name or no fame, nameless or fameless 無名).[11] In this short commentary, Zhuangzi deconstructs established beliefs in the areas of ontology, society, and linguistics or semiotics. Thus, wúmíng means to break the customary and privileged association between the sign and the meaning. It is then possible to invent new terms and phrases. New associations form. New meanings emerge. Again, the newly produced signification is deconstructed. Although this continuous process occurs, in Derrida's (1981a, p. 11) words, 'in the opening of saying and naming', it is not impossible for daos working with deconstructive effects within the cultural interior.

Becoming daofully otherwise

In this section, I explore the meaning of the daos of post-graphocentrism from the following three approaches: brush writing, ordinary life practices, and arts. These three approaches are interrelated.

. . . through the writing of wú

Calligraphy is a form of art and a traditional pedagogy of cultivating the Confucian-educated human being. It embraces Confucian and Daoist ideas simultaneously. The learning process of calligraphy can be divided into two phases. The first embodies Confucian spirit, whereas the second embraces Daoist insight. In the initiative phase, an apprentice needs to make great efforts to master the skills and codes, pay strict attention to every detail related to writing, and keep up with repeated practices. The preparation takes time and energy. As an intentional and telic practice, the difficult process of learning calligraphy is in accordance with the spirit of Confucianism. Confucius spent fourteen years journeying through different states looking for opportunities. Visiting governors of different states, Confucius hoped that his ideas about politics, ethics, society, and humanity would be considered for policy-making. He tried hard to pursue dreams of cosmopolitanism. Despite being rejected many times, Confucius as a person embodied the active spirit of diligence and persistence. The constant and earnest effort and defiance of hardship is what Confucius admires: 'The sage and the man of perfect virtue – how dare I rank myself with them? That I strive to become such without satiety, and teach others without weariness – this much can be said of me' (*Analects, Shu Er*, 7:34; trans. Legge, 1861a).[12]

Confucius never tires of learning and teaching. In contrast, he is always enthusiastic about these pursuits. Thus, he strives for self-cultivation, self-improvement, and self-enhancement. Confucius portrays himself thusly: 'He is simply a man, who in his eager pursuit of knowledge forgets his food, who in the joy of its attainment forgets his sorrows, and who does not perceive that old age is coming on' (*Analects, Shu Er*, 7:19; trans. Legge, 1861a).[13] This is the spirit that we discover in repeated practices of calligraphy practitioners. As the calligrapher master Wáng Xizhi says, to be skilful in writing one must practise 'countless times' (不得計其遍數也).

After one acquires skill in writing (and ethical virtues as well), practicing calligraphy is considered to be in harmony with dao. To be in harmony with dao is to do things spontaneously, naturally, and unintentionally – that is, in the state of being unconstrained and carefree. The state of being united with dao is seen in the graphic forms of characters and the inner peace of the calligrapher. In contrast with the aesthetic /moral values of unrighteousness, balance, equilibrium, and stableness cherished by Confucian artists, Daoists value naturalness, unpretentiousness, and inconspicuousness. Therefore, in the comments above, we can see why Fù highlights dullness, ugliness, disunity, and straightforwardness as artistically better than cleverness, pleasingness, slipperiness, and calculation – because the qualities of dullness, ugliness, disunity, and straightforwardness are more natural. How does the calligrapher express Daoist aesthetic qualities in writing? According to many ancient critics, there are two important techniques in writing that justly communicate the Daoist flavour. They are 'edge-hidden' (cángfeng) and 'blank-retention' (líubái) (Goldberg, 2004; Hua, 1997; Liu, 2010; Yen, 2005).

i   Edge-hidden

There are two types of techniques for holding the brush to contact the paper: 'edge-hidden' (cángfeng) and 'edge-exposure' (lòfeng). 'Edge-hidden' means that the tip or edge of the brush is hidden in the middle part of the stroke. When the brush contacts with the paper, the brush must be held upright rather than slanted from the side. In that case, the written words will look powerful and strong. This is referred to as the natural way of writing. As Tsài Yong (蔡邕, 133–192 CE) says: 'Calligraphy is generated from nature. There is nature, and so be ying and yáng. There is ying and yáng and so be the topos. The top and the tail [of the stroke] are hidden; the character is full of power. The exertion of writing [is as much as] the magnificence of the graphic forms' (Hua, 1997, p. 6; my translation).[14] Master calligraphers of different dynasties – including Wáng Xizhi (王羲之, 321–379 CE), Xú Hào (徐浩, 703–782 CE), Yán Zhenqing (顏真卿, 709–785 CE), Jiang Kwéi (姜夔, 1155–1211 CE), and many others – have declared 'edge-hidden' the rightful and proper way to use the brush,. In contrast, 'edge-exposure' is a technique through which the tip or edge of the brush shows on the stroke. This technique is criticised as 'ill',[15] 'poor',[16] 'soft', and 'eccentric'.[17]

136 Post-graphocentric education

As mentioned, there is a widespread belief in Chinese culture about the intertwining of morality and aesthetics. How a human being behaves morally is considered to correspond to what one expresses artistically. Concerning the brush technique, 'edge-hidden' (cángfeng) reflects 'the traditional Chinese idea about the proper bearing of a gentleman (junzǐ), a man with noble character' (Yen, 2005, p. 105). More importantly, a junzǐ does not show off his talents. Therefore, his humble and reserved character is more in keeping with the quality of 'edge-hidden' (cángfeng). The quality of modesty, humbleness, and keeping from being conspicuous is what Daoists value.

ii   Blank-retention

'Blank-retention' (líubái) is a technique of leaving blank space between lines and characters when writing or painting. Literally, 'líu' means 'to retain', 'to reserve', or 'to leave', and 'bái' means 'white'. The word also can mean 'void' or 'blank'. Simply speaking, líubái is to leave blank space, or not to fill vacant space with ink. Since the ink is black, the part of the paper not coated with black ink – not blackened – is white as well as blank. In Chinese arts, the blank is not left randomly or arbitrarily on the picture or in the text. Properly leaving the paper blank is a highly artistic and skilful technique based on great artistic, aesthetic, and moral ability. The proper blank communicates more profound and deep meaning than words or images visible in ink. Visually, the blank creates a space, an interruption, or a disconnection between the black line, blocks, or characters. Yet the discontinuity produces new meaning between intervals. As Goldberg (2004, pp. 181–182) states, 'it is through the visual, motorial, and tactile "imagination" that we give "body" to a calligraphic element in its constitutive role in the emergent configuration of the written character about its dynamic centre of motion. The written character is thus at once an expression of gestural movement and a constructed form.' The blank and the blackened dynamically come together to give meaning to the viewer. Líubái signifies by the absence of a signifier. The graphic vacuity within writing corresponds to what Derrida (1976, 2016) deliberates on 'supplements', including 'spacing, intervals, margins, and punctuation' (Butler, 2016). There is a meaning present by the absence of signifier.

Inner freedom is esteemed as the mindset that a master should accomplish. As the Eastern Han dynasty calligrapher Tsài Yong (133–192 CE) writes, the key to mastering calligraphy lies not in the calligrapher's tools and skills, but in one's inner freedom:

> Writing; releasing. In order to write one must release oneself from inner confinement. Let go the mind and heart. Then write. If one's heart and mind is obliged, one could not write well even if one has the best brush.
>
> (Hua, 1997, p. 5; my translation)[18]

In addition, the carefree calligrapher produces work that mirrors nature. As Tsài continues, excellent calligraphy embraces and reveals nature in every aspect. It is innate in the attitudes and postures of remarkable calligraphic works – e.g., 'sitting or walking, flying or moving, coming and going, lying down or getting up, being depressed or being joyful, insects' eating leaves, sharp swords and halberds, nice bows and arrows, water and fire, clouds and mists, the sun and the moon' (Hua, 1997, p. 6; my translation).[19] As described by calligraphers and critics, inner freedom accords with the Dao or daos and nature. Inner freedom, or self-release in Daoist words, is 'fasting of the mind'. 'Fast' literally means to abstain from food. 'Fasting of the mind' in Zhuangzi means keeping the mind free from all desires and deliberations. Zhuangzi states,

> Maintain a perfect unity in every movement of your will, You will not wait for the hearing of your ears about it, but for the hearing of your mind. You will not wait even for the hearing of your mind, but for the hearing of the spirit. Let the hearing (of the ears) rest with the ears. Let the mind rest in the verification (of the rightness of what is in the will). But the spirit is free from all pre-occupation and so waits for (the appearance of) things. Where the (proper) course is, there is freedom from all pre-occupation; such freedom is the fasting of the mind.
>
> (Zhuangzi, 4:2; trans. Legge, 1891)[20]

Fasting of the mind means entering a state of clarity, purity, stillness, and freedom from external attractions (Hung, 2015). A calligraphy master in such a state of mind writes as one who becomes harmonious with the ultimate dao. The master writes in a way that is unintentional but enlightened.

. . . through ordinary life practices

Zhuangzi's well-known story of the Cook Ding ingeniously relates how a master chef develops his extremely artful and natural practice of dismembering an ox from a novice. The Cook Ding described that when he first began to cut up an ox, he saw nothing but the (entire) carcase. After three years, he ceased to see it as a whole. Sixteen years after that, the Cook Ding entered state of being in harmony with dao. He says,

> Now I deal with it in a spirit-like manner, and do not look at it with my eyes. The use of my senses is discarded, and my spirit acts as it wills. Observing the natural lines, (my knife) slips through the great crevices and slides through the great cavities, taking advantage of the facilities thus presented. My art avoids the membranous ligatures, and much more the great bones. A good cook changes his knife every year; (it may have been injured) in cutting – an ordinary cook changes his every month – (it may have been) broken. Now my knife has been in use for nineteen years; it has cut up

several thousand oxen, and yet its edge is as sharp as if it had newly come from the whetstone.

(*Zhuangzi, Nourishing the Lord of Life*, 3:2; trans. Legge, 1891)[21]

The interlocutor ruler Wén Hùi praised the skill of the Cook Ding as impeccable and perfect and was inspired by his words for 'the nourishment of life'. Two implications can be drawn from this story.

First, the consonance between the notes of writing calligraphy and the story of the Cook Ding indicate that the supreme realm of a practice or vocation is to be in tune with daos, to be united with daos – a state that I term 'daoful'. The execution of a practice or a vocation in an artful and natural way is to reach the realm of daos. Therefore, to be in harmony with daos is to be both human (non-natural) and natural (non-human). The goal of being daoful is what we can find in calligraphic literature that embraces both Confucian and Daoist inspirations. As Ho (2005, p. 166) writes, 'The goal of learning is the attainment of *Dao* through dwelling in a practice, a view held by the founders of both Confucianism and Daoism'. The engagement of and aspiration for the daos is the most significant goal of self-cultivation in Chinese tradition. Writing calligraphy is one of the practices.

Second, reaching the realm of daos is to be simultaneously human (artful) and non-human (natural). From the Daoist perspective, this creates the nourishment of life. Being non/human seems to be a contradictory mode. Yet it is the state in which a human being is in harmony with daos through fully practising a profession or art. Be it cooking or writing, so long as one is entirely devoted with heart, mind, and body to a practice, one's life is nourished and enriched through attaining the daos. In this vein, any ordinary profession or practice could lead to the daos. The notion of daos sheds a new light on education in the sense that ordinary life practices, or even daily routines, are full of moments of capturing the daos. One simply needs to be attentive and concentrated, careful and mindful. It does not require heroic and ambitious enterprise to comprehend the daos or to be daoful.

... through arts

The arts are the third lens for examining post-graphocentric daos. As many scholars (Fenollosa & Pound, 1936; Liu, 1962; Murck & Fong, 1991; Stalling, 2010; Wu, 1969) have noted, the Chinese written character is a good medium for poetry. However, the character itself is viewed as a medium of visual poems, and thus visual arts. The works of Ezra Pound are the best exemplars. In addition, for Westerners like Fenollosa and Pound (1936), Chinese character writing is the exotic – but the exotic is, as they claim, the means of fructification. To Chinese-speaking people, post-graphocentrism offers a different lens for viewing the accustomed language anew. This is where we can find creativity and novelty for education and life.

In their pioneering article, Fenollosa and Pound (1936) regarded Chinese with great joy and admiration. They argued that Chinese is a better medium for poetry than Western languages. Their article started with a refutation of the Occidental debasement of Orientals, including Chinese and Japanese. Fenollosa then deliberates on the advantages of Chinese as a poetic language with sophistication and subtlety. Some features of Chinese are idea for conveying poetry. First, most Chinese characters are pictographs that can 'appeal to the eye' (Fenollosa & Pound, 1936, p. 6) without mediation. This is very similar to Leibniz's expression that Chinese 'speaks to the eye'. The Chinese character is a concrete image. Therefore, it is good to present the vividness of visual images. Two other characteristics make Chinese written language a good medium for poetry: the visual character keeps syncategrammatic [*sic*] words to a minimum; and the metaphors imply vivid visual images (Wu, 1969, p. 432). Such vividness and concreteness make the Chinese characters function as 'thought-pictures'. In the words of Fenollosa and Pound (1936, p. 9), 'they are alive'.

The visual vividness and concreteness of the Chinese written character makes Chinese script hardly equalled by spelling alphabet. Chinese script signifies without sound. Chinese writing can make sense to the viewer without stimulating auditory perception. A homophonic poem in classic Chinese by Yuán-Rèn Zhào (趙元任, 1892–1982) shows the visual appeal of Chinese written words that cannot be replaced by phonetic language.

施氏食獅史

石室詩士施氏, 嗜獅, 誓食十獅。氏時時適市視獅。十時, 適十獅適市。是時, 適施氏適市。氏視是十獅, 恃矢勢, 使是十獅逝世。氏拾是十獅屍, 適石室。石室濕, 氏使侍拭石室。石室拭, 氏始試食是十獅。食時, 始識是十獅屍, 實十石獅屍。試釋是事。

The Anecdote of Shi the Lion-Eater

In a stone den was a poet named Shi, who was addicted to eat lions, and had vowed to eat ten lions. He often went to the market to look for lions. At ten o'clock, ten lions had just been delivered to the market. At the very moment, Shi happened to arrive at the market. He saw those ten lions, and used his arrows to kill the lions. He brought the ten dead lions back to the stone den. The stone den was very damp. He had his servants to clean and dry the den. After the stone den was dried, he tried to eat the ten lions. When he started to eat, he realised that these ten lions were in fact stone lions. Try to explain what was happening.

(My translation)

This is indeed a ridiculous fictional story. The point is that it barely makes sense to listeners when it is read. Visual perceptivity plays a crucial role in understanding a story of such kind: homophony.

Shī Shì shí shī shǐ

Shíshì shīshì Shī Shì, shì shī, shì shí shí shī. Shì shíshí shì shì shì shī. Shí shí, shì shí shī shì shì. Shí shí, shì Shī Shì shì shì. Shì shì shì shí shī, shì shǐ shì, shǐ shì shí shī shìshì. Shì shí shì shí shī shì, shì shíshì. Shíshì shī, Shì shī shì shì shíshì. Shíshì shì, Shì shī shì shí shì shí shī. Shí shí, shǐ shí shì shí shī shì, shí shí shí shī shī. Shì shì shì shì.

(My translation)

A homophonic pun poem such as this aptly demonstrates the vividness, meaningfulness, spontaneity, and expressiveness of Chinese characters as visual signs. In this vein, the Chinese character plays a critical role in visual communication. Let me boldly suggest that the Chinese character itself is a type of visual art. The structure, the content, and the communicative function of the Chinese character are artistic.

Second, it is very interesting that the Chinese language contains a temporal element, even though it is strongly vision oriented. The spoken Chinese language is musical. As such, it arouses subtle feelings when heard. In writing the specific verse form of classical poetry – lùshi (律詩) or júejù (絕句) – the poet must obey specific rules concerning the number of characters on each line, the number of lines in each poem, and the tone patterns. The tone pattern of poems creates music when the poems are read. For some, the Chinese spoken language itself sounds musical, not matter what is read or said. Hence, the Chinese character is a visual art as well as an art of sound. It is not only the art of space but also the art of time.

Third, Chinese as a monosyllabic language is easy for the writer or author to arrange, both visually and musically. More deeply and importantly, the dispensability and flexibility of freely arranging characters in a piece of work is due to the 'simplicity in grammar' (Wu, 1969). The distinction between the subject and the predicate is relatively loose in comparison with Western languages. There is no inflection in Chinese grammar. As Wu (1969, p. 426) states, 'There are no tenses, no cases, no genders, no numbers, and in classic writings, even no punctuation.'

Moreover, in Chinese writing, a character can be a noun, a verb, or an adjective can be used interchangeably without any alteration in form. How it is used depends on the context. The most well-known example is in the chapter *Yán Yuan* of the *Analects*: 'jun jun, chéng chéng, fù fù, zǐ zǐ' (君君,臣臣,父父,子子。). Let us focus only on the first part. 'Jun' means 'king'. Literally, 'jun jun' means that a king is what a king should be or that a king should act like a king. Thus, the first character 君 is a noun, and the second is a verb. It is illuminating to see the flexibility and dispensability of the arrangement of characters with the simplicity of grammar that makes the Chinese language poetic and artistic. In contrast, although Western languages have more complex and rigorous grammatical rules that enable the expression of abstract ideas in great detail, the complicated and strict grammar rules create limitations. As mentioned in Chapter Five, Derrida uses *différance* (with an *a*) to replace *différence* (with an *e*) because the latter cannot refer 'either to *différer* as temporisation or to *différends* as *polemos*' (Derrida, 1982, p. 8). The linguistic, or grammatical, shortcoming drives the coinage of neographism. The creation of this new term produces new relationships and interplays between new and old terms and therefore elicits meanings. At the same time, new distinctions and boundaries are drawn. In contrast, even though Chinese − with its simple grammar − is thought to be a vague and ambiguous language, it offers rich possibilities of signification.

These three features − the visual vividness and concreteness of the written character, the temporal element, and the ease of arranging characters both visually and musically − make the Chinese language an ideal medium for poetry and arts. Further, the modern use of Chinese characters in arts demonstrates the potential and possibilities in new ways. Many contemporary artists create works by using and misusing, deconstructing and reconstructing characters.

In the remainder of this section, I discuss Xu Bing − one of the most provocative contemporary Chinese artists − as an example to demonstrate the intriguing relationship between writing, words, and daos. Xu Bing's works are full of imagination and creativity, and receive great attention and inspire responses from the audience. Words and writing play key roles in his arts. Chinese words are essential to Chinese culture and the personal life experience of the artist. As Xu Bing (2001, pp. 13–14) states, 'because the Chinese, language directly influences the methods of thinking and understanding of all Chinese people. To strike at the written word is to strike at the very essence of the culture. Any doctoring of the written word becomes in itself a transformation of the most inherent portion of a person's thinking. My experience with the written word has allowed me to understand this'. It is apparent that many of Xu Bing's works reflect writing and words. However, let us first focus on two very appealing and contentious works: *Tianshu* or *Book from the Sky* (1987–1991) and *New English Calligraphy Classroom* (1994–1998).

Tianshu is an installation piece first exhibited in 1988. I start with this installation because it is described as 'a breakthrough in thinking about language' from the artist (Erickson, 2001, p. 68). At first glimpse, it includes 'a grouping of books, scrolls, and panels printed in Chinese' (Erickson, 2001, p. 47). Yet under scrutiny, Chinese-literate viewers are sure to be stunned because not a word can be recognised. With *Tianshu*, Xu Bing dismantles characters and creates thousands of 'fake' unreadable characters. In reality, the characters he invented are totally incomprehensible to any Chinese-literate reader, including himself. Interestingly, the artist comments on his own work: 'Any explanation [of the *Book from the Sky*] is superfluous, because the work itself says nothing' (Cited from Erickson, 2001, p. 47). Does it really 'mean' nothing because it 'says' nothing?

More interesting is that the original title of this work is not *Tianshu* or *Book from the Sky*, but *Xishijian* (析世鑒), which means *A Mirror That Analyses the*

142 Post-graphocentric education

World (Wu, 1994). As the characters displayed are indeed 'nonsense writing', this installation is contradictorily intended to be a mirror that reflects and analyses the world. The critic Wu (1994, p. 411) says aptly: 'As a "mirror", it reflects while reversing this world; as a piece of "nonsense writing", it deconstructs and reconstructs what makes this world legible, conceivable, and therefore, meaningful.' There is an internal tension between the nonsense and the mirror – both are parts of the pseudo-character. The nonsense writing, in Wu's (1994) view, destroys the signified but not the signifier. Xu Bing polarises the visuality of the signifier by keeping the specious and deceptive form without the referent. Nevertheless, the sense or comprehensibility of the characters is strongly viewer dependent. For those able to read Chinese, the fake characters are nonsensical and funny. For those who do not understand Chinese, these signs are foreign and exotic, but not ridiculous.

In later years, Xu Bing created *New English Calligraphy Classroom* (1994–1998). This installation demonstrates English words in Chinese form – every word is written within a square and calligraphic form. The artist set up a calligraphy classroom for his audience to write English words with brush pens and ink for the exhibition. Through this installation, the artist breaks the rules of Western phonetic orthography and the continuity of speech. However, the words 'New English' have the appearance of a Chinese character without the vividness or the feature of imitating nature. These words are invented without any relevance to the Six Principles. *New English* is a hybrid, the result of mixing different cultures. In this vein, perhaps, *New English* can be called 'Chinglish' or 'Engnese'.

These two series of works interestingly contrast in a nuanced and paradoxical way: the East and the West meet, confront, and negotiate with each other. The pseudo-characters of the *Tianshu* are like normal Chinese written words at first glance, but they are meaningless when carefully read. In contrast, the words of *New English Calligraphy Classroom* look like unreadable pseudo-characters but are actually comprehensible and intelligible to attentive viewers. The contrast between these two installations forces the viewer to question what sense means, what sign means, and, more deeply, what meaning means.

Another work by Xu Bing is worth notice. *Guidaqiang* or *Ghosts Pounding the Wall* (1990–1991) consists of 29 rubbings of a section of the Great Wall by means of a traditional Chinese method of print-making. The title of the installation comes from a critique of the earlier *Tianshu*. In Chinese, 'guidaqiang' or 'ghosts pounding the wall' is a folk phrase used to criticise ridiculous or stupid things, people, or objects that no one can understand. The work *Tianshu* is criticised as absurd, stupid, or senseless as the idea of ghosts pounding the wall. Xu Bing did not respond to this criticism but instead appropriated the phrase to name his next work. This naming signifies two ironic rebellions and reversals: by naming his new work *Guidaqiang*, the artist turns an attack into approval. The confrontation is reversed into an encounter. The opposition becomes a negotiation. A dialogue without words occurs between different sides. This is

Post-graphocentric education 143

a rebellion as well as a resistance, but it is neither a fight nor a conflict. It is an ironic gesture with widely open hands.

The second rebellion is more relevant to language. As mentioned at the beginning of the book, the origin of the Chinese character comes from the legend about Cang Jié. As related in the literature, ghosts 'wailed in the night' after written characters were invented by the legendary figure Cang Jié. Ghosts are worried about being impeached or reprimanded by the written records. They fear losing the power of controlling the universe's secrets. It seems that the power of the written word is stronger than that of supernatural spectres. The interesting and revealing point is that written words are powerful enough to supersede the ghosts of the universe. Are the pseudo-characters 'real' words if they are meaningless? Do they have similarly strong power? And how about the New English words written in the shapes of Chinese character squares? Are they similarly powerful? According to Wu Hung (1994), Xu Bing seems to sympathise with the wailing ghosts: 'Ever since human beings created those picture-like yet non-pictorial words, they began a process during which they have become increasingly complex, increasingly exhausted, and increasingly perplexed by their own writings' (Xu Bing, cited from Wu, 1994, p. 414). Xu Bing does not give a straightforward answer to my questions above, but he acknowledges that the creation of rebellious arts elicits more and more confusion, bewilderment, and fatigue. Overall, XuBing's artistic creation interestingly and dialectically embodies both graphocentrism and post-graphocentrism, and thus enlightens our understanding of the paradoxical daos – full of inexhaustible possibilities.

Let us turn to Xu Bing's Landscript works which demonstrate the proximity of language and nature. In these works, 'the Chinese character for "tree", 木, is used to depict a tree, the character for "mountain", 山, to depict a mountain, the character for "water", 水, to depict water, and so on.' (Vainker, 2013, p. 116). This way of painting – and writing – reflects the historical pictographic belief in the origin of word – by imitating nature. Language and nature are corresponding to each other. Apart from the Landscript works, Xu Bing's installation *The Living Word* or *The Bird Has Flown* displays spectacular dynamics of the word. This piece of work is composed of hundreds of pieces of coloured acrylic sheeting in different forms of Chinese character for bird. As the artist explained as follows: 'the dictionary definition of niao (bird) is written on the gallery floor in the simplified text created by Mao. The niao characters then break away from the confines of the literal definition and take flight through the installation space. As they rise into the air, the characters gradually change from the simplified text to standardized Chinese text and finally to the ancient Chinese pictograph for "bird". The characters are rainbow coloured to create a magical, fairy-tale quality'(Xu, 2011). Weintraub also provide a very pertinent and vivid deccription about *The Living Word*: 'Viewing the work from bottom to top, the acrylic forms slowly metamorphose from the modern Chinese character for "bird" at ground level to more traditional calligraphic forms of the

144 Post-graphocentric education

character, and finally take the shape of ancient pictograms based on natural bird forms at the top of the piece' (Weintraub, 2011, August). It is mesmerising to see the becoming of the flatly displayed characters into three-dimensional and physical objects with thickness and mass. It seems that the pictographic quality and the movement of the rising word 鳥 for 'bird' bring life to the deadly written word.

For me, Xu Bing's art embodies both graphocentrism and post-graphocentrism, the Dao and daos. One the one hand, Xu Bing (2013, p. 124) says: 'For in fact, the nature, the thinking, the way of looking at things, the aesthetic appreciation, artistic core and even the physiological rhythm – indeed almost every aspect of the Chinese people – is connected with the "pattern of Chinese characters"'. Overall, why China becomes what it is today has to do with the written word. In the artist's mind, deep in Chinese culture is a strong attachment and obsession to the written word, which in turn nourishes his creation. There is a graphocentric thought in Xu Bing's art and view. On the other hand, the artist's work is pregnant with post-graphocentric meanings. The creative and novel use of the written word challenges and questions the established understanding of language and symbol. In so doing the spirit of post-graphocentrism and the implied unlimited daos are enfolded.

Xu Bing's work manifests the deconstructive sense of daos. His arts can be seen as one of the fructifications of post-graphocentric culture in the ongoing process of construction, deconstruction, and reconstruction of daos. There have been studies about the comparison between Xu Bing and Derrida. Xu Bing (2014) admits his ignorance about Derrida's theory, even though they were invited in the same event in 2000. It seems that it was the only occasion that they met each other in person. There was a rare trace of interpersonal communication. Years later, Xu Bing's assistant handed him an envelope on which was written 'To Mr. Jacques Derrida'. At that time, Derrida already passed away. The envelope had never been sent out.

Whether there was interaction or an interpersonal relationship between Derrida and Xu Bing is not important to me. What matters is the consonance between Derrida's deconstruction and Xu Bing's art. A certain degree of vicariousness occurs between them, or between their philosophies. Xu Bing's view of art is deconstructive, even though he insists that he is very much [Chinese] culture bound and that he knows very little about Derrida. He states,

> I love using the written word to create works of art. My creations are words but yet simultaneously are not words. They look familiar, but you cannot name them. They have been disguised to look different internally and externally.
>
> (Xu, 2001, p. 18)

By turning the familiar into the strange, Xu Bing creates nonsense writing. And yet, the nonsense writing means more than the character appears. That is why

Post-graphocentric education 145

it incites and fuels ceaseless debates. Does it challenge the meaning of writing? Does it question the nature of the Chinese character as a visual sign, or the nature of language? Is the ridiculing of fake words or new words a criticism of tradition? Does the art mock the authority – in what aspect, or in every aspect? Is it a tribute to or an epitaph of the written character? We are hesitant to give a definite answer. It is not either/or, nor both. However, it is fascinating that the works of Xu Bing embody the notion of Derrida's *différance* in the following sense that

> Already we have had to delineate *that différance is not*, does not exist, is not a present-being (*on*), in any form; and we will be led to delineate also everything *that* it *is not*, that is, *everything;* and consequently that it has neither existence nor essence.
>
> (Derrida, 1982, p. 6)

Xu Bing's work vividly embodies the idea of *différance*. His words strike us powerfully on the enigmatic interplay of dao and deconstruction.

> These masked 'words', like computer viruses, have a purpose in the human mind. In the space between understanding and misunderstanding, as concepts are flipped, customary modes of thought are thrown into confusion, creating obstacles to connections and expression. It is by opening up these unopened spaces that we may revisit the origins of thought and comprehension.
>
> (Xu, 2001, pp. 18–19)

Xu Bing uses the very powerful and vivid analogy of a virus to describe the pseudo-words. Interestingly, the etymology of the word 'virus' originates from Latin *virus*, meaning 'poison, sap of plants, slimy liquid, a potent juice' (Harper, n.d.a). The virus is poisonous and noxious. The fake word, like the virus, infects, vexes, torments the mind, and thereby puzzles, ruins, corrupts, and undoes the accustomed and purported structures. Likewise, Derrida plays with words in a similar fashion when he coins the new vocabulary of *différance* (1982) or writes the words of 'writing', 'encasing', and 'screening' into 'wriTing', 'encAsIng', and 'screeNing' (1981b, p. 344). The playing with words is to unsettle the discourses that have been 'pervaded by the metaphysics of presence, the speculative attribution of a substance, or a subject to every possible concept' (Butler, 2016, p. xvi). Yet the 'pervasion' is also a sort of infection that goes unnoticed until a different virus invades the mind of the host to agitate, decompose, and deconstruct the established institution. Both Derrida and Xu Bing display the paradoxical dynamics of daos that disrupt the order and hierarchy of speaking and writing. The paradoxical daos and deconstruction seduce us to reconsider the process of the interaction, confrontation, and collusion between phonic and graphic elements that form speech and writing.

146 Post-graphocentric education

Crossing the boundaries of dao and deconstruction

Language has long been believed a distinctive part of being human. For phonocentrists, spoken language is the key. For graphocentrists, it is the written language. I suggest that different cultures have different inclinations. For example, phonocentrism dominates the West, while graphocentrism governs the East. Even so, the phonocentric West does not and cannot discard the idea of graphocentrism. Immanuel Kant (2003, p. 13) says, 'In the earliest records of even very civilised nations we still find a distinct taint of barbarianism, and yet how much culture is presupposed for mere writing to be possible! So much so that, with regard to civilised people, the beginning of the art of writing might be called the beginning of the world'. Although Kant may not mean non-phonetic writing, his view implies the recognition of writing as a visual sign to a certain degree. In the East, the power of visual words to capture meaning is noticeable and strong. The artist Xu Bing (Erickson, 2001, p. 59) claims that the written language 'particularly but not exclusively' is 'the key to being human, and . . . the crux of human culture'. Although he repeats that he is bound to the culture of writing, his art displays sharp criticism and severe questioning of this relationship. Perhaps he does not intend to do so, but the incorporation of dao or daos in the arts, is not always under control of the artist.

There are ongoing dialectics, paradoxes, and dichotomies (e.g., human/non-human, culture/nature, civilisation/barbarianism, male/female, spoken word/written word, sense/nonsense, phonocentrism/graphocentrism, East/West, Logos/Dao, Logos/deconstruction, Dao/dao, solemn/playful, tragedy/comics, etc.) that have been imposed upon us from every facet of life. But these opposites, which are supposed to be exclusive from each other, indeed penetrate, permeate, and affect each other in the subtlest ways. Seriousness can be found in frivolous events, or ridiculousness in sombre occasions. This is where the unbearable lightness or the evanesent graveness lies. The Zen or Chan didactics of koàn (公案), the Daoist wú-practices, and the strategy of deconstruction are intended to reveal the paradoxical meanings of human understanding and experiences by disengaging what we are attached to, by estranging what we are familiar with, by demystifying what has been divinised, by regarding what has been despised, by condemning what has been extolled, by letting go of what has been firmly held. The activity of daos or deconstruction is to create, to produce, to perform, to manifest, to play – to act playfully – différance through the continuously changing relationships among language, speech, and writing. The movement of play of différance is spontaneously beyond control, calculation, and limits, even though through human history is rife with attempts and conflicts of controlling, domination, and exploitation. Play is an unimpeded and free movement. Play as an act could be part of human nature, but – it varies according to different cultures (Huzinga, 1949). Human beings can be understood as Human the Player (*Homo Ludens*). For me, what deserves more attention is the

Post-graphocentric education 147

relationship between play and education. The word *school*, from Latin *schola*, means 'intermission of work, leisure for learning'. Likewise, the Greek *skhole* means 'spare time, leisure, rest ease; idleness; that in which leisure is employed' but also 'a place for lectures, school' (Harper, n.d.b). *Education*, from the Latin *educates*, means 'bring up, rear, educate' (Harper, n.d.c). A school as a place of leisure is also a place of bringing up and rearing. Education takes time. The concepts of education, school, and play, which share the essential meaning of leisure, are closely related in the sense that education is undertaken through play and, conversely, play is engaged in education. The dao-deconstructive pedagogy, or the Zen/Chán koàn, embodies artistic playfulness. A Zen/Chán teacher uses 'a blow or shout or even a few quiet words' to 'startle students into letting go' (Loy, 2007, p. 118). Yet this does not suggest that a blow or shout or even a few quiet words must be the method of teaching about Zen/Chán. Actually, there are no specifically regulated or standard steps or procedures of teaching about or playing dao-deconstruction. Anything that is normalised, standardised, or canonised needs to be shaken or questioned, challenged or broken. Unexpectedness is central to dao-deconstruction. This is where education occurs through play, or where play takes place in education.

Notes

1　三十輻, 共一轂, 當其無, 有車之用。埏埴以為器, 當其無, 有器之用。鑿戶牖以為室, 當其無, 有室之用。故有之以為利, 無之以為用。(道德經11章)
2　方可方不可, 方不可方可; 因是因非, 因非因是。是以聖人不由, 而照之于天。(莊子內篇齊物論2:5)
3　君君, 臣臣, 父父, 子子。(論語顏淵, 12:11)
4　惡! 惡可?大多政, 法而不諜, 雖固, 亦无罪。雖然, 止是耳矣, 夫胡可以及化! 猶師心者也。(莊子內篇人間世1.4.1)
5　若一志, 无聽之以耳而聽之以心, 无聽之以心而聽之以氣。聽止於耳, 心止於符。氣也者, 虛而待物者也。唯道集虛。虛者, 心齋也。(莊子內篇人間世1.4.2)
6　顏回曰: 「回益矣。」仲尼曰: 「何謂也?」曰: 「回忘仁義矣。」曰: 「可矣, 猶未也。」他日復見, 曰: 「回益矣。」曰: 「何謂也?」曰: 「回忘禮樂矣。」曰: 「可矣, 猶未也。」他日復見, 曰: 「回益矣。」曰: 「何謂也?」曰: 「回坐忘矣。」仲尼蹴然曰: 「何謂坐忘?」顏回曰: 「墮肢體, 黜聰明, 離形去知, 同於大通, 此謂坐忘。」仲尼曰: 「同則無好也, 化則無常也。而果其賢乎! 丘也請從而後也。」(莊子內篇大宗師, 1.6.9)
7　孟子見梁惠王。王曰: 「叟不遠千里而來, 亦將有以利吾國乎?」孟子對曰:「王何必曰利?亦有仁義而已矣。...」(孟子梁惠王上, 1A.1)
8　子路問成人。子曰: 「若臧武仲之知, 公綽之不欲, 卞莊子之勇, 冉求之藝, 文之以禮樂, 亦可以為成人矣。」(論語憲問, 14:12)
9　天降下民, 作之君, 作之師。(孟子梁惠王下, 1B.10)
10　至人無己, 神人無功, 聖人無名。(莊子內篇逍遙遊, 1.1.3)
11　Some scholars such as Burton Watson (1968) and James Legge (1985) translate 聖人無名 as 'the sage has no fame'. This translation does have good consistency and coherency with the former two kinds of *wú* in devaluing the worldly fame and fortunes but it could ignore the linguistic or semiotic aspect. The translation of *míng* as fame puts the focus on the social aspect.
12　若聖與仁, 則吾豈敢?抑為之不厭, 誨人不倦, 則可謂云爾已矣。(論語述而, 7:34)

13 其為人也, 發憤忘食, 樂以忘憂, 不知老之將至云爾。(論語述而, 7:19)
14 父書肇於自然, 自然既立, 陰陽生焉；陰陽既生, 形勢出矣。藏頭護尾, 力在其中, 下筆用力, 肌膚之麗。(蔡邕, 九勢)
15 常欲筆鋒在畫中, 則左右皆無病矣。(姜夔, 續書譜用筆) (Hua, 1997, p. 359) 用筆之勢, 特須藏鋒, 鋒若不藏, 字則有病。(徐浩, 論書) (Hua, 1997, p. 252)
16 夫臨文用筆之法...或有藏鋒者大, 側筆者乏。(王羲之, 筆勢論觀形章第八) (Hua, 1997, p. 31)
17 筆軟則奇怪生焉。(蔡邕, 九勢) (Hua, 1997, p. 6)
18 書者, 散也。欲書先散懷抱, 任情恣性, 然後書之。若迫於事, 雖中山兔毫, 不能佳也。(蔡邕, 書論) (Hua, 1997, p. 5)
19 若坐若行, 若飛若動, 若往若來, 若臥若起, 若愁若喜, 若蟲食木葉, 若利劍長戈, 若強弓硬矢, 若水火, 若雲霧, 若日月。(蔡邕, 書論) (Hua, 1997, p. 6)
20 若一志, 无聽之以耳而聽之以心, 无聽之以心而聽之以氣。聽止於耳, 心止於符。氣也者, 虛而待物者也。唯道集虛。虛者, 心齋也。(莊子, 人間世, 4:2)
21 方今之時, 臣以神遇, 而不以目視, 官知止而神欲行。依乎天理, 批大郤, 導大窾, 因其固然。技經肯綮之未嘗, 而況大軱乎！良庖歲更刀, 割也；族庖月更刀, 折也。今臣之刀十九年矣, 所解數千牛矣, 而刀刃若新發於硎。(莊子, 養生主, 3:2)

References

Ames, T. R., & Hall, L. D. (2003). *Daodejing: Making this life significant*. New York, NY: Ballantine.

Burik, S. (2010). Thinking on the edge: Heidegger, Derrida, and the Daoist gateway (Men 門), *Philosophy East & West*, *60*(4), 499–516.

Butler, J. (2016). Introduction. In J. Derrida (Ed.), *Of grammatology*, newly revised translation (pp. vii–xxiv). Baltimore, MD: Johns Hopkins University Press.

Derrida, J. (1976). *Of grammatology*. Trans. G. C. Spivak. Baltimore, MD: John Hopkins University Press.

Derrida, J. (1981a). *Positions*. Chicago, IL: University of Chicago Press.

Derrida, J. (1981b). *Dissemination*. Chicago, IL: University of Chicago Press.

Derrida, J. (1982). *Margins of philosophy*. Chicago, IL: University of Chicago Press.

Derrida, J. (2016). *Of grammatology*. Trans. G. C. Spivak. Introduction by J. Butler. Baltimore, MD: John Hopkins University Press.

Erickson, B. (2001). *The art of Xu Bing: words without meaning, meaning without words*. Washington, DC: Smithsonian Institution.

Fenollosa, E., & Pound, E. (1936). *The Chinese written character as a medium for poetry*. San Francisco, CA: City Lights Books.

Goldberg, S. J. (2004). The primacy of gesture: phenomenology and the art of Chinese calligraphy. In A.-T. Tymieniecka (Ed.), *Analecta Husserliana LXXXI* (pp. 175–186). London, UK: Springer.

Hall, L. D., & Ames, T. R. (1998). *Thinking from the Han: Self, truth, and transcendence in Chinese and Western culture*. Albany, NY: State University of New York Press.

Harper, D. (n.d.a). Virus. *The online etymology dictionary*. Retrieved August 20, 2016, from www.etymonline.com/index.php?allowed_in_frame=0&search=virus

Harper, D. (n.d.c). Educate. *The online etymology dictionary*. Retrieved August 26, 2016, from www.etymonline.com/index.php?term=educate

Harper, D. (n.d.b). School. *The online etymology dictionary*. Retrieved August 26, 2016, from www.etymonline.com/index.php?allowed_in_frame=0&search=school

Ho, W. P. (2005). The Chinese approach to learning: The paradigmatic case of Chinese calligraphy. In C. Ota & C. Erriker (Eds.), *Spiritual education: Literary, empirical, and pedagogical approaches* (pp. 154–174). Brighten, UK: Sussex Academic Press.

Hua, C-R. 華正人(1997). *Selected essays on calligraphy over history, vol. 1–2*歷代書法論文選上下冊. Taipei: Hua Cheng臺北: 華正書局.

Hung, R. (2015). To be as not to be: In search of an alternative humanism in the light of early Daoism and deconstruction. *Journal of Philosophy of Education, 49*(3), 418–434.

Huzinga, J. (1949). *Homo Ludens: A study of the play-element in culture*. London, UK: Routledge & Kegan Paul.

Kant, I. (2003). *On education*. Trans. A. Churton. Mineola, NY: Dover Publications.

Legge, J. (1861a). *The chinese classics, volume 1: The analects*. Retrieved March 15, 2017, from http://ctext.org/analects

Legge, J. (1891). *The writings of Chuang Tzu*. Retrieved March 15, 2017, from http://ctext.org/zhuangzi

Legge, J. (Trans.). (1985). *The works of Mencius*, Clarendon. Retrieved August 27, 2015, from Donald Sturgeon (Ed.), *Chinese text project*. http://ctext.org/mengzi

Liu, C. 劉鑒毅 (2010). A study on "Yung Pi" of the calligraphy theory in the late Qing dynasty晚清書學用筆論. *Thesis of Department of Painting and Calligraphy*書畫藝術學刊, *8*, 83–124.

Liu, J. J.Y. (1962). *The art of Chinese poetry*. Chicago, IL: Chicago University Press.

Loy, D. R. (2007). Lacking ethics. In Y. Wang (Ed.), *Deconstruction and the ethical in Asian thought* (pp. 113–128). London, UK: Routledge.

Murck, A., & Fong, W. (1991). *Words and images: Chinese poetry, calligraphy, and painting*. New York, NY: Metropolitan Museum of Art.

Nelson, E. S. (2009). Responding with *Dao*: Early Daoist ethics and the environment, *Philosophy East and West, 59*(3), 294–316.

Stalling, J. (2010). *Poetics of emptiness: Transformations of Asian thought in American poetry*. New York, NY: Fordham University Press.

Vainker, S. J. (2013). Landscript. In S. J. Vainker (Ed.), *Landscape/Landscript: Nature as language in the art of Xu Bing* (pp. 116–119). Oxford, UK: Ashmolean Museum of Art and Archaeology.

Watson, B. (Trans.). (1968). *Zhuang Tzu: Basic writings*. New York, NY: Columbia University Press.

Watson, B. (Trans.). (1970). *The complete works of Chuang-Tzu*. New York, NY: Columbia University Press.

Weintraub, M. (2011, August). *On view now | back to the future: Xu Bing, "The Living Word," and the legacy of 1989*. Retrieved March 29, 2017, from http://magazine.art21.org/2011/08/04/on-view-now-back-to-the-future-xu-bing-the-living-word-and-the-legacy-of-1989/#.WJfpzPIYMRc

Wu, H. (1994). A "Ghost Rebellion": Notes on Xu Bing's "Nonsense Writing" and other works. *Public Culture, 6*, 411–411.

Wu, J. S. (1969). Chinese language and Chinese thought. *Philosophy East and West, 19*(4), 423–434.

Xu, B. (2001). The living word. Trans. A. L. Huss. In B. Erickson (Ed.), *The art of Xu Bing: Words without meaning, meaning without words* (pp. 13–20). Washington, DC: Smithsonian Institution.

Xu, B. (2011, July). *Xu Bing: The living word*. July 19 through October 2, 2011. Retrieved from www.themorgan.org/exhibitions/xu-bing?id=54

Xu, B. (2013). Landscript series. In S. J. Vainker (Ed.), *Landscape/landscript: Nature as language in the art of Xu Bing* (pp. 120–129). Oxford, UK: Ashmolean Museum of Art and Archaeology.

Xu, B.徐冰 (2014). To Mr. Jacques Derrida. TO：雅克•德里達先生. *Today Literary Magazine*今天文學雜誌, *Summer, No. 105*, 48–51. Translation by Samuel Moore. Retrieved March 15, 2017, from www.xubing.com/index.php/site/texts

Yen, Y. (2005). *Calligraphy and power in contemporary Chinese society*. New York, NY: Routledge Curzon.

Epilogue
Playing the word

> Think of exclamations alone, with their completely different functions.
> Water!
> Away!
> Ow!
> Help!
> Fine!
> No!
> Are you inclined still to call these words 'names of objects'?
> —(Wittgenstein, 1958, §27)

Words matter. We human beings, in East or West, are enchanted, haunted, and made anxious by words, be they spoken or written. The sixteenth-century Chinese fantasy novel *Journey to the West* (Wu, 1993) tells a story about a Buddhist pilgrimage made by a monk named Xúan Zàng (also known as Táng Monk and Tripitaka) and his three disciples. It is a long and dangerous journey, for many demons, supernatural creatures, and animal spirits come attack them and hunt the monk. The adventure is full of exciting fights. The fighters employ the magical techniques of Dao, sometimes by using magical instruments. The 'Purple Gold Red Gourd' (紫金紅葫蘆) and the 'Jade Vase' (淨玉瓶) are mentioned in the thirty-fifth chapter. When one holds either of the instruments and calls the name of the enemy, the enemy who responds will be sucked in. Then the container is sealed with the tape bearing the words 'As Quickly Commanded by the Old Master' (太上老君急急如律令奉敕). In one and three-quarter hours, the captured enemy will be reduced to pus. How powerful the word is! In this anecdote, the word appears in divergent forms, spoken and written. The magical power of the word is bilateral. The spoken word first shows its power in calling and answering, in naming and responding. Speech communicates between the one who utters and the one who receives and responds to the utterance by voice. The next magic happens when the tape with written words is used to seal the vase or jar. The written word, silently but powerfully, changes and ends the form of life. The acquisition of words, the ability to use words, is

152 Epilogue

a privilege. Central to the anecdote is the implication that humans experience deep-seated uneasiness and anxiety, respect and desire, with respect to the word.

Similar angst is found in both East and West. *Inkheart*, authored by Cornelia Funke, is a popular teen fantasy novel published in 2003. The story chronicles the adventure of Maggie and her father, Mortimer. Both father and daughter have a special gift: the magical power to 'read' characters out of stories. When they read stories aloud, the fictitious characters come out of the books and become real persons in the flesh. The voice gives life to the written word. From the literary tradition, it is the effect of Western phonocentrism, more or less. And yet the voice alone does not work. When Maggie and Mortimer try to change the plot, they cannot only 'say' it. They must read the written words. Again, the spoken and written words collaborate to change the world. In Western language, it seems that phonocentrism intertwined with the metaphysics of presence dominate thinking, and graphic elements indeed lurk and operate here. In the East, the written word appears to dominate, though underlying phonetic elements have an effect.

We trust words, and yet we cast doubt upon them lest we be subjugated by them. The spoken word or the written word, regardless of the enchantment, should be always be treated with strict vigilance. The mistrust of language is not a rejection of language but a gesture of carefulness and watchfulness about language. The spoken or written word should not be consecrated, reified, or worshiped. On the contrary, the word is to be questioned and interrogated, scrutinised and examined. This is what we discover in both Western deconstruction and Eastern artful daos:

> Whether we take the signified or the signifier, language has neither ideas nor sounds that existed before the linguistic system, but only conceptual and phonic differences that have issued from the system.
>
> (Derrida, 1982, p. 11)

There is no independent signifier. A sign, whether audio or visual, is situated and contextualised in a system, in a language. It is able to signify because it is related to and interplays with other signs. Echoing Derrida in the West and the modern (or post-modern) Xu Bing in the East, the ancient Zhuangzi has a similar view that there is neither absolute right nor absolute wrong. So-called frivolous knowledge is as important as so-called serious knowledge. Words of influential people such as the sage kings are of no greater value than the words of commoners such as porters and pedlars. Implied in this scepticism or relativism is a notion that the rendering of a comparison or a judgement is based on the indispensability of at least two different entities, terms, concepts, names, or words. A comparison needs at least two entities that are not identical, and two terms that can be used to refer to the entities. To compare A with B means to relate A to B, to consider the similarities and differences between them. Zhuangzi reveals the triviality and insignificance of making comparisons between world affairs, as well as the subtle and profound interrelationship and interdependence of entities in epistemological, ethical, and metaphysical aspects.

The mistrust in and continuous re-evaluation of language in Derrida and Daoist philosophers remind us of the concept of language-game. Through the concept of language-game, Wittgenstein questions the traditional metaphysical belief in the correspondence between language and reality. We have discovered a similar critique of deconstruction and daos. New vocabularies, new terms, neologism (or neographism), pseudo-characters – whether named or invented by Derrida, Xu Bing, or others – are various modes of playing the word. The relationship between names and objects, between the signifier and the signified, is never stabilised or secured. On the contrary, it is in an ongoing process of becoming. Life is a game of playing of, in, by, and with words. It is possible to play words in new ways, but these new ways of playing and new rules of the game involve questioning and criticising the status quo, including everything that has been approved or disapproved, esteemed or marginalised, and every criterion used to test or evaluate the world. We venture to write and speak but need to be brave to cast doubt upon, resist, overturn, and rebel against the word that we have written down and spoken out. Play words.

References

Derrida, J. (1982). *Margins of philosophy*. Chicago, IL: University of Chicago Press.

Funke, C. (2003). *Inkheart*. Trans. A. Bell. New York, NY: Scholastic.

Wittgenstein, L. (1958). *Philosophical investigation*. Oxford, UK: Basil Blackwell.

Wu, Cheng'en (1993). *Journey to the West*. Trans. W. J. F. Jenner. Beijing, China: Foreign Languages Press.

Index

Abel-Rémusat, Jean Pierre 101
active organs, practice 91–92
Addiss, Stephen 113
aesthetic morality 61–66
aesthetics, morality (intertwining) 61–66
Ames, Roger T. 117
An, Liu 17
Analects 19–21, 24, 29–30; emphasis
    108–109; jūnzi description 45; texts,
    requirement 59; virtue, articulation 64
Ancient Dao 108, 114
Anecdote of Shi the Lion-Eater, The 139
Annals of Chín Shi Huáng 47
anonymity, assurance 58
Anshíh, Wang 59
appellation: emergence 32; legitimation 29;
    rectification, comparison 33
Aristotle 3, 91
artistic activity 67
arts, usage 138–145
Asking About Shén 25, 63
As Quickly Commanded by the Old
    Master 151
associative compounds 96

Bacon, Francis 1
ba-gū-wén (eight-legged essay) 59
benevolence 63
benevolence (love) 70
benevolence (rén), dignity 72
bias 2–7
bì huì (tabooing) 47
Bing, Xu 141–146, 152
bird-call 98
blank-retention 136–137
Boltz, William G. 13, 105
Book from the Sky (Bing) 141

Book of Poetry 48
Bryan, Patrick 113

calligrapher: moral emblem 61–62;
    self-development 53
calligraphic works, attitudes/postures 136
calligraphy: aesthetic quality 62; codes
    46–47, 65, 82; constitution 68; depiction
    63; generation 135; learning 50;
    pedagogical code 46–47; practice 51,
    66, 68; utensils, invention 65; writing,
    discipline 46
cángfeng (edge-hidden) 135–136
Cang Jié 143
capitalisation, economic function 6
cardinal heart-minds 79
Carving the Literary Dragon 101
cave allegory 13
Centre ruler (Chaos) 123
cháng (long) 97
chángdao 111
cháng dao, translation 113
cháng (constant), translation 113
Chaos 123
chaotic natures 122–123
*Character Book Seeking for Official
    Emoluments* 55–56
character, calligraphic forms 143–144
characters, invention 94, 99
Chartier, Roger 24
chéng chéng 140
Cheng, Ju Lyū 49
chi (force) 62, 68
Chiéh, Tsang 17, 18
Chih-T'ui, Yen 21
China: hereditary nobility, absence 54; Jesuit
    studies 4

Index   155

Chín empire, states unity 81
Chinese: anti-barbarian attitude 83; characters, complication 4; characters, origin 105; folk culture, influence 114; folk tradition 38; grammar, inflection (absence) 140; graphocentric humanism, contrast 71; graphocentric tradition 38; graphocentrism 16; logocentrism 101; paradox 6–7; spiritual culture, exegeticism 92; thinkers, perspective 35; tradition, truth (origin) 103; word, visual sensibility 26; written character, vividness/concreteness 139; written system, importation 9
Chinese culture: power 69; pulses 119
Chinese language: imperfection 9–10; Western languages, quantitative differences 2; word, signification 10
Chinese prejudice 89–94; blindness 93; paradox 5, 93
Ching dynasty 48, 49, 81; criticism 63; examination system, changes 59
Chíng dynasty, written characters (usage) 96–97
Chong, Wáng 17, 37
Chŏu, Chan 65
chung (loyalty/faithfulness) 75
Chung-ying, Cheng 118
Chunqiu (Spring and Autumn Annals) 56
Chun Qiu Făn Lù 32
Chun Qiu Zŭo Zhuàn 47
civil imperial examinations, implementation 57
Classical Prose Movement (kŭ wén movement) 58
College de France 101
commonplace 119
communication, language (usage) 4
compound ideographs 96
conceptual metaphors 12–13
Confucian doctrines, Sòng dynasty inheritance 60
Confucianism: core teachings 29; Dao, orthodoxy 114; disciples 115–116; spirit 134–135
Confucian-Mohist period, positive dao period 118
Confucius 19–23; Húi, dialogue 132–133; humility 38; speech attitude 21; thinkers 29; virtue 19–20
Confucius, doctrines: insights 63–64; mastery 56–57; speech, usage 20

congenic order 115
Contra Physiognomy (Xúnzi) 31
Cook Ding, story 137–138
correcting names 29
cosmopolitanism, dreams (pursuit) 134–135
courteousness 63
Cratylus (Plato) 91
Crisp, Roger 93
"cultural" character 45
cultural shock 1

dăi 48
Dao (dao) 111–116; accordance 62; boundaries, crossing 146–147; concept 118; deconstructive sense 144; discussions 114; harmony 133–134, 137–138; logos comparison 89, 109; logos function 100–104; metaphysics 127; myriad Daos 116–123; non-Logos 111; notions 138; origin 118; orthodoxy 114; paradox 121–122; paradoxical dynamics 145; realm, reaching 138; truth 103–104; word, usage 101
Daocentrism, metaphysics 127
Dao-deconstruction 108
Daodejing 26, 93, 100, 117, 121, 129
daoful, goal 138
daofully, becoming 134–145
daoful, term (usage) 128
Daoism 20, 99; philosophy 118; principles 68; religion 114; self-deconstruction 131–132; values 45, 66
Dao-logocentrism 89
Dào, term (usage) 93–94
Dàoxúe (Dao-learning) 59; orthodoxy 60
Dao Yuan (Way's Origin, The) 114
DàXúe 115
dé (goodness) 62
death penalties 48
deconstruction 129; boundaries, crossing 146–147; concept, usage 111; proposal 109–112; seduction 145
defect 119–120
deferential desire, achievement 131
deferring, différance phase 129
delay 128
delegation 128
derivative cognates 96
Derrida, Jacques 2–8, 16, 19, 24, 80, 144; communication examination 82; différance 134; echo 152–153; Of Grammatology 3, 91; New Essays 93;

156 Index

nonphonetic scripts 97; phonocentrism/logocentrism/ethnocentrism, alliance 90; presence, terms 38; spoken language supplement 37; writing, manifestation 28

Descartes, Rene 13, 90

detour 128

dí (tribe) 83

dialectics 146

dichotomy 146; reversal 130

dièn shìh (palace examination) 57

différance 109–110, 115, 119, 122; elements 128; idea 145; notion 145; play, movement 146–147; usage 141

différends/différents 110

differ()nce 109

discontinuity 136

discourse 13

Divine Mind 93

Divine, The 119

Dong-guozi 119

dualist ideas, hierarchy 90

dual opposition 129

Duàn, Shu 68

Duke Huán 47

Duke of Wèi 22

Duke of Zhou 33, 34

Duke Zhao of Lǔ 22

Duke Zhou 47

dú zun rú shù 56

Eastern Asia, credentialism 60

Eastern Han Dynasty 25–26, 136; criticism 18; Xúan (scholar) 98

Eastern Hàn period 56–57

edge-hidden 135–136

education, meaning 128

elenchus 71–72

Ellul, Jacques 10–11

Emile (Rousseau) 91

empire naming taboo (gúo huì) 47

emptiness 128

enlightenment 12

Essai (Warburton) 24, 28

Essay on the Origin of Language, The (Rousseau) 91–92

Essays on Art (Xizaǐ) 63

ethical-ontological distinctions 90

ethical-political concerns 130–131

ethnocentrism 92; phonocentrism/logocentrism, alliance 90

European hallucination 5

external excitement, chasing 121

eye, appeal/speaking 139

fǎn 49–50

Fánwùliúxíng (All Things Are Forms in Flux) 114

Fǎnyán 63

fate, call 98

Father, Dao 108, 114

Fei, Hán 22–23

Feng, Fong 51

Fenollosa, Ernest 92, 138

filial piety 56

Five Classics 56

former kings: Dao 114; separation 79

form imitation 96

Four Treasures 64

Four Treasures of the Study 46, 51

Free and Easy Wondering (Zhuangzi) 134

fresh blood 54–55

friend, Dao 116

frivolous knowledge, importance 152–153

fructification 138

fù fù 140

Funke, Cornelia 152

Ganlu Zìshu (Character Book Seeking for Official Emoluments) 55

gentle-folk, association 76

Gernet, Jacques 8

Ghosts Pounding the Wall (Bing) 142–143

ghosts, worry 142–143

glib talk, devaluation 19–20

gong (courteousness) 75

Gongquán, Liě 49

Gongquǎn, Liǔ 63, 65

Gong, Wei Ling 20

Gong Yě Cháng 114

Gong, Zhòng 70

Gòng, Zǐ 20

good person, Dao 114

goodwill, implication 76

grammar: rules, impact 141; simplicity 140

graphic elements, phonic elements (collusion) 145

graphic forms, magnificence 135

graphic orthography 54–56

graphocentric context 100

graphocentric education 44

graphocentric ethics 61

graphocentric holism 61; impact 66–68

graphocentric worldview 35–39

graphocentrism 16, 45, 146; embodiment 144; logocentrism, relationship 94–104; paradox 89; problems, overcoming 111

grapholiteracy 81; cultivation 82

Great Being 119

Great Grand Dao 114–115, 124

Great One 117

Greco-Christian tradition, logos 104

gǔ (skeleton/bone) 75

Gǔanzi 34–35

gǔa yán (few words) 71

Gù, Ban 26, 251

Guidaqiang (Bing) 142–143

gǔo (fruit) 97

gúo huì (empire naming taboo) 47

Gúozījian 60

Hall, David L. 117

Han Dynasty 25

Hàn dynasty 56; fall 57

Hánfeizǐ 23, 28

Hànlin Academy, examinations 60

Hán Yù 58

Hào, Chéng 59

Hào, Xú 50, 135

harmonious society, description *(Analects)* 130

harmony 63

heart-mind, voice 102–103

heart of compassion/shame 72–73

Heaven, Dao 108, 117

Hegel, Georg Wilhelm Friedrich 3–4, 92–93; language perspective 9–10; metaphysics 94

Heidegger, Martin 3, 94

hénchàng 112

Héngxian (Primordial Constant) 114

hereditary nobility, absence 54

hierarchy, reversal 130–131

hieroglyphist prejudice 93

Homo Ludens (Human the Player) 146–147

hsiang-chü li-hsüan (district recommendation upon village selection) 56

Hsiéh, Liú 101–102; inconsistency, problem 103

Hu (Northern Ocean ruler) 123

Hùa 49

hùa 7

Huáng, Chín Shi 47

Hui, Xí Zì 39

Húi, Yán 132; Confucius, dialogue 132–133

hùi (kindness) 47, 75

Húinánzǐ 17–18

human behaviours, regulation 78

human culture 146

humanity, beginning 72

human specificity, spoken language basis 11

human spoken language 11

Human the Player 146–147

Humiliation of the Words, The (Ellul) 10–11

Húmíng (examinees name) 58

Húmíng (names of examinees) 58

Hung, Wu 143

Husserl, Edmund 3, 90

Idea 10

ideogram 11

ideographic language 1

ideographic radicals, usage 97

ideographic system, word representation 2

ideographs 95; simple/compound ideographs 96

iekariukedjutu (writing/translation) 6

image: capture 27; idea 27

imperfection, dualities 119–120

Imperial Academy 60

imperial civil examinations 54, 56–61; system, control 54; usage 54–61

imperial examination: passing 127–128; system, appearance 56

inalterability, characteristics 35–36

inconspicuousness, valuation 135

Inkheart (Funke) 152

internal goodwill 76

invisible/insensible 130

Ivanhoe, Philip 113

Jade Vase 151

Jéi, Cang 67

Ji, Lù 27–28

jiǎjiè 96

Jié, Cang 17, 27

Jì Fǎ 32

Jin 47

Jìn, Xian 24

Jin, Xie 49, 52

Jǐng 56

jìng (respectfulness) 76

Jín period, Nine Grade Referee system 57

Jìnshìh degree, candidate testing 59

158 Index

Jìnshìh examination 57–58; difficulty 58; focus, change 59
Jìnshìh examination, mandate 57
Jìn Xin 20
Journey to the West (Wu) 151
Judging Calligraphy (Chang) 68
jun jun 140
junzǐ 45, 62, 64, 74, 127; bearing 136; cultivation 109; Dao 108, 114; perspective 115–116; xiǎorén, comparison 63
justice, doing (impossibility) 110

kaiqiào (having holes open) 123
kana (phonogram) 11
kana (syllabic symbols) 13
kanji (ideogram) 11
kanji (ideographic symbol) 13
Kant, Immanuel 146
Key to Calligraphy, The (Cheng) 49
kingdom, sovereignty (initiation) 37
King Wŭ 33–34
knowledge, principle 78
koàn, Zen/Chan didactics 146–147
kòngsheng (tribute students) 60
Kundera, Milan 109
kŭ wén movement 58
kwan (generosity) 75
Kwéi, Jiang 49, 135–136

Landscript 143
language: impact 141; limits 121; means 131; mistrust/re-evaluation 153; paradox 103–104; perspective (Hegel) 9–10; usage, difficulty 121–122
lǎo 73
Laozi 47, 58, 100; Dao 113; Dao, notion 117; justice, doing (impossibility) 110
learning, goal 138
Legge, James 112, 116
Leibniz, Gottfried Wilhelm 92, 139
Les differents 110
Letting Be, and Exercising Forbearance 122
Leví-Strauss, Claude 5–6, 19, 44, 80
lexical-etymological clarification 94
lǐ (rites) 30, 31, 61; performing 69
lǐ (rules of propriety) 75; manifestation 75
Líang, king Hùi 133
licensing examinations 55
life practices, usage 137–138
Li Ji 77–78
Lǐ Jì (Book of Rites) 22, 32

Lǐjì (Book of Rites, The) 29–30, 56, 115
Li Lou 115
lín 49–50
linguistic metaphors 12–13
literacy, classification 80–81
literary inquisition 47
literary persecution 48
literate culture 8–9
literati-bureaucrats, selection 55
líu (to retain) 136
líubái 136
lìu shu 95, 96
Liŭtǐ 49
Living Word, The (Weintraub) 143–144
Locke, John 10
lòfeng (edge-exposure) 135
logic 94
logocentrism 92; graphocentrism, relationship 94–104; phonocentrism/ethnocentrism, alliance 90
logographic language 1
logo-graphocentrism 104
logo-phonocentrism 104; presence 92; problems, discovery 110–111; property 93
logo-phono-ethnocentrism 92, 109
logo-phono-graphocentrism 104
logos (Logos) 2–7; concept 93; Dao, comparison 89, 109; function 100–104; normalisation 116–117; translation 101; usage 89–94
Lombardo, Stanley 113
Longxi, Zhang 100
lower class, literacy 55
Lu, Ji 24
Lù, Zǐ 30, 71
Lŭ (ruler), Confucius admiration 74
Lùnhéng (Critical Essays) 17, 37
LǔshìChunqiu 34

magisterial naming taboo (xiàn huì) 47
making stripes 6
mán (southern tribe) 83
Master, Dao 108
materiality, valuation 24
meaning, conveyance (failure) 27–28
mediation, economic function 6
Mémoire sur la ve et les ouvrages de Lao-tseu (Abel-Rémusat) 101
mén (gate) 97
Mencius 19, 20, 33, 47; barbarians, doctrines 82–83; Dao, discussions 114; morality,

origin 64; rén (benevolence) 77; text requirement 59

Mèngfǔ, Zhào 52, 65; criticism 66

Men of Filial Piety and Incorruptibility, recruitment 56

Menzi 70

metaphorical diversion 3

metaphysics: Chinese version 38–39; history 3, 94

mildness 63

mind, fasting 132, 137

míng: explanation 98; function 30; name/appellation 29, 94, 98; origin 30; zì, synonym 98

mǐng (keenness) 75

ming (naming) 117

Ming dynasty 49

Míng dynasty 58; examinations, changes 59

Míng-jin examination 57–58; cancellation 59

minister, Dao 116

minister-subject, Dao 116

Ministry of the Personnel, office allocation 57

Mirror That Analyses the World, A (Wu) 141

mó 49–50

moral aesthetics 61–66

morality: innateness 64; origin 64

moral self, cultivation 53

moral situations, acquaintance 68

moral writing subject, cultivation 61

Mountain Bàodó, calligraphy practice location 52

mù (tree) 97

Mu, Chíen 54, 59–61

Mù, Xiàng 63

Mullis, Eric 67, 68

myriad Daos 116–123

Nambikwara: gifts, exchange 19; written language, absence 5

name-call 98

names: case instability 113; correction 29, 34; graph, relationship 99–100; identification 30–32; rectification 34

national-level examination 57

natural chaos 122–123

naturalness, valuation 135

natural world, phrases (usage) 67–68

Neo-Confucianism 58–59

neographism 109

New English Calligraphy Classroom (Bing) 141–142

New Essays (Derrida) 5, 93

niao (bird) 143

Nine Grade Referee system 57

no-action 120, 129

no-desire 129

no-knowledge 122–123

non-action, justification 122–123

non-coercive action 131

non-I 131

non-linguistic entities, signification 92

non-literate culture 8–9

non-phonetic expression 3

non-phonetic language 104

nonphonetic scripts 97

non-phonetic writing, criticism 92

non-self 131

nonsense writing 142

Normal Course for Rulers and Kings (Zhuangzi) 123

Northern dynasty, Nine Grade Referee system 57

Northern Ocean, ruler 123

Northern Sòng dynasty 50; literati, oeuvre 59

nothingness 128

Nourishing the Lord of Life (Zhuangzi) 137–138

objects, hierarchy 28

Occidental debasement, refutation 139

ocularcentric culture 25

ocularcentrism 12–13

Of Grammatology (Derrida) 3, 91

Olson, Hope A. 35

On Calligraphy (Shì) 63

On Drinking (Qían) 127, 131

One Dao 116–117

Ong, Walter 36–37

On Interpretation 91

On the Calligraphy of Xiao Zǐyún (Shì) 68

opposing groups, formulation 90

Outer Congeries of Sayings 28

Pagoda of Divine Relics 39

Pagoda of Respectful Words 39

paradoxes 146

paradoxical daos, seduction 145

passive organs, practice 91–92

perfection, dualities 119–120

perfect unity, maintenance 137

160 Index

personal character traits, development 53
personal favouritism, prevention 58
pervasion 145
petty man (little man), translation 63
Phaedrus (Plato) 36–37, 91
phallagocentrism 92
phonetic compounds (production), ideographic radicals (usage) 97
phonetic expression, derivative 3
phonetic language 4; societies 1
phonetic-semantic compounds 96; making 99–100
phonetic system 2
phonetic writing, metaphysics 92
phonic elements, graphic elements (collusion) 145
phonocentrism 3
phonocentrism, logocentrism/ ethnocentrism (alliance) 90
phono-logocentrism, implication 4
physicality, attention 22, 24
physical likeness, idea 27
pictographs 95; form imitation 96
pingcháng 112
Plato 3, 36–37, 72, 90, 113–114; cave allegory 13; metaphysics 94
polyphonic use 97
polysemia 110
polysemic use 97
pó-shìh 56
Post, Emily 76
post-graphocentric approach 28
post-graphocentric culture, fructifications 144
post-graphocentric daos, examination 138
post-graphocentric education 127
post-graphocentric meanings 144
post-graphocentric thrust 124; momentum 128
post-graphocentrism 108; embodiment 144; problems, overcoming 111
postponement 128
Pound, Ezra 138
power, mechanism 82
presence: form 6; metaphysics, Chinese version 38–39
pre-Socratic Greeks 3
Prince Chǔ Yúan 26
propriety, rules 78
purity 63
Purple Gold Red Gourd 151

Q, Ah 82, 83
Qían, Táo 127, 128, 131
Qín (imperial dynasty) 55
Quesnay, François 54
Qu Li 78

ratio, meaning 99
realistic depiction 97
rebus characters 96
rebus use 97
Recluse Poet 128
Record of Famous Paintings of the History, A (Chang) 18
rectification, appellation (comparison) 33
rectifying names 29
referral 128
rén (benevolence) 69–73; concept 70; manifestation 76; virtue 76
rén, deficiency 19–20
Rénzong (emperor) 65
reprieve 128
resemblance, idea 27
reserving 128
Rites of Zhou 62
róng (southern tribe) 83
Rousseau, Jean Jacques 3, 90–92
Royal Society 4
rú (Confucian literati) 45–46, 131
ruler, Dao 116
Rú scholars, principles/learning 31
Ryden, Edmund 113

sages naming taboo (shèn huì) 47
Saussure, Ferdinand de 2
school, etymology 147
science: concept 3, 94; scientificity 3
Scribe's Records 55
self: cultivation 53; deconstruction 131–132
self-consciousness, presence 100
self-cultivation, process 115, 131
self-deconstruction 131
self-realisation/self-fulfillment, dependence 74
serious knowledge 152–153
Seventh Letter (Plato) 91, 113
Shan, Fù 65
shàng (up) 97
Shang Dynasty 33
Shàng Shu (Book of Documents) 103
shen (body) 53
Shèn, Xǔ 12, 23, 37, 99
shèn huì (sages naming taboo) 47

Index 161

Shénzong of Sòng, reign 59
shì 75
Shih (Book of Poetry) 56
shìh (aristocrats) 45–46
shìh zì zhĕ 11
Shūjì 47
Shíjì (Scribe's Records) 55
Shì, Su 50, 52, 63; calligraphy statement 65
Shu (Book of Documents) 56
shu (script) 99
Shu (Southern Ocean ruler) 123
Shu, Dŏn Zhòng 32
Shu, Hàn 26
shu, usage 48
shudào (Dao of writing) 46
Shu Er 134–135
shufă (calligraphy writing) 46
Shùn 33; Dao 108, 114
Shuowén 69–70, 73, 96
ShuowénJiĕzì 37
Shuo wén jiĕ zì 95–96
Shuowén Jiĕzì (Chinese character dictionary) 7, 12, 17, 23, 98, 111
shūwén 27–28
sign-function 6
signification 10
signifiers, impact 3–4
si huì (private naming taboo) 47
simple character, usage 96–97
simple ideographs 96
sinographs, usage 82
Six Categories of Scribal Acts 96
Six Principles 142
social hierarchy, deconstruction 133
social order, grounding 130
social practices, existence 118
Society for Cherishing Written Characters 39
Socrates 37; method 72
Sòng dynasty 47; fairness, importance 59; imperial examinations 58; imperial examinations, differences 59
Southern dynasty, Nine Grade Referee system 57
Southern Ocean ruler 123
Southern Sòng 49
spacing 110
speech: dismissal 17; embodiment 102–103; insignificance 20; logos, usage 89–94; negative attitudes (Confucius) 21
spiritual Beings, offerings 77

spoken language: dependence 102–103; human specificity basis 11; writing process, conversion 8
spoken word, usage 1
Spring/War period 47
Ssu-yŭ, Tèng 21
State Wei 132
subjectification 127–128, 130; process, deconstruction 129
Suí dynasty 54, 81; imperial examination system, appearance 56
Súi dynasty 45; civil imperial examination implementation 57; rise 57
Suírénshi (Flinter) 33
Sunqían, Wáng 50
Sŭoyùan (locking of examination halls) 58
Supreme Master 133

tabooing (bì huì) 47
Tàiyishengshŭi (Great One Birthed Water, The) 114
Taizong, Tang 52
Tàizong, Táng 67–68
Tang (emperor) 33
Tang Dynasty 17
Táng dynasty 68
Táng dynasty, examinations 55–58; differences 59
Táng Monk 151
Táng ZhíYán (tales) 58
Táng ZhíYán (tales) 58
Tao 101
Tao Te Ching 71
Tàzŭ (emperor) 60
temporisation/temporalisation 110
Ténglù (transcription) 58
Teng Wen Gong 114–116
Téng Wén Gong l' 33
terminology, correction 34
Teuth, myth 91
texts, search 16
Thamus, praise 36–37
Theuth, Thamus praise 36–37
thinking: Chinese approach 12–13; education, spoken/written word (usage) 1
Thirteen Classics 74
thought-pictures 139
Three Kingdoms 45
tĭ (body) 75
Tianshu (Bing) 141–143
time, becoming-space 110
Tín, Shèn Ji 39

162 Index

Tín, Xí Zì 39
Ting, Chá Sì 48
tíng shìh (court examination) 57
to be void 128
to be without 128
Tractatus Logico-Philosophicus (Wittgenstein) 121
treacherous doctrine 31
tribute students 60
Tripitaka 151
Tristes Tropiques (Leví-Strauss) 19, 44
true human, humaneness 79–80
True King institutes 31–32
trustworthiness 63
truth 116; origin 103–104; speaking 112
truthfulness, corruption 18
tsèwèn (bamboo slips) 56–57
tsèwèn (questioning by bamboo slips) 56
Tzŭ, Lăo 71

Ultimate Reality 116–117
Unbearable Lightness of Being, The (Kundera) 109
unpretentiousness, valuation 135
uprightness 63
useless pieces 116

value-oppositions, setup 90
Varga, Aron Kibédi 11
vein/venation 102
verbal eloquence, mistrust 21
verifiability, characteristics 35–36
virtue 72, 77; articulation 64; meaning 74–75; value (Confucius) 19–20
virus, etymology 145
visibility, characteristics 35–36
visual culture 25
visual perceptivity, importance 139
voice 2–7, 13

wànwù 119
Warburton, William 24, 28
Warring State, writing (power) 22–23
way-making (dao) 117
Way of Heaven, The 104
wéi 48
wéi míng sũo zhǐ 48
Wèi period, Nine Grade Referee system 57
wén 7–8, 21; line/stripe 94; origin 102; zì, relationship 99
wén (vein/venation) 99
Wén Fù (Essay on Literature) 27–28

Wèn, Xiàn 20
wénxiàn 21
Wénxin Diaolóng 101–102
wénzì 7, 102
wén zì 12
wén zì yù 48
Western Enlightenment 100
Western Han Dynasty 32, 33
Western languages, Chinese language (quantitative differences) 2
Western logocentrism 101
Western ocularcentrism 12–13
Western phonetic orthography 142
Western phonocentric episteme 100
Western phonocentric tradition 37
Western phonocentrism 72; contrast 71; effect 152
Western visual culture, focus 12–13
Whaíguàn, Chang 68
Whims in Spring Rain (Jìn) 49
Wilkins, John 4
wisdom 63
wit, Laozi renunciation 121
Wittfogel, Karl August 54
Wittgenstein, Ludwig 121, 151
women, Dao 116
word: collection 104; correctness 109; invention 67; issues 7–13; playing 151; representation 2; selection 60; signification 10; spoken word, usage 1; term, indication 30; trust 152; understanding 13; visual recognition, relationship 11; written word, usage 1
worldliness, valuation 24
writing: ability, discrimination 89–90; action, impact 22; cessation 53; concept 3, 94; didactics 46, 48–53; discipline 46; disciplines, institutionalisation 111; experience 5; graphic vacuity 136; instantaneousness 6; institutionalisation, imperial civil examination (impact) 54–61; invention 7; issues 7–13; logos, usage 89–94; nonsense writing 142; power 22–23, 89; restriction 46–48; rise 17; situation 80; skill, acquisition 135; utensils 65
"Writing Lesson, A" (Leví-Strauss) 5–6
writing subject 45; automaton 78–80; cessation 80–83; construction 80; cultivation 9, 44, 66–68, 127–128; perfecting, virtues 69–80
written characters, usage 96–97

written word: doctoring 141; power 143; usage 1

wú: concept 120; Daoist concept 28; meaning 128–129; term, usage 131; writing, usage 134–137

Wu, Joseph 96–97

wú-concepts, signification 130–131

Wǔ Dú (Five Vermin) 33

wúmíng (fameless) 134

Wǔ of Hàn 56

wú-practices 128–134; elements 129

wúwéi 120, 129, 131

wúwǔo 129, 131

wú yán (no words) 71

wúyù 120, 129, 131

wúzhi 120, 129, 131

xià (under) 97

Xia Dynasty 33

xiàn 21

Xiang, Liu 34

xiàng xíng 96

xiàn huì (magisterial naming taboo) 47

Xian Jìn 114

Xianzhi, Wáng 52

xiào (filial piety) 56, 69, 73–75

Xiào Jīng (contents) 74

Xìao-líen (Men of Filial Piety and Incorruptibility) 56

xiǎorén, junzi (comparison) 63

Xìcí (Commentary) 103

xin (heart-mind) 64

xìn (trustfulness) 75

xin, ideas 95

xíng sheng 96

xinzhai (mind-fasting) 132

Xióng, Yáng 25, 33, 38, 63

Xishijian 141

xiu (mend/repair) 53

Xiu, Ouyáng 59

xiu-shen (self, cultivation) 53

Xizaǐ, Liú 63, 68

Xizhi, Wáng 62, 68, 135

Xìzhi, Wáng 52

Xi, Zhu 59, 77

Xúan, Zhèng 98

Xúe Ér 71, 73, 114

Xun, Lu 82

Xúnzǐ 31–33, 41

yán 7, 103

yán (utterance, language, word) 30

Yáng of Súi, Jìnshìh examination mandate 57

Yán Hùo 71

Yánti 49

Yan Yuan 70

Yán Yuan 71

Yán Yuan (Analects) 140–141

Yáo 33; Dao 108, 114

Yáo Yue 76

yèh (music) 30

Yellow Emperor 17, 33, 67

Yen, Prime Minister letter 23

Yèn-Yūan, Chang 18

yì (idea) 95

yì (righteousness) 31, 64, 69, 75

yí (southern tribe) 83

Yì, Ba 21

Yì, Ba 75

Yi, Chéng 59

Yìjing 103

Yìjing (Book of Changes) 56

Yijing Wáng Bì 26–27

Yong, Tsài 136–137

Yǒuchaóshì (Nest-Dweller) 33

Yòu, Gou 17–18, 73

Young, Michael 81

yóu yú yì (wander the arts) 62

yǔ (rain) 96

Yu (sage king) 33

Yù, Hán 58

Yu, Jiyuan 117

Yúan dynasty, Rénzong (emperor) 65

Yuanmíng, Táo 128

Yúansun, Yán 55

Yuan, Yán 84

Yuánzhang, Zhu 48

Yungzhèng (emperor) 48

Zàng, Xúan 151

Zen/Chán koàn 147

ZengzǐWén 22

Zhang, Zi 74

Zhào, Yúan-Rèn 139

Zhèng (to correct/rectify) 29

Zhèngmíng 32, 34–35

zhèngmíng 26, 29; idea 30; types 34

Zhèng míng, indication 34

Zhèngtú, pursuit 60

Zhenqing, Yán 63, 65, 135

Zhenquin, Yán (calligraphic style) 49

zhī 48

zhì (wisdom) 69

Zhi, Chang 52

zhǐ shì 96
Zhitui, Yán 21
zhong (loyalty) 69
Zhongni, countenance (change) 133
zhòngsheng 119
Zhongshu, Qian 100, 113
zhu 48
Zhuang, Liǔ 22
Zhuangzi (Zhuangzi) 98, 101, 104, 121; Dao 109; representation 118–119
zhūan zhù 96–97

zì 7, 11, 29, 94; míng, synonym 98; usage 97–100; wén, relationship 99
Zi Chǔ 47
zǐ, combination 73
Zǐ Lù 71
ZìLù 29
Zǐyún, Xiao 68
Zǐ, Zhang 74
zǐ zǐ 140
zùowàng (sitting and forgetting) 132
Zǔo Zhuàn 47